MAR

MW01110418

L O N D O N   P R I D E

OR

WHEN THE WORLD WAS YOUNGER

Volume 1

Elibron Classics
www.elibron.com

Elibron Classics series.

© 2005 Adamant Media Corporation.

ISBN 1-4021-9115-4 (paperback)
ISBN 1-4212-9672-1 (hardcover)

This Elibron Classics Replica Edition is an unabridged facsimile
of the edition published in 1897 by Bernhard Tauchnitz,
Leipzig.

COLLECTION

OF

BRITISH AUTHORS

TAUCHNITZ EDITION.

VOL. 3179.

LONDON PRIDE. BY M. E. BRADDON.

IN TWO VOLUMES.

VOL. I.

LONDON PRIDE

OR

WHEN THE WORLD WAS YOUNGER

BY

M. E. BRADDON,

AUTHOR OF

"LADY AUDLEY'S SECRET," "VIXEN," "ISHMAEL," ETC.

COPYRIGHT EDITION.

IN TWO VOLUMES.—VOL. I.

LEIPZIG

BERNHARD TAUCHNITZ

1897.

CONTENTS

OF VOLUME I.

———

LONDON PRIDE.

CHAPTER I.

A HARBOUR FROM THE STORM.

THE wind howled across the level fields, and flying
showers of sleet rattled against the old leathern coach as
it drove through the thickening dusk. A bitter winter,
this year of the Royal tragedy.

A rainy summer, and a mild rainy autumn had been
followed by the hardest frost this generation had ever
known. The Thames was frozen over, and tempestuous
winds had shaken the ships in the Pool, and the steep
gable ends and tall chimney-stacks on London Bridge.
A never-to-be-forgotten winter, which had witnessed the
martyrdom of England's King, and the exile of her chief
nobility, while a rabble Parliament rode roughshod over
a cowed people. Gloom and sour visages prevailed, the
maypoles were down, the play-houses were closed, the
bear-gardens were empty, the cock-pits were desolate;
and a saddened population, impoverished and depressed by the sacrifices that had been exacted and the

tyranny that had been exercised in the name of Liberty, were ground under the iron heel of Cromwell's red-coats.

The pitiless journey from London to Louvain, a journey of many days and nights, prolonged by accident and difficulty, had been spun out to uttermost tedium for those two in the heavily moving old leathern coach. Who and what were they, these wearied travellers, journeying together silently towards a destination which promised but little of pleasure or luxury by way of welcome—a destination which meant severance for those two?

One was Sir John Kirkland, of the Manor Moat, Bucks, a notorious Malignant, a grey-bearded cavalier, aged by trouble and hard fighting; a soldier and servant who had sacrificed himself and his fortune for the King, and must needs begin the world anew now that his master was murdered, his own goods confiscated, the old family mansion, the house in which his parents died and his children were born, emptied of all its valuables, and left to the care of servants, and his master's son a wanderer in a foreign land, with little hope of ever winning back crown and sceptre.

Sadness was the dominant expression of Sir John's stern, strongly marked countenance, as he sat staring out at the level landscape through the unglazed coach window, staring blankly across those wind-swept Flemish fields where the cattle were clustering in sheltered corners, a monotonous expanse, crossed by ice-bound dykes that looked black as ink, save where the last rays of the setting sun touched their iron hue with blood-red splashes. Pollard willows indicated the edge of one field, gaunt poplars marked the boundary of another, alike leafless and unbeautiful, standing darkly out against the dim grey sky. Night was hastening towards the travellers, narrowing and blotting out that level landscape, field, dyke, and leafless wood.

Sir John put his head out of the coach window, and looked anxiously along the straight road, peering through the shades of evening in the hope of seeing the crocketed spires and fair cupolas of Louvain in the distance. But he could see nothing save a waste of level pastures and the gathering darkness. Not a light anywhere, not a sign of human habitation.

Useless to gaze any longer into the impenetrable night. The traveller leant back into a corner of the carriage with folded arms, and, with a deep sigh, composed himself for slumber. He had slept but little for the last week. The passage from Harwich to Ostend in a fishing-smack had been a perilous transit, prolonged by adverse winds. Sleep had been impossible on board that wretched craft; and the land journey had been fraught with vexation and delays of all kinds—stupidity of postillions, dearth of horseflesh, badness of the roads —all things that can vex and hinder.

Sir John's travelling companion, a small child in a cloak and hood, crept closer to him in the darkness, nestled up against his elbow, and pushed her little cold hand into his leathern glove.

"You are crying again, father," she said, full of pity. "You were crying last night. Do you always cry when it grows dark?"

"It does not become a man to shed tears in the daylight, little maid," her father answered gently.

"Is it for the poor King you are crying—the King
those wicked men murdered?"

"Ay, Angela, for the King; and for the Queen and
her fatherless children still more than for the King, for
he has crowned himself with a crown of glory, the
diadem of martyrs, and is resting from labour and
sorrow, to rise victorious at the great day, when his
enemies and his murderers shall stand ashamed before
him. I weep for that once so lovely lady—widowed,
discrowned, needy, desolate—a beggar in the land where
her father was a great king. A hard fate, Angela, father
and husband both murdered."

"Was the Queen's father murdered too?" asked the
silver-sweet voice out of darkness, a pretty piping note
like the song of a bird.

"Yes, love."

"Did Bradshaw murder him?"

"No, dearest, 'twas in France he was slain—in Paris;
stabbed to death by a madman."

"And was the Queen sorry?"

"Ay, sweetheart, she has drained the cup of sorrow.
She was but a child when her father died. She can
but dimly remember that dreadful day. And now she
sits, banished and widowed, to hear of her husband's
martyrdom; her elder sons wanderers, her young
daughter a prisoner."

"Poor Queen!" piped the small sweet voice, "I am
so sorry for her."

Little had she ever known but sorrow, this child of
the Great Rebellion, born in the old Buckinghamshire
manor house, while her father was at Falmouth with the
Prince—born in the midst of civil war, a stormy petrel,

bringing no message of peace from those unknown skies whence she came, a harbinger of woe. Infant eyes love bright colours. This baby's eyes looked upon a house hung with black. Her mother died before the child was a fortnight old. They had christened her Angela. "Angel of Death," said the father, when the news of his loss reached him, after the lapse of many days. His fair young wife's coffin was in the family vault under the parish church of St. Nicholas in the Vale, before he knew that he had lost her.

There was an elder daughter, Hyacinth, seven years the senior, who had been sent across the Channel in the care of an old servant at the beginning of the troubles between King and Parliament.

She had been placed in the charge of her maternal grandmother, the Marquise de Montrond, who had taken ship for Calais when the Court left London, leaving her royal mistress to weather the storm. A lady who had wealth and prestige in her own country, who had been a famous beauty when Richelieu was in power, and who had been admired by that serious and sober monarch, Louis the Thirteenth, could scarcely be expected to put up with the shifts and shortcomings of an Oxford lodging-house, with the ever-present fear of finding herself in a town besieged by Lord Essex and the rebel army.

With Madame de Montrond, Hyacinth had been reared, partly in a mediæval mansion, with a portcullis and four squat towers, near the Château d'Arques, and partly in Paris, where the lady had a fine house in the Marais. The sisters had never looked upon each other's faces, Angela having entered upon the troubled scene

after Hyacinth had been carried across the Channel to
her grandmother. And now the father was racked with
anxiety lest evil should befall that elder daughter in
the war between Mazarin and the Parliament, which
was reported to rage with increasing fury.

Angela's awakening reason became conscious of a
world where all was fear and sadness. The stories she
heard in her childhood were stories of that fierce war
which was reaching its disastrous close while she was
in her cradle. She was told of the happy peaceful
England of old, before darkness and confusion gathered
over the land; before the hearts of the people were
set against their King by a wicked and rebellious Parliament.

She heard of battles lost by the King and his
partisans; cities besieged and taken; a flash of victory
followed by humiliating reverses; the King's party always
at a disadvantage; and hence the falling away of the
feeble and the false, the treachery of those who had
seemed friends, the impotence of the faithful.

Angela heard so often and so much of these things
—from old Lady Kirkland, her grandmother, and from
the grey-haired servants at the manor—that she grew
to understand them with a comprehension seemingly
far beyond her tender years. But a child so reared is
inevitably older than her years. This little one had
never known childish pleasures or play, childish companions or childish fancies.

She roamed about the spacious gardens, full of
saddest thoughts, burdened with all the cares that
weighed down that kingly head yonder; or she stood
before the pictured face of the monarch with clasped

hands and tearful eyes, looking up at him with the
adoring compassion of a child prone to hero-worship—
thinking of him already as saint and martyr—whose
martyrdom was not yet consummated in blood.

King Charles had presented his faithful servant, Sir
John Kirkland, with a half-length replica of one of his
Vandyke portraits, a beautiful head, with a strange in-
ward look—that look of isolation and aloofness which
we who know his story take for a prophecy of doom—
which the sculptor Bernini had remarked, when he
modelled the royal head for marble. The picture hung
in the place of honour in the long narrow gallery at the
Manor Moat, with trophies of Flodden and Zutphen arranged against the blackened oak panelling above it.
The Kirklands had been a race of soldiers since the
days of Edward III. The house was full of war-like
decorations—tattered colours, old armour, memorials of
fighting Kirklands who had long been dust.

There came an evil day when the rabble rout of
Cromwell's crop-haired soldiery burst into the manor
house to pillage and destroy, carrying off curios and
relics that were the gradual accumulation of a century
and a half of peaceful occupation.

The old Dowager's grey hairs had barely saved her
from outrage on that bitter day. It was only her utter
helplessness and afflicted condition that prevailed upon
the Parliamentary captain, and prevented him from
carrying out his design, which was to haul her off to
one of those London prisons at that time so gorged
with Royalist captives that the devilish ingenuity of the
Parliament had devised floating gaols on the Thames,
where persons of quality and character were herded to-

gether below decks, to the loss of health, and even of
life.

Happily for old Lady Kirkland, she was too lame
to walk, and her enemies had no horse or carriage in
which to convey her; so she was left at peace in her
son's plundered mansion, whence all that was valuable
and easily portable was carried away by the Round-
heads. Silver plate and family plate had been sacrificed
to the King's necessities.

The pictures, not being either portable or readily
convertible into cash, had remained on the old panelled
walls.

Angela used to go from the King's picture to her
father's. Sir John's was a more rugged face than the
Stuart's, with a harder expression; but the child's heart
went out to the image of the father she had never seen
since the dawn of consciousness. He had made a hurried journey to that quiet Buckinghamshire valley soon
after her birth—had looked at the baby in her cradle,
and then had gone down into the vault where his young
wife was lying, and had stayed for more than an hour
in cold and darkness alone with his dead. That lovely
French wife had been his junior by more than twenty
years, and he had loved her passionately—had loved
her and left her for duty's sake. No Kirkland had
ever faltered in his fidelity to crown and king. This
John Kirkland had sacrificed all things, and, alone with
his beloved dead in the darkness of that narrow charnel
house, it seemed to him that there was nothing left for
him except to cleave to those fallen fortunes and
patiently await the issue.

He had fought in many battles and had escaped

with a few scars; and he was carrying his daughter to Louvain, intending to place her in the charge of her great-aunt, Madame de Montrond's half sister, who was head of a convent in that city, a safe and pious shelter, where the child might be reared in her mother's faith.

Lady Kirkland, the only daughter of the Marquise de Montrond, one of Queen Henrietta Maria's ladies-in-waiting, had been a papist, and, although Sir John had adhered steadfastly to the principles of the Reformed Church, he had promised his bride, and the Marquise, her mother, that if their nuptials were blessed with off-spring, their children should be educated in the Roman faith — a promise difficult of performance in a land where a stormy tide ran high against Rome, and where Popery was a scarlet spectre that alarmed the ignorant and maddened the bigoted. And now, duly provided with a safe conduct from the regicide, Bradshaw, he was journeying to the city where he was to part with his daughter for an indefinite period. He had seen but little of her, and yet it seemed as hard to part thus as if she had prattled at his knees and nestled in his arms every day of her young life.

At last across the distance, against the wind-driven clouds of that stormy winter sky, John Kirkland saw the lights of the city—not many lights or brilliant of their kind, but a glimmer here and there—and behind the glimmer the dark bulk of masonry, roofs, steeples, watchtowers, bridges.

The carriage stopped at one of the gates of the city, and there were questions asked and answered, and papers shown, but there was no obstacle to the entrance of the travellers. The name of the Ursuline

Convent acted like a charm, for Louvain was papist to
the core in these days of Spanish dominion. It had
been a city of refuge nearly a hundred years ago for
all that was truest and bravest and noblest among
English Roman Catholics, in the cruel days of Queen
Elizabeth, and Englishmen had become the leading
spirits of the University there, and had attracted the
youth of Romanist England to the sober old Flemish
town, before the establishment of Dr. Allan's rival
seminary at Douai. Sir John could have found no safer
haven for his little ewe lamb.

The tired horses blundered heavily along the stony
streets, and crossed more than one bridge. The town
seemed pervaded by water, a deep narrow stream like
a canal, on which the houses looked, as if in feeble
mockery of Venice—houses with steep crow-step gables,
some of them richly decorated; narrow windows for the
most part dark, but with here and there the yellow
light of lamp or candle.

The convent faced a broad open square, and had a
large walled garden in its rear. The coach stopped in
front of a handsome doorway, and after the travellers
had been scrutinised and interrogated by the portress
through an opening in the door, they were admitted
into a spacious hall, paved with black and white marble,
and adorned with a statue of the Virgin Mother, and
thence to a parlour dimly lighted by a small oil lamp,
where they waited for about ten minutes, the little girl
shivering with cold, before the Superior appeared.

She was a tall woman, advanced in years, with a
handsome, but melancholy countenance. She greeted
the cavalier as a familiar friend.

"Welcome to Flanders!" she said. "You have fled from that accursed country where our Church is despised and persecuted——"

"Nay, reverend kinswoman, I have fled but to go back again as fast as horses and sails can carry me. While the fortunes of my King are at stake, my place is in England, or it may be in Scotland, where there are still those who are ready to fight to the death in the royal cause. But I have brought this little one for shelter and safe keeping, and tender usage, trusting in you who are of kin to her as I could trust no one else —and, furthermore, that she may be reared in the faith of her dead mother."

"Sweet soul!" murmured the nun. "It was well for her to be taken from your troubled England to the kingdom of the saints and martyrs."

"True, reverend mother; yet those blasphemous levellers who call us 'Malignants' have dubbed themselves 'Saints.'"

"Then affairs go no better with you in England, I fear, Sir John?"

"Nay, madam, they go so ill that they have reached the lowest depth of infamy. Hell itself hath seen no spectacle more awful, no murder more barbarous, no horrider triumph of wickedness, than the crime which was perpetrated this day se'nnight at Whitehall."

The nun looked at him wistfully, with clasped hands, as one who half apprehended his meaning.

"The King!" she faltered, "still a prisoner?"

"Ay, reverend lady, but a prisoner in Paradise, where angels are his guards, and saints and martyrs his companions. He has regained his crown; but it is the

crown of martyrdom, the aureole of slaughtered saints.
England, our little England that was once so great
under the strong rule of that virgin-queen who made
herself the arbiter of Christendom, and the wonder of
the world——"

The pious lady shivered and crossed herself at this
praise of the heretic queen—praise that could only
come from a heretic.

"Our blessed and peaceful England has become a
den of thieves, given over to the ravening wolves of
rebellion and dissent, the penniless soldiery who would
bring down all men's fortunes to their own level, seize
all, eat and drink all, and trample crown and peerage
in the mire. They have slain him, reverend mother,
this impious herd—they gave him the mockery of a
trial—just as his Master, Christ, was mocked. They
spurned and spat upon him, even as our Redeemer was
spurned; and then, on the Sabbath day, they cried
aloud in their conventicles, "Lord, hast Thou not smelt
a sweet savour of blood?" Ay, these murderers gloried
in their crime, bragged of their gory hands, lifted them
up towards heaven as a token of righteousness!"

The cavalier was pacing to and fro in the dimness
of the convent parlour, with quick, agitated steps, his
nostrils quivering, grizzled brows bent over angry eyes,
his hand trembling with rage as it clutched his sword-
hilt.

The reverend mother drew Angela to her side, took
off the little black silk hood, and laid her hand caressingly on the soft brown hair.

"Was it Cromwell's work?" she asked.

"Nay, reverend mother, I doubt whether of his own

accord Cromwell would have done this thing. He is a villain, a damnable villain—but he is a glorious villain. The Parliament had made their covenant with the King at Newport—a bargain which gave them all, and left him nothing—save only his broken health, grey hairs, and the bare name of King. He would have been but a phantom of authority, powerless as the royal spectres Æneas met in the under-world. They had got all from him—all save the betrayal of his friends. There he budged not, but was firm as rock."

"'Twas likely he remembered Strafford, and that he prospered no better for having flung a faithful dog to the wolves," said the nun.

"Remembered Strafford? Ay, that memory has been a pillow of thorns through many a sleepless night. No, it was not Cromwell who sought the King's blood—though it has been shed with his sanction. The Parliament had got all, and would have been content, but the faction they had created was too strong for them. The levellers sent their spokesman—one Pride, an ex-drayman, now colonel of horse—to the door of the House of Commons, who arrested the more faithful and moderate members, imposed himself and his rebel crew upon the House, and hurried on that violation of constitutional law, that travesty of justice, which compelled an anointed King to stand before the lowest of his subjects—the jacks-in-office of a mutinous commonalty —to answer for having fought in defence of his own inviolable rights."

"Did they dare condemn their King?"

"Ah, madam, they found him guilty of high treason, in that he had taken arms against the Parliament. They sentenced their royal master to death—and seven days ago London saw the spectacle of judicial murder—a blameless King slain by the minion of an armed rabble!"

"But did the people—the English people—suffer this in silence? The wisest and best of them could surely be assembled in your great city. Did the citizens of London stand placidly by to see this deed accomplished?"

"They were like sheep before the shearer. They were dumb. Great God! can I ever forget that sea of white faces under the grey winter sky, or the universal groan that went up to heaven when the stroke of the axe sounded on the block, and men knew that the murder of their King was consummated; and when that anointed head with its grey hairs, whitened with sorrow, mark you, not with age, was lifted up, bloody, terrible, and proclaimed the head of a traitor? Ah, reverend mother, ten such moments will age a man by ten years. Was it not the most portentous tragedy which the earth has ever seen since He who was both God and Man died upon Calvary? Other judicial sacrifices have been, but never of a victim as guiltless and as noble. Had you but seen the calm beauty of his countenance as he turned it towards the people! Oh, my King, my master, my beloved friend, when shall I see that face in Paradise, with the blood washed from that royal brow, with the smile of the redeemed upon those lips!"

He flung himself into a chair, covered his face with those weather-stained hands, which had broadened by much grasping of sword and pistol, pike and gun, and sobbed aloud, with a fierce passion that convulsed the strong muscular frame. Of all the King's servants this

one had been the most steadfast, was marked in the
black book of the Parliament as a notorious Malignant.
From the raising of the standard on the castle-hill at
Nottingham—in the sad evening of a tempestuous day,
with but scanty attendance, and only evil presages—to
the treaty at Newport, and the prison on the low
Hampshire coast, this man had been his master's constant companion and friend; fighting in every battle,
cleaving to King and Prince in spite of every opposing
influence, carrying letters between father and son in the
teeth of the enemy, humbling himself as a servant, and
performing menial labours, in those latter days of bitter-
ness and outrage, when all courtly surroundings were
denied the fallen monarch.

And now he mourned his martyred King more bitterly
than he would have mourned his own brother.

The little girl slipped from the reverend mother's
lap, and ran across the room to her father.

"Don't cry, father!" she murmured, with her own
eyes streaming. "It hurts me to see you."

"Nay, Angela," he answered, clasping her to his
breast. "Forgive me that I think more of my dead
King than of my living daughter. Poor child, thou hast
seen nothing but sorrow since thou wert born; a land
racked by civil war; Englishmen changed into devils; a
home ravaged and made desolate; threatenings and
curses; thy good grandmother's days shortened by
sorrow and rough usage. Thou wert born into a house
of mourning, and hast seen nothing but black since thou
hadst eyes to notice the things around thee. Those
tender ears should have heard only loving words. But
it is over, dearest; and thou hast found a haven within

these walls. You will take care of her, will you not, madam, for the sake of the niece you loved?"

"She shall be the apple of my eye. No evil shall come near her that my care and my prayers can avert. God has been very gracious to our order—in all troublous times we have been protected. We have many pupils from the best families of Flanders—and some even from Paris, whence parents are glad to remove their children from the confusion of the time. You need fear nothing while this sweet child is with us; and if in years to come she should desire to enter our order———"

"The Lord forbid!" cried the cavalier. "I want her to be a good and pious papist, madam, like her sweet mother; but never a nun. I look to her as the staff and comfort of my declining years. Thou wilt not abandon thy father, wilt thou, little one, when thou shalt be tall and strong as a bulrush, and he shall be bent and gnarled with age, like the old medlar on the lawn at the Manor? Thou wilt be his rod and staff, wilt thou not, sweetheart?"

The child flung her arms round his neck and kissed him. It was her only answer, but that mute reply was a vow.

"Thou wilt stay here till England's troubles are over, Angela, and that base herd yonder have been trampled down. Thou wilt be happy here, and wilt mind thy book, and be obedient to those good ladies who will teach thee; and some day, when our country is at peace, I will come back to fetch thee."

"Soon," murmured the child, "soon, father?"

"God grant it may be soon, my beloved! It is hard for father and children to be scattered, as we are scattered; thy sister Hyacinth in Paris, and thou in Flanders, and I in England. Yet it must needs be so for a while!"

"Why should not Hyacinth come to us and be reared with Angela?" asked the reverend mother.

"Nay, madam, Hyacinth is well cared for with your sister, Madame de Montrond. She is as dear to her maternal grandmother as this little one here was to my good mother, whose death last year left us a house of mourning. Hyacinth will doubtless inherit a considerable portion of Madame de Montrond's wealth, which is not insignificant. She is being brought up in the precincts of the Court."

"A worldly and a dangerous school for one so young," said the nun, with a sigh. "I have heard my father talk of what life was like at the Louvre when the Béarnais reigned there in the flower of his manhood, newly master of Paris, flushed with hard-won victory, and but lately reconciled to the Church."

"Methinks that great captain's court must have been laxer than that of Queen Anne and the Cardinal. I have been told that the child-king is being reared, as it were, in a cloister, so strict are mother and guardian. My only fear for Hyacinth is the troubled state of the city, given over to civil warfare only less virulent than that which has desolated England. I hear that the Fronde is no war of epigrams and pamphlets, but that men are as earnest and bloodthirsty as they were in the League. I shall go from here to Paris to see my first-born before I make my way back to London."

"I question if you will find her at Paris," said the reverend mother. "I had news from a priest in the

diocese of the Coadjutor. The Queen-mother left the city
secretly with her chosen favourites in the dead of the
night on the sixth of this month, after having kept the
festival of Twelfth Night in a merry humour with her
Court. Even her waiting-women knew nothing of her
plans. They went to St. Germain, where they found
the château unfurnished, and where all the Court had to
sleep upon was a few loads of straw. Hatred of the
Cardinal is growing fiercer every day, and Paris is in a
state of siege. The Princes are siding with Mathieu Molé
and his Parliament, and the Provincial Parliaments are
taking up the quarrel. God grant that it may not be in
France as it has been with you in your unhappy England;
but I fear the Spanish Queen and her Italian minister
scarce know the temper of the French people."

"Alas, good friend, we have fallen upon evil days, and
the spirit of revolt is everywhere; but if there is trouble
at the French Court, there is all the more need that I
should make my way thither, be it at St. Germain or
at Paris, and so assure myself of my pretty Hyacinth's
safety. She was so sweet an infant when my good and
faithful steward carried her across the sea to Dieppe.
Never shall I forget that sad moment of parting, when
the baby arms were wreathed round my sweet saint's
neck; she so soon to become again a mother, so brave
and patient in her sorrow at parting with her first-born.
Ah, sister, there are moments in this life that a man
must needs remember, even amidst the wreck of his
country." He dashed away a tear or two, and then
turned to his kinswoman with outstretched hands and
said, "Good night, dear and reverend mother; good
night and good-bye. I shall sleep at the nearest inn,

and shall be on the road again at daybreak. Good-bye, my soul's delight."

He clasped his daughter in his arms, with something of despair in the fervour of his embrace, telling himself, as the soft cheek was pressed against his own, how many years might pass ere he would again so clasp that tender form and feel those innocent kisses on his bearded lips. She and the elder girl were all that were left to him of love and comfort, and the elder sister had been taken from him while she was a little child. He would not have known her had he met her unawares; nor had he ever felt for her such a pathetic love as for this guilt-less death-angel, this baby whose coming had ruined his life, whose love was nevertheless the only drop of sweetness in his cup.

He plucked himself from that gentle embrace, and walked quickly to the door.

"You will apply to me for whatever money is needed for the child's maintenance and education," he said, and in the next moment was gone.

CHAPTER II.

WITHIN CONVENT WALLS.

MORE than ten years had come and gone since that
bleak February evening when Sir John Kirkland carried
his little daughter to a place of safety, in the old city
of Louvain, and in all those years the child had grown
like a flower in a sheltered garden, where cold winds
never come. The bud had matured into the blossom
in that mild atmosphere of piety and peace; and now,
in this fair springtide of 1660, a girlish face watched
from the convent casement for the coming of the father
whom Angela Kirkland had not looked upon since she
was a child, and the sister she had never seen.

They were to arrive to-day, father and sister, on a
brief visit to the quiet Flemish city. Yonder in England there had been curious changes since the stern
Protector turned his rugged face to the wall, and laid
down that golden sceptre with which he had ruled as
with a rod of iron. Kingly title would he none; yet
where kings had chastised with whips, he had chastised
with scorpions. Ireland could tell how the little finger
of Cromwell had been heavier than the arm of the
Stuarts. She had trembled and had obeyed, and had
prospered under that scorpion rule, and England's
armaments had been the terror of every sea while
Cromwell stood at the helm; but now that strong brain

and bold heart were in the dust, and it had taken
England little more than a year to discover that
Puritanism and the Rump were a mistake, and that to
the core of her heart she was loyal to her hereditary
King.

She asked not what manner of man this hereditary
ruler might be; asked not whether he were wise or
foolish, faithful or treacherous. She forgot all of tyranny
and of double-dealing she had suffered from his for-
bears. She forgot even her terror of the scarlet spectre,
the grim wolf of Rome, in her disgust at Puritan fervour
which had torn down altar-rails, usurped church pulpits,
destroyed the beauty of ancient cathedrals. Like a
woman or a child, she held out her arms to the unknown, in a natural recoil from that iron rule which
had extinguished her gaiety, silenced her noble liturgy,
made innocent pleasures and elegant arts things forbidden. She wanted her churches, and her theatres,
her cock-pits and taverns, and bear-gardens and maypoles back again. She wanted to be ruled by the law,
and not by the sword; and she longed with a romantic
longing for that young wanderer who had fled from her
shores in a fishing-boat, with his life in his hand, to return in a glad procession of great ships dancing over
summer seas, eating, drinking, gaming, in a coat worth
scarce thirty shillings, and with empty pockets for his
loyal subjects to make haste and fill.

Angela had the convent parlour all to herself this
fair spring morning. She was the favourite pupil of the
nuns, had taken no vows, pledged herself to no novi-
ciate, ever mindful of her promise to her father. She
had lived as happily and as merrily in that abode of

piety as she could have lived in the finest palace in
Europe. There were other maidens, daughters of the
French and Flemish nobility, who were taught and
reared within those sombre precincts, and with them
she had played and worked and laboured at such
studies as became a young lady of quality. Like that
fair daughter of affliction, Henrietta of England, she
had gained in education by the troubles which had
made her girlhood a time of seclusion. She had been
first the plaything of those elder girls who were finish-
ing their education in the convent, her childishness ap-
pealing to their love and pity; and then, after being
the plaything of the nuns and the elder pupils, she became the favourite of her contemporaries, and in a
manner their queen. She was more thoughtful than
her class-fellows, in advance of her years in piety and
intelligence; and they, knowing her sad story—how she
was severed from her country and kindred, her father
a wanderer with his King, her sister bred up at a
foreign Court—had first compassionated and then admired her. From her twelfth year upwards her intellectual superiority had been recognised in the convent, alike by the nuns and their pupils. Her aptitude
at all learning, and her simple but profound piety, had
impressed everybody. At fourteen years of age they
had christened her "the little wonder;" but later, seeing
that their praises embarrassed and even distressed her,
they had desisted from such loving flatteries, and were
content to worship her with a silent adulation.

Her father's visits to the Flemish city had been few
and far apart, fondly though he loved his motherless
girl. He had been a wanderer for the most part

during those years, tossed upon troubled seas, fighting
with Condé against Mazarin and Anne of Austria, and
reconciled with the Court later, when peace was made,
and his friends the Princes were forgiven; an exile from
France of his own free will when Louis banished his
first cousin, the King of England, in order to truckle to
the triumphant usurper. He had led an adventurous
life, and had cared very little what became of him in a
topsy-turvy world. But now all things were changed.
Richard Cromwell's brief and irresolute rule had
shattered the Commonwealth, and made Englishmen
eager for a king. The country was already tired of
him whose succession had been admitted with blank
acquiescence; and Monk and the army were soon to
become masters of the situation. There was hope that
the General was rightly affected, and that the King
would have his own again; and that such of his followers as had not compounded with the Parliamentary
Commission would get back their confiscated estates;
and that all who had suffered in person or pocket
for loyalty's sake would be recompensed for their
sacrifices.

It was five years since Sir John's last appearance at
the convent, and Angela's heart beat fast at the thought
that he was so near. She was to see him this very
day; nay, perhaps this very hour. His coach might
have passed the gate of the town already. He was
bringing his elder daughter with him, that sister whose
face she had never seen, save in a miniature, and who
was now a great lady, the wife of Baron Fareham, of
Chilton Abbey, Oxon, Fareham Park, in the County of
Hants, and Fareham House, London, a nobleman who:e

estates had come through the ordeal of the Parliamentary Commission with a reasonable fine, and to
whom extra favour had been shown by the Commissioners, because he was known to be at heart a Republican. In the meantime, Lady Fareham had a
liberal income allowed her by the Marquise, her grandmother, and she and her husband had been among
the most splendid foreigners at the French Court, where
the lady's beauty and wit had placed her conspicuously
in that galaxy of brilliant women who shone and
sparkled about the sun of the European firmament—
Le roi soleil, or "the King," par excellence, who took
the blazing sun for his crest. The Fronde had been
a time of pleasurable excitement to the high-spirited
girl, whose mixed blood ran like quicksilver, and who
delighted in danger and party strife, stratagem and intrigue. The story of her courage and gaiety of heart
in the siege of Paris, she being then little more than a
child, had reached the Flemish convent long after the
acts recorded had been forgotten at Paris and St. Germain.

Angela's heart beat fast at the thought of being restored to these dear ones, were it only for a short span.
They were not going to carry her away from the convent; and, indeed, seeing that she so loved her aunt,
the good reverend mother, and that her heart cleaved
to those walls and to the holy exercises which filled so
great a part of her life, her father, in replying to a
letter in which she had besought him to release her
from her promise and allow her to dedicate herself to
God, had told her that, although he could not surrender
his daughter, to whom he looked for the comfort of his

closing years, he would not urge her to leave the Ursulines until he should feel himself old and feeble, and in need of her tender care. Meanwhile she might be a nun in all but the vows, and a dutiful niece to her kind aunt, Mother Anastasia, whose advanced years and failing health needed all consideration.

But now, before he went back to England, whither he hoped to accompany the King and the Princes ere the year was much older, Sir John Kirkland was coming to visit his younger daughter, bringing Lady Fareham, whose husband was now in attendance upon His Majesty in Holland, where there were serious negotiations on hand—negotiations which would have been full of peril to the English messengers two years ago, when that excellent preacher and holy man, Dr. Hewer, of St. Gregory, was beheaded for having intelligence with the King, through the Marquess of Ormond.

The parlour window jutted into the square over against the town hall, and Angela could see the whole length of the narrow street along which her father's carriage must come.

The tall, slim figure and the fair, girlish face stood out in full relief against the grey stone mullion, bathed in sunlight. The graceful form was undisguised by courtly apparel. The soft brown hair fell in loose ringlets, which were drawn back from the brow by a band of black ribbon. The girl's gown was of soft grey woollen stuff, relieved by a cambric collar covering the shoulders, and by cambric elbow-sleeves. A coral and silver rosary was her only ornament; but face and form needed no aid from satins or velvets, Venetian lace or Indian filagree.

The sweet, serious face was chiefly notable for eyes of darkest grey, under brows that were firmly arched and almost black. The hair was a dark brown, the complexion somewhat too pale for beauty. Indeed, that low-toned colouring made some people blind to the fine and regular modelling of the high-bred face; while there were others who saw no charm in a countenance which seemed too thoughtful for early youth, and therefore lacking in one of youth's chief attractions—gladness.

The face lighted suddenly at this moment, as four great grey Flanders horses came clattering along the narrow street and into the square, dragging a heavy painted wooden coach after them. The girl opened the casement and craned out her neck to look at the arrival. The coach stopped at the convent door, and a footman alighted and rang the convent bell, to the interested curiosity of two or three loungers upon the steps of the town hall over the way.

Yes, it was her father, greyer but less sad of visage than at his last visit. His doublet and cloak were handsomer than the clothes he had worn then, though they were still of the same fashion, that English mode which he had affected before the beginning of the troubles, and which he had never changed.

Immediately after him there alighted a vision of beauty, the loveliest of ladies, in sky-blue velvet and pale grey fur, and with a long white feather encircling a sky-blue hat, and a collar of Venetian lace veiling a bosom that scintillated with jewels.

"Hyacinth!" cried Angela, in a flutter of delight.

The portress peered at the visitors through her spyhole, and being satisfied that they were the expected guests, speedily opened the iron-clamped door.

There was no one to interfere between father and daughter, sister and sister, in the convent parlour. Angela had her dear people all to herself, the Mother Superior respecting the confidences and outpourings of love, which neither father nor children would wish to be witnessed even by a kinswoman. Thus, by a rare breach of conventual discipline, Angela was allowed to receive her guests alone.

The lay-sister opened the parlour door and ushered in the visitors, and Angela ran to meet her father, and fell sobbing upon his breast, her face hidden against his velvet doublet, her arms clasping his neck.

"What, mistress, hast thou so watery a welcome, now that the clouds have passed away, and every loyal English heart is joyful?" cried Sir John, in a voice that was somewhat husky, but with a great show of gaiety.

"Oh, sir, I have waited so long, so long for this day. Sometimes I thought it would never come, that I should never see my dear father again."

"Poor child! it would have been only my desert hadst thou forgotten me altogether. I might have come to you sooner, pretty one; indeed, I would have come, only things went ill with me. I was down-hearted and hopeless of any good fortune in a world that seemed given over to psalm-singing scoundrels; and till the tide turned I had no heart to come nigh you. But now fortunes are mended, the King's and mine, and you have a father once again, and shall have a home by-and-by, the house where you were born, and where your angel-mother made my life blessed. You are like her,

Angela!" holding back the pale face in his strong hands, and gazing upon it earnestly. "Yes, you favour your mother; but your face is over sad for your years. Look at your sister here! Would you not say a sunbeam had taken woman's shape and come dancing into the room?"

Angela looked round and greeted the lady, who had stood aside while father and daughter met. Yes, such a face suggested sunlight and summer, birds, butterflies, all things buoyant and gladsome. A complexion of dazzling fairness, pearly, transparent, with ever-varying carnations; eyes of heavenliest blue, liquid, laughing, brimming with *espièglerie;* a slim little nose with an upward tilt, which expressed a contemptuous gaiety, an inquiring curiosity; a dimpled chin sloping a little towards the full round throat; the bust and shoulders of a Venus, the waist of a sylph, set off by the close-fitting velvet bodice, with its diamond and turquoise buttons; hair of palest gold, fluffed out into curls that were traps for sunbeams; hands and arms of a milky whiteness emerging from the large loose elbow-sleeves—a radiant apparition which took Angela by surprise. She had seen Flemish vraus in the richest attire, and among them there had been women as handsome as Helena Forment; but this vision of a fine lady from the court of the "roi soleil" was a revelation. Until this moment, the girl had hardly known what grace and beauty meant.

"Come and let me hug you, my dearest Puritan," cried Hyacinth, holding out her arms. "Why do you suffer your custodians to clothe you in that odious grey, which puts me in mind of lank-haired psalm-singing scum, and all their hateful works? I would have you sparkling in white satin and silver, or blushing in brocade powdered with forget-me-nots and rosebuds. What would Fareham say if I told him I had a Puritan in grey woollen stuff for my sister? He sends you his love, dear, and bids me tell you there shall be always an honoured place in our home for you, be it in England or France, in town or country. And why should you not fill that place at once, sister? Your education is finished, and to be sure you must be tired of these stone walls and this sleepy town."

"No, Hyacinth, I love the convent and the friends who have made it my home. You and Lord Fareham are very kind, but I could not leave our reverend mother; she is not so well or so strong as she used to be, and I think she likes to have me with her, because though she loves us all, down to the humblest of the lay-sisters, I am of her kin, and seem nearest to her. I don't want to forsake her; and if it was not against my father's wish I should like to end my days in this house, and to give my thoughts to God."

"That is because thou knowest nought of the world outside, sweetheart," protested Hyacinth. "I admire the readiness with which folks will renounce a banquet they have never tasted. A single day at the Louvre or the Palais Royal would change your inclinations at once and for ever."

"She is too young for a court life, or a town life either," said Sir John. "And I have no mind to remove her from this safe shelter till the King shall be firm upon his throne, and our poor country shall have settled into a stable and peaceful condition. But there must be no vows, Angela, no renunciation of kindred and home. I look to thee for the comfort of my old age!"

"Dear father, I will never disobey you. I shall remember always that my first duty is to you; and when you want me, you have but to summon me; and whether you are at home or abroad, in wealth and honour, or in exile and poverty, I will go to you, and be glad and happy to be your daughter and your servant."

"I knew thou wouldst, dearest. I have never forgotten how the soft little arms clung about my neck, and how the baby lips kissed me, in this same parlour, when my heart was weighed down by a load of iron, and there seemed no ray of hope for England or me. You were my comforter then, and you will be my comforter in the days to come. Hyacinth here is of the butterfly breed. She is fair to look upon, and tender and loving; but she is ever on the wing. And she has her husband and her children to cherish, and cannot be burdened with the care of a broken-down greybeard."

"Broken-down! Why, you are as brave a gallant as the youngest cavalier in the King's service," cried Hyacinth. "I would pit my father against Montagu or Buckingham, Buckhurst or Roscommon — against the gayest, the boldest of them all, on land or sea. Broken-down, forsooth! We will hear no such words from you, sir, for a score of years. And now you will want all your wits to take your proper place at Court as sage counsellor and friend of the new King. Sure he will need his father's friends about him to teach him statecraft—he who has led such a gay, good-for-nothing life as a penniless rover, with scarce a sound coat to his back."

"Nay, Hyacinth, the King will have no need of us old Malignants. We have had our day. He has shrewd Ned Hyde for counsellor, and in that one long head there is craft enough to govern a kingdom. The new Court will be a young Court, and the fashion of it will be new. We old fellows, who were gallant and gay enough in the forties, when we fought against Essex and his tawny scarves, would be but laughable figures at the Court of a young man bred half in Paris, and steeped in French fashions and French follies. No, Hyacinth, it is for you and your husband the new day dawns. If I get back to my old meads and woods and the house where I was born, I will sit quietly down in the chimney corner, and take to cattle-breeding, and a pack of harriers, for the diversion of my declining years. And when my Angela can make up her mind to leave her good aunt she shall keep house for me."

"I should love to be your housekeeper, dearest father. If it please Heaven to restore my aunt to health and strength, I will go to you with a heart full of joy," said the girl, hanging caressingly upon the old cavalier's shoulder.

Hyacinth flitted about the room with a swift, birdlike motion, looking at the sacred images and prints, the *tableau* over the mantelpiece, which told, with much flourish of penmanship, the progress of the convent pupils in learning and domestic virtues.

"What a humdrum, dismal room!" she cried. "You should see our convent parlours in Paris. At the Carmelites, in the Rue Saint Jacques, *par exemple,* the

Queen-mother's favourite convent, and at Chaillot, the house founded by Queen Henrietta—such pictures, and ornaments, and embroidered hangings, and tapestries worked by devotees. This room of yours, sister, stinks of poverty, as your Flemish streets stink of garlic and cabbage. Faugh! I know not which is worse!"

Having thus delivered herself of her disgust, she darted upon her younger sister, laid her hands upon the girl's shoulders, and contemplated her with mock seriousness.

"What a precocious young saint thou art, with no more interest in the world outside this naked parlour than if thou wert yonder image of the Holy Mother. Not a question of my husband, or my children, or of the last fashion in hood and mantle, or of the new laced gloves, or the French King's latest divinity."

"I should dearly like to see your children, Hyacinth," answered her sister.

"Ah! they are the most enchanting creatures, the girl a perpetual sunbeam, ethereal, elfish, a being of life and movement, and with a loquacity that never tires; the boy a lump of honey, fat, sleek, lazily beautiful. I am never tired of admiring them, when I have time to see them. Papillon—an old friend of mine has surnamed her Papillon because she is never still—was five years old on March 19. We were at St. Germain on her birthday. You should have seen the toys and trinkets and sweetmeats which the Court showered upon her—the King and Queen, Monsieur, Mademoiselle, the Princess Henrietta, her godmother—everybody had a gift for the daughter of La folle Baronne Fareham. Yes, they are lovely creatures, Angela; and I am miserable to think that it may be half a year before I see their sweet faces again."

"Why so long, sister?"

"Because they are at the Château de Montrond, grandmother's place near Dieppe, and because Fareham and I are going hence to Breda to meet the King, our own King Charles, and help lead him home in triumph. In London the mob are shouting, roaring, singing, for their King; and Montagu's fleet lies in the Downs, waiting but the signal from Parliament to cross to Holland. He who left his country in a scurvy fishing-boat will go back to England in a mighty man-of-war, the *Naseby*—mark you, the *Naseby*—christened by that Usurper, in insolent remembrance of a rebel victory; but Charles will doubtless change that hated name. He must not be put in mind of a fight where rebels had the better of loyal gentlemen. He will sail home over those dancing seas, with a fleet of great white-winged ships circling round him like a flight of silvery doves. Oh, what a turn of fortune's wheel! I am wild with rapture at the thought of it!"

"You love England better than France, though you must be almost a stranger there," said Angela, wonderingly, looking at a miniature which her sister wore in a bracelet.

"Nay, love, 'tis in Paris I am an insignificant alien, though they are ever so kind and flattering to me. At St. Germain I am only Madame de Montrond's granddaughter—the wife of a somewhat morose gentleman who was cleverer at winning battles than at gaining hearts. At Whitehall I shall be Lady Fareham, and shall enjoy my full consequence as the wife of an

English nobleman of ancient lineage and fine estate, for, I am happy to tell you, his lordship's property suffered less than most people's in the rebellion, and anything his father lost when he fought for the good cause will be given back to the son now the good cause is triumphant, with additions, perhaps—an earl's coronet instead of a baron's beggarly pearls. I should like Papillon to be Lady Henrietta."

"And you will send for your children, doubtless, when you are sure all is safe in England?" said Angela, still contemplating the portrait in the bracelet, which her sister had unclasped while she talked. "This is Papillon, I know. What a sweet, kind, mischievous face!"

"Mischievous as a Barbary ape—kind, and sweet as the west wind," said Sir John.

"And your boy?" asked Angela, reclasping the bracelet on the fair, round arm, having looked her fill at the mutinous eyes, the brown, crisply curling hair, dainty, pointed chin, and dimpled cheeks. "Have you his picture, too?"

"Not his; but I wear his father's likeness somewhere betwixt buckram and Flanders lace," answered Hyacinth, gaily, pulling a locket from amidst the splendours of her corsage. "I call it next my heart; but there is a stout fortification of whalebone between heart and picture. You have gloated enough on the daughter's impertinent visage. Look now at the father, whom she resembles in little, as a kitten resembles a tiger."

She handed her sister an oval locket, bordered with diamonds, and held by a slender Indian chain; and Angela saw the face of the brother-in-law whose kindness and hospitality had been so freely promised to her.

She explored the countenance long and earnestly.

"Well, do you think I chose him for his beauty?" asked Hyacinth. "You have devoured every lineament with that serious gaze of yours, as if you were trying to read the spirit behind that mask of flesh. Do you think him handsome?"

Angela faltered: but was unskilled in flattery, and could not reply with a compliment.

"No, sister; surely none have ever called this countenance handsome; but it is a face to set one thinking."

"Ay, child, and he who owns the face is a man to set one thinking. He has made me think many a time when I would have travelled a day's journey to escape the thoughts he forced upon me. He was not made to bask in the sunshine of life. He is a stormy petrel. It was for his ugliness I chose him. Those dark stern features, that imperious mouth, and a brow like the Olympian Jove. He scared me into loving him. I sheltered myself upon his breast from the thunder of his brow, the lightning of his eye."

"He has a look of his cousin Wentworth," said Sir John. "I never see him but I think of that murdered man—my father's friend and mine—whom I have never ceased to mourn."

"Yet their kin is of the most distant," said Hyacinth. "It is strange that there should be any likeness."

"Faces appear and reappear in families," answered her father. "You may observe that curiously recurring likeness in any picture-gallery, if the family portraits cover a century or two. Louis has little in common with his grandfather; but two hundred years hence there may be a prince of the royal house whose every feature shall recall Henry the Great.

The portrait was returned to its hiding-place, under perfumed lace and cobweb lawn, and the reverend mother entered the parlour, ready for conversation, and eager to hear the history of the last six weeks, of the collapse of that military despotism which had convulsed England and dominated Europe, and was now melting into thin air as ghosts dissolve at cock-crow, of the secret negotiations between Monk and Grenville, now known to everybody; of the King's gracious amnesty and promise of universal pardon, save for some score or so of conspicuous villains, whose hands were dyed with the Royal Martyr's blood.

She was full of questioning: and, above all, eager to know whether it was true that King Charles was at heart as staunch a papist as his brother the Duke of York was believed to be, though even the Duke lacked the courage to bear witness to the true faith.

Two lay-sisters brought in a repast of cakes and syrups and light wines, such delicate and dainty food as the pious ladies of the convent were especially skilled in preparing, and which they deemed all-sufficient for the entertainment of company! even when one of their guests was a rugged soldier like Sir John Kirkland. When the light collation had been tasted and praised, the coach came to the door again, and swallowed up the beautiful lady and the old cavalier, who vanished from Angela's sight in a cloud of dust, waving hands from the coach window.

CHAPTER III.

LETTERS FROM HOME.

THE quiet days went by, and grew into years, and time was only marked by the gradual failure of the reverend mother's health; so gradual, so gentle a decay, that it was only when looking back on St. Sylvester's Eve that her great-niece became aware how much of strength and activity had been lost since the Superior knelt in her place near the altar, listening to the solemn music of the midnight Mass that sanctified the passing of the year. This year the reverend mother was led to her seat between two nuns, who sustained her feeble limbs. This year the meek knees, which had worn the marble floor in long hours of prayer during eighty pious years, could no longer bend. The meek head was bowed, the bloodless hands were lifted up in supplication, but the fingers were wasted and stiffened, and there was pain in every movement of the joints.

There was no actual malady, only the slow death in life called old age. All the patient needed was rest and tender nursing. This last her great-niece supplied, together with the gentlest companionship. No highly trained nurse, the product of modern science, could have been more efficient than the instinct of affection had made Angela. And then the patient's temper was so

amiable, her mind, undimmed after eighty-three years of
life, was a mirror of God. She thought of her fellow-
creatures with a Divine charity; she worshipped her
Creator with an implicit faith. For her in many a
waking vision the heavens opened and the spirits of departed saints descended from their abode in bliss to
hold converse with her. Eighty years of her life had
been given to religious exercises and charitable deeds.
Motherless before she could speak, she had entered the
convent as a pupil at three years of age, and had taken
the veil at seventeen. Her father had married a great
heiress, whose only child, a daughter, was allowed to
absorb all the small stock of parental affection; and
there was no one to dispute Anastasia's desire for the
cloister. All she knew of the world outside those walls
was from hearsay. A rare visit from her lovely half-sister,
the Marquise de Montrond, had astonished her with the
sight of a distinguished Parisienne, and left her wondering. She had never read a secular book. She knew not
the meaning of the word pleasure, save in the mild
amusements permitted to the convent children —
"children" till they left the convent as young women
—on the evening of a saint's day; a stately dance of
curtsyings and waving arms; a little childish play,
dramatising some incident in the lives of the saints. So
she lived her eighty years of obedience and quiet usefulness, learning and teaching, serving and governing. She
had lived through the Thirty Years' War, through the
devastations of Wallenstein, the cruelties of Bavarian
Tilly, the judicial murder of Egmont and Horn. She
had heard of villages burnt, populations put to the sword,
women and children killed by thousands. She had con-

versed with those who remembered the League; she had
seen the nuns weeping for Edward Campion's cruel fate;
she had heard Masses sung for the soul of murdered
Mary Stuart. She had heard of Raleigh's visions of
conquest and of gold, setting his prison-blanched face
towards the West, in the afternoon of life, to encounter
bereavement, treachery, sickening failure, and go back to
his native England to expiate the dreams of genius with
the blood of a martyr. And through all the changes
and chances of that eventful century she had lived apart,
full of pity and wonder, in a charmed circle of piety
and love.

Her room, in these peaceful stages of the closing
scene, was a haven of rest. Angela loved the seclusion
of the panelled chamber, with its heavily mullioned casement facing the south-west, and the polished oak floor,
on which the red and gold of the sunset were mirrored,
as on the dark stillness of a moorland tarn. For her
every object in the room had its interest or its charm.
The associations of childhood hallowed them all. The
large ivory crucifix, yellow with age, dim with the kisses
of adoring lips; the delf statuettes of Mary and Joseph,
flaming with gaudy colour; the figure of the Saviour and
St. John the Baptist, delicately carved out of boxwood, in
a group representing the baptism in the river Jordan, the
holy dove trembling on a wire over the Divine head; the
books, the pictures, the rosaries: all these she had gazed
at reverently when all things were new, and the convent
passages places of shuddering, and the service of the
Mass an unintelligible mystery. She had grown up within
those solemn walls; and now, seeing her kinswoman's
life gently ebbing away, she could but wonder what she

would have to do in this world when another took the Superior's place, and the tie that bound her to Louvain would be broken.

The lady who would in all probability succeed Mother Anastasia as Superior was a clever, domineering woman, whom Angela loved least of all the nuns—a widow of good birth and fortune, and a thorough Fleming; stolid, bigoted, prejudiced, and taking much credit to herself for the wealth she had brought to the convent, apt to talk of the class-room and the chapel her money had helped to build and restore as "my class-room," or "my chapel."

No; Angela had no desire to remain in the convent when her dear kinswoman should have vanished from the scene her presence sanctified. The house would be haunted with sorrowful memories. It would be time for her to claim that home which her father had talked of sharing with her in his old age. She could just faintly remember the house in which she was born—the moat, the fish-pond, the thick walls of yew, the peacocks and lions cut in box, of which the gardener who clipped them was so proud. Faintly, faintly, the picture of the old house came back to her; built of grey stone, and stained with moss, grave and substantial, occupying three sides of a quadrangle, a house of many windows, few of which were intended to open, a house of dark passages, like these in the convent, and flights of shallow steps, and curious turns and twistings here and there. There were living birds that sunned their spreading tails and stalked in slow stateliness on the turf terraces, as well as those peacocks clipped out of yew. The house lay in a Buckinghamshire valley, shut round and sheltered by hills and coppices, where there was an abundance of game. Angela had seen the low, cavern-like larder hung with pheasants and hares.

Her heart yearned towards the old house, so distinctly pictured by memory, though perchance with some differences from the actual scene. The mansion would seem smaller to her, doubtless, beholding it with the eyes of womanhood, than childish memory made it. But to live there with her father, to wait upon him and tend him, to have Hyacinth's children there, playing in the gardens as she had played, would be as happy a life as her fancy could compass.

All that she knew of the march of events during those tranquil years in the convent came to her in letters from her sister, who was a vivacious letter-writer, and prided herself upon her epistolary talent—as indeed upon her general superiority, from a literary standpoint, to the women of her day.

It was a pleasure to Lady Fareham in some rare interval of solitude—when the weather was too severe for her to venture outside the hall door, even in her comfortable coach, and when by some curious concatenation she happened to be without visitors—to open her portfolio and prattle with her pen to her sister, as she would have prattled with her tongue to the visitors whom snow or tempest kept away. Her letters written from London were apt to be rare and brief, Angela noted; but from his lordship's mansion near Oxford, or at the Grange between Fareham and Winchester—once the property of the brothers of St. Cross—she always sent a budget. Few of these lengthy epistles contained anything bearing upon Angela's own existence—except

the oft-repeated entreaty that she would make haste and
join them—or even the flippant suggestion that Mother
Anastasia should make haste and die.   They were of the
nature of news-letters; but the news was tinctured by
the feminine medium through which it came, and there
was a flavour of egotism in almost every page.   Lady
Fareham wrote as only a pretty woman, courted, flattered,
and indulged by everybody about her, ever since she
could remember, could be forgiven for writing.   People
had petted her and worshipped her with such uniform
subservience that she had grown to thirty years of age
without knowing that she was selfish, accepting homage
and submission as a law of the universe, as kings and
princes do.

Only in one of those letters was there that which
might be called a momentous fact, but which Angela
took as easily as if it had been a mere detail, to be
dismissed from her thoughts when the letter had been
laid aside.

It was a letter with a black seal, announcing the
death of the Marquise de Montrond, who had expired
of an apoplexy at her house in the Marais, after a
supper party at which Mademoiselle, Madame de Longueville, Madame de Montausier, the Duchesse de Bouillon,
Lauzun, St. Evremond, cheery little Godeau, Bishop of
Vence, and half a dozen other famous wits had been
present, a supper bristling with royal personages.   Death
had come with appalling suddenness while the lamps of
the festival were burning, and the cards were still upon
the tables, and the last carriage had but just rolled
under the *porte cochère*.

"It is the manner of death she would have chosen,"

wrote Hyacinth. "She never missed confession on the
first Sunday of the month; and she was so generous to
the Church and to the poor that her director declared
she would have been too saintly for earth, but for the
human weakness of liking fine company. And now,
dearest, I have to tell you how she has disposed of her
fortune; and I hope, if you should think she has not
used you generously, you will do me the justice to believe that I have neither courted her for her wealth
nor influenced her to my dear sister's disadvantage.
You will consider, *très chère,* that I was with her from
my eighth year until the other day when Fareham
brought me to England. She loved me passionately in
my childhood, and has often told me since that she
never felt towards me as a grandmother, but as if she
had been actually my mother, being indeed still a young
woman when she adopted me, and by strangers always
mistaken for my mother. She was handsome to the
last, and young in mind and in habits long after youth
had left her. I was said to be the image of what she
was when she rivalled Madame de Hautefort in the
affections of the late King. You must consider, sweetheart, that he was the most moral of men, and that
with him love meant a passion as free from sensual
taint as the preferences of a sylph. I think my good
grandmother loved me all the better for this fancied
resemblance. She would arrange her jewels about my
hair and bosom, as she had worn them when Buckingham came wooing for his master; and then she would
bid her page hold a mirror before me and tell me to
look at the face of which Queen Anne had been jealous,
and for which Cinq Mars had run mad. And then she

would shed a tear or two over the years and the charms
that were gone, till I brought the cards and cheered her
spirits with her favourite game of primero.

"She had her fits of temper and little tantrums
sometimes, Ange, and it needed some patience to restrain
one's tongue from insolence; but I am happy to remember that I ever bore her in profound respect, and
that I never made her seriously angry but once—which
was when I, being then almost a child, went out into the
streets of Paris with Henri de Malfort and a wild party,
masked, to hear Beaufort address the populace in the
market-place, and when I was so unlucky as to lose the
emerald cross given her by the great Cardinal, for whom,
I believe, she had a sneaking kindness. Why else should
she have so hated his Eminence's very much favoured
niece, Madame de Combalet?

"But to return to that which concerns my dear sister.
Regarding me as her own daughter, the Marquise has
lavished her bounties upon me almost to the exclusion
of my own sweet Angela. In a word, dearest, she
leaves you a modest income of four hundred louis—or
about three hundred pounds sterling—the rental of two
farms in Normandy; and all the rest of her fortune she
bequeaths to me, and Papillon after me, including her
house in the Marais—sadly out of fashion now that
everybody of consequence is moving to the Place Royale
—and her château near Dieppe; besides all her jewels,
many of which I have had in my possession ever since
my marriage. My sweet sister shall take her choice of a
carcanet among those old-fashioned trinkets. And now,
dearest, if you are left with a pittance that will but serve
to pay for your gloves and fans at the Middle Exchange,

and perhaps to buy you an Indian nightgown in the
course of the year—for your Court petticoats and man-
tuas will cost three times as much—you have but to
remember that my purse is to be yours, and my home
yours, and that Fareham and I do but wait to welcome
you either to Fareham House, in the Strand, or to Chiltern
Abbey, near Oxford. The Grange near Fareham I never
intend to re-enter if I can help it. The place is a
warren of rats, which the servants take for ghosts. If
you love water you will love our houses, for the river
runs near them both; indeed, when in London, we
almost think ourselves in Venice, save that we have a
spacious garden, which I am told few of the Venetians
can command, their city being built upon an assemblage
of minuscule islets, linked together by innumerable
bridges."

Angela smiled as she looked down at her black
gown—the week-day uniform of the convent school, exchanged for a somewhat superior grey stuff on Sundays
and holidays—smiled at the notion of spending the rent
of two farms upon her toilet. And how much more
ridiculous seemed the assertion that to appear at King
Charles's Court she must spend thrice as much! Yet
she could but remember that Hyacinth had described
trains and petticoats so loaded with jewelled embroidery
that it was a penance to wear them—lace worth hundreds of pounds—plumed hats that cost as much as a
year's maintenance in the convent.

Mother Anastasia expressed considerable displeasure
at Madame de Montrond's disposal of her wealth.

"This is what it is to live in a Court, and to care
only for earthly things!" she said. "All sense of justice

4*

is lost in that world of vanity and self-love. You are as
near akin to the Marquise as your sister; and yet, because she was familiar with the one and not with the
other—and because her vain, foolish soul took pleasure
in a beauty that recalled her own perishable charms, she
leaves one sister a great fortune and the other a pittance!"

"Dear aunt, I am more than content——"

"But I am not content for you, Angela. Had the
estate been divided equally you might have taken the
veil, and succeeded to my place in this beloved house,
which needs the accession of wealth to maintain it in
usefulness and dignity."

Angela would not wound her aunt's feelings by one
word of disparagement of the house in which she had
been reared; but, looking along the dim avenue of the
future, she yearned for some wider horizon than the
sky, barred with tall poplars which rose high above the
garden wall that formed the limit of her daily walks.
Her rambles, her recreations, had all been confined
within that space of seven or eight acres, and she thought
sometimes with a sudden longing of those hills and valleys of fertile Buckinghamshire, which lay so far back
in the dawn of her mind, and were yet so distinctly
pictured in her memory.

And London—that wonderful city of which her sister
wrote in such glowing words! the long range of palaces
beside the swift-flowing river, wider than the Seine
where it reflects the gloomy bulk of the Louvre and the
Temple! Were it only once in her life, she would like
to see London—the King, the two Queens, Wh tehall,
and Somerset House. She would like to see all the
splendour of Court and city; and then to taste the

placid retirement of the house in the valley, and to be her father's housekeeper and companion.

Another letter from Hyacinth announced the death of Mazarin.

"The Cardinal is no more. He died in the day of success, having got the better of all his enemies. A violent access of gout was followed by an affection of the chest which proved fatal. His sick-room was crowded with courtiers and sycophants, and he was selling sinecures up to the day of his death. Fareham says his death-bed was like a money-changer's counter. He was passionately fond of hocca, the Italian game which he brought into fashion, and which ruined half the young men about the Court. The counterpane was scattered with money and playing cards, which were only brushed aside to make room for the last Sacraments. My Lord Clarendon declares that his spirits never recovered from the shock of his Majesty's restoration, which falsified all his calculations. He might have made his favourite niece Queen of England; but his Italian caution restrained him, and the beautiful Hortense has to put up with a new-made duke—a title bought with her uncle's money—to whom the Cardinal affianced her on his death-bed. He was a remarkable man, and so profound a dissembler that his pretended opposition to King Louis' marriage with his niece Olympe Mancini would have deceived the shrewdest observer, had we not all known that he ardently desired the union, and that it was only his fear of Queen Anne's anger which prevented it. Her Spanish pride was in arms at the notion, and she would not have stopped short at revolution to prevent or to revenge such an alliance.

"This was perhaps the only occasion upon which she ever seriously opposed Mazarin. With him expires all her political power. She is now as much a cypher as in the time of the late King, when France had only one master, the great Cardinal. He who is just dead, Fareham says, was but a little Richelieu; and he recalls how when the great Cardinal died people scarce dared tell one another of his death, so profound was the awe in which he was held. He left the King a nullity, and the Queen all powerful. She was young and beautiful then, you see; her husband was marked for death, her son was an infant. All France was hers—a kingdom of courtiers and flatterers. And now she is old and ailing; and Mazarin being gone, the young King will submit to no minister who claims to be anything better than a clerk or a secretary. Colbert he must tolerate —for Colbert means prosperity—but Colbert will have to obey. My friend, the Duchesse de Longueville, who is now living in strict retirement, writes me the most exquisite letters; and from her I hear all that happens in that country which I sometimes fancy is more my own than the duller climate where my lot is now cast. Fifteen years at the French Court have made me in heart and mind almost a Frenchwoman; nor can I fail to be influenced by my maternal ancestry. I find it difficult sometimes to remember my English, when conversing with the clodhoppers of Oxfordshire, who have no French, yet insist, for finery's sake, upon larding their rustic English with French words.

"All that is most agreeable in our court is imitated from the Palais Royal and the Louvre.

"'Whitehall is but the shadow of a shadow,' says

Fareham, in one of his philosophy fits, preaching upon the changes he has seen in Paris and London. And, indeed, it is strange to have lived through two revolutions, one so awful in its final catastrophe that it dwarfs the other, yet both terrible; for I, who was a witness of the sufferings of Princes and Princesses during the two wars of the Fronde, am not inclined to think lightly of a civil war which cost France some of the flower of her nobility, and made her greatest hero a prisoner and an exile for seven years of his life.

"But oh, my dear, it was a romantic time! and I look back and am proud to have lived in it. I was but twelve years old at the siege of Paris; but I was in Madame de Longueville's room, at the Hôtel de Ville, while the fighting was going on, and the officers, in their steel cuirasses, coming in from the thick of the strife. Such a confusion of fine ladies and armed men—breast-plates and blue scarves—fiddles squeaking in the salon, trumpets sounding in the square below!"

* * * * *

In a letter of later date Lady Fareham expatiated upon the folly of her sister's spiritual guides.

"I am desolated, *ma mie,* by the absurd restriction which forbids you to profit by my New Year's gift. I thought, when I sent you all the volumes of la Scudèry's enchanting romance, I had laid up for you a year of enjoyment, and that, touched by the baguette of that exquisite fancy, your convent walls would fall, like those of Jericho at the sound of Jewish trumpets, and you would be transported in imagination to the finest society in the world—the company of Cyrus and Mandane—under which Oriental disguise you are shown every

feature of mind and person in Condé and his heroic
sister, my esteemed friend, the Duchesse de Longueville. As I was one of the first to appreciate Mademoiselle Scudèry's genius, and to detect behind the
name of the brother the tender sentiments and delicate
refinement of the sister's chaster pen, so I believe I was
the first to call the Duchesse 'Mandane,' a sobriquet
which soon became general among her intimates.

"You are not to read 'Le Grand Cyrus,' your aunt
tells you, because it is a romance! That is to say, you
are forbidden to peruse the most faithful history of your
own time, and to familiarise yourself with the persons
and minds of great people whom you may never be so
fortunate as to meet in the flesh. I myself, dearest
Ange, have had the felicity to live among these princely
persons, to revel in the conversations of the Hôtel de
Rambouillet—not, perhaps, as our grandmother would
have told you, in its most glorious period—but at least
while it was still the focus of all that is choicest in letters and in art. Did we not hear M. Poquelin read his
first comedy before it was represented by Monsieur's
company in the beautiful theatre at the Palais Royal,
built by Richelieu, when it was the Palais Cardinal?
Not read 'Le Grand Cyrus,' and on the score of
morality! Why, this most delightful book was written
by one of the most moral women in Paris—one of the
chastest—against whose reputation no word of slander
has ever been breathed! It must, indeed, be confessed
that Sapho is of an ugliness which would protect her even
were she not guarded by the ægis of genius. She is
one of those fortunate unfortunates who can walk through
the furnace of a Court unscathed, and leave a reputa-

tion for modesty in an age that scarce credits virtue in woman.

"I fear, dear child, that these narrow-minded restrictions of your convent will leave you of a surpassing ignorance, which may cover you with confusion when you find yourself in fine company. There are accomplishments without which youth is no more admired than age and grey hairs; and to sparkle with wit or astonish with learning is a necessity for a woman of quality. It is only by the advantages of education that we can show ourselves superior to such a hussy as Albemarle's gutter-bred duchess, who was the faithless wife of a sailor or barber—I forget which—and who hangs like a millstone upon the General's neck now that he has climbed to the zenith. To have perfect Italian and some Spanish is as needful as to have fine eyes and complexion nowadays. And to dance admirably is a gift indispensable to a lady. Alas! I fear that those little feet of yours—I hope they *are* small—have never been taught to move in a coranto or a contre-danse, and that you will have to learn the alphabet of dancing at an age when most women are finished performers. The great Condé, while winning sieges and battles that surpassed the feats of Greeks and Romans, contrived to make himself the finest dancer of his day, and won more admiration in high-bred circles by his graceful movements, which everyone could understand and admire, than by prodigies of valour at Dunkirk or Nordlingen."

The above was one of Lady Fareham's most serious letters. Her pen was exercised, for the most part, in a lighter vein. She wrote of the Court beauties, the Court jests—practical jokes some of them, which our finer minds of to-day would consider in execrable taste—such jests as we read of in Grammont's memoirs, which generally aimed at making an ugly woman ridiculous, or an injured husband the sport and victim of wicked lover and heartless wife. No sense of the fitness of things constrained her ladyship from communicating these Court scandals to her guileless sister. Did they not comprise the only news worth anybody's attention, and relate to the only class of people who had any tangible existence for Lady Fareham? There were millions of human beings, no doubt, living and acting and suffering on the surface of the earth, outside the stellary circles of which Louis and Charles were the suns; but there was no interstellar medium of sympathy to convey the idea of those exterior populations to Hyacinth's mind. She knew of the populace, French or English, as of something which was occasionally given to become dangerous and revolutionary, which sometimes starved and sometimes died of the plague, and was always unpleasing to the educated eye.

Masquerades, plays, races at Newmarket, dances, duels, losses at cards—Lady Fareham touched every subject, and expatiated on all; but she had usually more to tell of the country she had left than of that in which she was living.

"Here everything is on such a small scale, *si mesquin!*" she wrote. "Whitehall covers a large area, but it is only a fine banqueting hall and a labyrinth of lodgings, without suite or stateliness. The pictures in the late King's cabinet are said to be the finest in the world, but they are a kind of pieces for which I care

very little—Flemish and Dutch chiefly—with a series of
cartoons by Raphael, which connoisseurs affect to admire, but which, did they belong to me, I would gladly
exchange for a set of Mortlake tapestries.

"His Majesty here builds ships, while the King of
France builds palaces. I am told Louis in spending
millions on the new palace at Versailles, an ungrateful
site—no water, no noble prospect as at St. Germain, no
population. The King likes the spot all the better,
Madame tells me, because he has to create his own
landscape, to conjure lakes and cataracts out of dry
ground. The buildings have been but two years in
progress, and it must be long before these colossal
foundations are crowned with the edifice which Louis
and his architect, Mansart, have planned. Colbert is
furious at this squandering of vast sums on a provincial
palace, while the Louvre, the birthplace and home of
dynasties, remains unfinished.

"The King's reason for disliking St. Germain—a
château his mother has always loved—has in it something childish and fantastic, if, as my dear duchess declares, he hates the place only because he can see
the towers of St. Denis from the terrace, and is thus
hourly reminded of death and the grave. I can hardly
believe that a being of such superior intelligence could
be governed by any such horror of man's inevitable end.
I would far sooner attribute the vast expenditure of
Versailles to the common love of monarchs and great
men for building houses too large for their necessities.
Indeed, it was but yesterday that Fareham took me to
see the palace—for I can call it by no meaner name
—that Lord Clarendon is building for himself in the

open country at the top of St. James's Street. It promises to be the finest house in town, and, although not
covering so much ground as Whitehall, is judged far
superior to that inchoate mass in its fine proportions
and the perfect symmetry of its saloons and galleries.
There is a garden a-making, projected by Mr. Evelyn,
a great authority on trees and gardens. A crowd of
fine company had assembled to see the newly finished
hall and dining parlour, among them a fussy person,
who came in attendance upon my Lord Sandwich, and
who was more voluble than became his quality as a
clerk in the Navy Office. He was periwigged and dressed
as fine as his master, and, on my being civil to him,
talked much of himself and of divers taverns in the city
where the dinners were either vastly good or vastly ill.
I told him that as I never dined at a tavern the subject
was altogether beyond the scope of my intelligence, at
which Sandwich and Fareham laughed, and my per-
tinacious gentleman blushed as red as the heels of his
shoes. I am told the creature has a pretty taste in
music, and is the son of a tailor, but professes a genteel
ancestry, and occasionally pushes into the best company.

"Shall I describe to you one of my latest conquests,
sweetheart? 'Tis a boy—an actual beardless boy of
eighteen summers; but such a boy! So beautiful, so
insolent, with an impudence that can confront Lord
Clarendon himself, the gravest of noblemen, who, with
the sole exception of my Lord Southampton, is the one
man who has never crossed Mrs. Palmer's threshold,
or bowed his neck under that splendid fury's yoke. My
admirer thinks no more of smoking these grave nobles,

men of a former generation, who learnt their manners at the court of a serious and august King, than I do of teasing my falcon. He laughs at them, jokes with them in Greek or in Latin, has a ready answer and a witty quip for every turn of the discourse; will even interrupt his Majesty in one of those anecdotes of his Scottish martyrdom which he tells so well and tells so often. Lucifer hmiself could not be more arrogant or more audacious than this bewitching boy-lover of mine, who writes verses in English or Latin as easy as I can toss a shuttle-cock. I doubt the greater number of his verses are scarce proper reading for you or me, Angela; for I see the men gather round him in corners as he murmurs his latest madrigal to a chosen half-dozen or so; and I guess by their subdued tittering that the lines are not over modest; while by the sidelong glances the listeners cast round, now at my Lady Castlemaine, and anon at some other goddess in the royal pantheon, I have a shrewd notion as to what alabaster breast my witty lover's shafts are aimed at.

"This youthful devotee of mine is the son of a certain Lord Wilmot, who fought on the late King's side in the troubles. This creature went to the university of Oxford at twelve years old—as it were, straight from his go-cart to college, and was master of arts at fourteen. He has made the grand tour, and pretends to have seen so much of this life that he has found out the worthlessness of it. Even while he wooes me with a most romantic ardour, he affects to have outgrown the capacity to love.

"Think not, dearest, that I outstep the bounds of matronly modesty by this airy philandering with my

young Lord Rochester, or that my serious Fareham is
ever offended at our pretty trifling.   He laughs at the
lad as heartily as I do, invites him to our table, and is
amused by his monkeyish tricks.   A woman of quality
must have followers; and a pert, fantastical boy is the
safest of lovers.   Slander itself could scarce accuse Lady
Fareham, who has had soldier-princes and statesmen at
her feet, of an unworthy tenderness for a jackanapes of
seventeen; for, indeed, I believe his eighteenth birthday
is still in the womb of time.   I would with all my heart
thou wert here to share our innocent diversions; and I
know not which of all my playthings thou wouldst
esteem highest, the falcon, my darling spaniels, made
up of soft silken curls and intelligent brown eyes, or
Rochester.   Nay, let me not forget the children, Papillon and Cupid, who are truly very pretty creatures,
though consummate plagues.   The girl, Papillon, has a
tongue which Wilmot says is the nearest approach to
perpetual motion that he has yet discovered; and the
boy, who was but seven last birthday, is full of mischief,
in which my admirer counsels and abets him.

"Oh, this London, sweetheart, and this Court! How
wide those violet eyes would open couldst thou but look
suddenly in upon us after supper at Basset, or in the
park, or at the playhouse, when the orange girls are
smoking the pretty fellows in the pit, and my Lady
Castlemaine is leaning half out of her box to talk to the
King in his!   I thought I had seen enough of festivals
and dances, stage-plays and courtly diversions beyond
sea; but the Court entertainments at Paris or St.
Germain differed as much from the festivities of Whitehall as a cathedral service from a dance in a booth at

Bartholomew Fair.   His Majesty of France never forgets
that he is a king.   His Majesty of England only re-
members his kingship when he wants a new subsidy, or
to get a Bill hurried through the Houses.   Louis at
four-and-twenty was serious enough for fifty.   Charles at
thirty-four has the careless humour of a schoolboy.   He
is royal in nothing except his extravagance, which has
squandered more millions than I dare mention since he
landed at Dover.

"I am growing almost as sober as my solemn spouse,
who will ever be railing at the King and the Duke, and
even more bitterly at the favourite, his Grace of Buckingham, who is assuredly one of the most agreeable men
in London.   I asked Fareham only yesterday why he
went to Court, if his Majesty's company is thus distasteful to him.   "It is not to his company I object, but to
his principles," he answered, in that earnest fashion of
his which takes the lightest questions *au grand serieux.*
"I see in him a man who, with natural parts far above
the average, makes himself the jest of meaner intellects,
and the dupe of greedy courtesans; a man who, trained
in the stern school of adversity, overshadowed by the
great horror of his father's tragical doom, accepts life as
one long jest, and being, by a concatenation of circumstances bordering on the miraculous, restored to the
privileges of hereditary monarchy, takes all possible
pains to prove the uselessness of kings.   I see a man
who, borne back to power by the irresistible current of
the people's affections, has broken every pledge he gave
that people in the flush and triumph of his return.   I
see one who, in his own person, cares neither for Paul
nor Peter, and yet can tamely witness the persecution

of his people because they do not conform to a State
religion—can allow good and pious men to be driven
out of the pulpits where they have preached the Gospel
of Christ, and suffer wives and children to starve because the head of the household has a conscience. I
see a king careless of the welfare of his people, and
the honour and glory of his reign; affecting to be a
patriot, and a man of business, on the strength of an
extravagant fancy for shipbuilding; careless of everything
save the empty pleasure of an idle hour. A king who
lavishes thousands upon wantons and profligates, and
who ever gives not to the most worthy, but to the most
importunate."

"I laughed at this tirade, and told him, what indeed
I believe, that he is at heart a Puritan, and would better
consort with Baxter and Bunyan, and that frousy crew,
than with Buckhurst and Sedley, or his brilliant kinsman, Roscommon."

From her father directly, Angela heard nothing, and
her sister's allusions to him were of the briefest, anxiously
as she had questioned that lively letter-writer. Yes, her
father was well, Hyacinth told her; but he stayed mostly
at the Manor Moat. He did not care for the Court
gaieties.

"I believe he thinks we have all parted company
with our wits," she wrote. "He seldom sees me but to
lecture me, in a sidelong way, upon my folly; for his
railing at the company I keep hits me by implication. I
believe these old courtiers of the late King are Puritans
at heart; and that if Archbishop Laud were alive he
would be as bitter against the sins of the town as any
of the cushion-thumping Anabaptists that preach to the

elect in back rooms and blind alleys. My father talks
and thinks as if he had spent all his years of exile in
the cave of the Seven Sleepers. And yet he fought
shoulder to shoulder with some of the finest gentlemen
in France—Condé, Turenne, Gramont, St. Evremond,
Bussy, and the rest of them. But all the world is
young, and full of wit and mirth, since his Majesty came
to his own; and elderly limbs are too stiff to trip in our
new dances. I doubt my father's mind is as old-
fashioned, and of as rigid a shape as his Court suit, at
sight of which my best friends can scarce refrain from
laughing."

This light mention of a parent whom she reverenced
wounded Angela to the quick; and that wound was
deepened a year later, when she was surprised by a
visit from her father, of which no letter had forewarned
her. She was walking in the convent garden, in her
hour of recreation, tasting the sunny air, and the beauty
of the many-coloured tulips in the long narrow borders,
between two espalier rows trained with an exquisite
neatness, and reputed to bear the finest golden pippins
and Bergamot pears within fifty miles of the city. The
trees were in blossom, and a wall of pink and white
bloom rose up on either hand above the scarlet and
amber tulips.

Turning at the end of the long alley, where it met a
wall that in August was flushed with the crimson velvet
of peaches and nectarines, Angela saw a man advancing
from the further end of the walk, attended by a lay
sister. The high-crowned hat and pointed beard, the
tall figure in a grey doublet crossed with a black sword-
belt, the walk, the bearing, were unmistakable. It might

have been a figure that had stepped out of Vandyke's
canvas.   It had nothing of the fuss and flutter, the
feathers and ruffles, the loose flow of brocade and velvet,
that marked the costume of the young French Court.

Angela ran to receive her father, and could scarce
speak to him, she was so startled, and yet so glad.

"Oh, sir, when I prayed for you at Mass this morning,
how little I hoped for so much happiness! I had a letter
from Hyacinth only a week ago, and she wrote nothing
of your intentions.   I knew not that you had crossed
the sea."

"Why, sweetheart, Hyacinth sees me too rarely, and
is too full of her own affairs, ever to be beforehand with
my intentions; and, although I have been long heartily
sick of England, I only made up my mind to come to
Flanders less than a week ago.   No sooner thought of
than done.   I came by our old road, in a merchant
craft from Harwich to Ostend, and the rest of the way
in the saddle.   Not quite so fast as they used to ride
that carried his Majesty's post from London to York, in
the beginning of the troubles, when the loyal gentlemen
along the north road would galop faster with despatches
and treaties than ever they rode after a stag.   Ah, child,
how hopeful we were in those days; and how we all
told each other it was but a passing storm at Westminster, which could all be lulled by a little civil con-
cession here and there on the King's part!   And so it
might, perhaps, if he would but have conceded the right
thing at the right time—yielded but just the inch they
asked for when they first asked—instead of shilly-shally-
ing till they got angry, and wanted ells instead of inches.

'Tis the stitch in time, Angela, that saves trouble, in politics as well as in thy petticoat."

He had flung his arm round his daughter's neck as they paced slowly side by side.

"Have you come to stay at Louvain, sir?" she asked, timidly.

"Nay, love, the place is too quiet for me. I could not stay in a town that is given over to learning and piety. The sound of their everlasting carillon would tease my ear with the thought, 'Lo, another quarter of an hour gone of my poor remnant of days, and nothing to do but to doze in the sunshine or fondle my spaniel, fill my pipe, or ride a lazy horse on a level road, such as I have ever hated.'"

"But why did you tire of England, sir? I thought the King would have wanted you always near him. You, his father's close friend, who suffered so much for Royal friendship. Surely he loves and cherishes you! He must be a base, ungrateful man if he do not."

"Oh, the King is grateful, Angela, grateful enough and to spare. He never sees me at Court but he has some gracious speech about his father's regard for me. It grows irksome at last, by sheer repetition. The turn of the sentence varies, for his Majesty has a fine stand-ing army of words, but the gist of the phrase is always the same, and it means, 'Here is a tiresome old Put to whom I must say something civil for the sake of his ancient vicissitudes.' And then his phalanx of foppery stares at me as if I were a Topinambou; and since I have seen them mimic Ned Hyde's stately speech and manners, I doubt not before I have crossed the ante-room I have served to make sport for the crew, since

5*

their wit has but two phases—ordure and mimickry. Look not so glum, daughter. I am glad to be out of a Court which is most like——such places as I dare not name to thee."

"But to have you disrespected, sir; you, so brave, so noble! You who gave the best years of your life to your royal master!"

"What I gave I gave, child. I gave him youth— that never comes back—and fortune, that is not worth grieving for. And now that I have begun to lose the reckoning of my years since fifty, I feel I had best take myself back to that roving life in which I have no time to brood upon losses and sorrows."

"Dear father, I am sure you must mistake the King's feelings towards you. It is not possible that he can think lightly of such devotion as yours."

"Nay, sweetheart, who said he thinks lightly? He never thinks of me at all, or of anything serious under God's sky. So long as he has spending money, and can live in a circle of bright eyes, and hear only flippant tongues that offer him a curious incense of flattery spiced with impertinence, Charles Stuart has all of this life that he values. And for the next—a man who is shrewdly suspected of being a papist, while he is attached by gravest vows to the Church of England, must needs hold heaven's rewards and hell's torments lightly."

"But Queen Catherine, sir—does not she favour you? My aunt says she is a good woman."

"Yes, a good woman, and the nearest approach to a cypher to be found at Hampton Court or Whitehall. Young Lord Rochester has written a poem upon 'Nothing.' He might have taken Queen Catherine's

name as a synonym. She is nothing; she counts for
nothing. Her love can benefit nobody; her hatred, were
the poor soul capable of hating persistently, can do no
one harm."

"And the King—is he so unkind to her?"

"Unkind! No. He allows her to live. Nay, when
for a few days—the brief felicity of her poor life—she
seemed on the point of dying, he was stricken with
remorse for all that he had not been to her, and was
kind, and begged her to live for his sake. The polite
gentleman meant it for a compliment—one of those
pious falsehoods that men murmur in dying ears—but
she took him at his word and recovered; and she is
there still, a little dark lady in a fine gown, of whom
nobody takes any notice, beyond the emptiest formality
of bent knees and backward steps. There are long
evenings at Hampton Court in which she is scarce
spoken to, save when she fawns upon the fortunate lady
whom she began by hating. Oh, child, I should not
talk to you of these things; but some of the disgust that
has made my life bitter bubbles over in spite of me.
I am a wanderer and an exile again, dear heart. I
would sooner trail a pike abroad than suffer neglect at
home. I will fight under any flag so long as it flies not
for my country's foe. I am going back to my old friends
at the Louvre, to those few who are old enough to care
for me; and if there come a war with Spain, why my
sword may be of some small use to young Louis, whose
mother was always gracious to me in the old days at
St. Germain, when she knew not in the morning whether
she would go safe to bed at night. A golden age of
peace has followed that wild time; but the Spanish

king's death is like to light the torch and set the war-
dogs barking. Louis will thrust his sword through the
treaty of the Pyrenees if he see the way to a throne
t'other side of the mountains."

"But could a good man violate a treaty?"

"Ambition knows no laws, sweet, nor ever has since
Hannibal."

"Then King Louis is no better a man than King
Charles?"

"I cannot answer for that, Angela; but I'll warrant
him a better king from the kingly point of view. Scarce
had death freed him from the Cardinal's leading-strings
than he snatched the reins of power, showed his
ministers that he meant to drive the coach. He has a
head as fit for business as if he had been the son of a
woollen-draper. Mazarin took pains to keep him ignorant
of everything that a king ought to know; but that shrewd
judgment of his taught him that he must know as much
as his servants, unless he wanted them to be his masters.
He has the pride of Lucifer, with a strength of will and
power of application as great as Richelieu's. You will
live to see that no second Richelieu, no new Mazarin,
will arise in his reign. His ministers will serve him,
and go down before him, like Nicolas Fouquet, to whom
he has been implacable."

· "Poor gentleman! My aunt told me that when his
judges sentenced him to banishment from France, the
King changed the sentence to imprisonment for life."

"I doubt if the King ever forgave those fêtes at
Vaux, which were designed to dazzle Mademoiselle la
Vallière, whom this man had the presumption to love.
One may pity so terrible a fall, yet it is but the ruin of

a bold sensualist, who played with millions as other men play with tennis balls, and who would have drained the exchequer by his briberies and extravagances if he had not been brought to a dead stop. The world has been growing wickeder, dearest, while this fair head has risen from my knee to my shoulder; but what have you to do with its wickedness? Here you are happy and at peace——"

"Not happy, father, if you are to hazard your life in battles and sieges. Oh, sir, that life is too dear to us, your children, to be risked so lightly. You have done your share of soldiering. Everybody that ever heard your name in England or in France knows it is the name of a brave captain—a leader of men. For our sakes, take your rest now, dear sir. I should not sleep in peace if I knew you were with Condé's army. I should dream of you wounded and dying. I cannot bear to think of leaving my aunt now that she is old and feeble; but my first duty is to you, and if you want me I will go with you wherever you may please to make your home. I am not afraid of strange countries."

"Spoken like my sweet daughter, whose baby arms clasped my neck in the day of despair. But you must stay with the reverend mother, sweetheart. These bones of mine must be something stiffer before they will consent to rest in the chimney corner, or sit in the shade of a yew hedge while other men throw the bowls. When I have knocked about the world a few years longer, and when Mother Anastasia is at rest, thou shalt come to me at the Manor, and I will find thee a noble husband, and will end my days with my children and grandchildren. The world has so changed since the forties, that I shall think I have lived centuries instead of decades, when the farewell hour strikes. In the mean time I am pleased that you should be here. The Court is no place for a pure maiden, though some sweet saints there be who can walk unsmirched in the midst of corruption."

"And Hyacinth? She can walk scatheless through that Court furnace. She writes of Whitehall as if it were Paradise."

"Hyacinth has a husband to take care of her; a man with a brave headpiece of his own, who lets her spark it with the fairest company in the town, but would make short work of any fop who dared attempt the insolence of a suitor. Hyacinth has seen the worst and the best of two Courts, and has an experience of the Palais Royal and St. Germain which should keep her safe at Whitehall."

Sir John and his daughter spent half a day together in the garden and the parlour, where the traveller was entertained with a collation and a bottle of excellent Beaujolais before his horse was brought to the door. Angela saw him mount, and ride slowly away in the melancholy afternoon light, and she felt as if he were riding out of her life for ever. She went back to her aunt's room with an aching heart. Had not that kind lady, her mother in all the essentials of maternal love, been so near the end of her days, and so dependent on her niece's affection, the girl would have clung about her father's neck, and implored him to go no more a-soldiering, and to make himself a home with her in England.

CHAPTER IV.

THE VALLEY OF THE SHADOW.

THE reverend mother lingered till the beginning of summer, and it was on a lovely June evening, while the nightingales were singing in the convent garden, that the holy life slipped away into the Great Unknown. She died as a child falls asleep, the saintly grey head lying peacefully on Angela's supporting arm, the last look of the dying eyes resting on that tender nurse with infinite love.

She was gone, and Angela felt strangely alone. Her contemporaries, the chosen friend who had been to her almost as a sister, the girls by whose side she had sat in class, had all left the convent. At twenty-one years of age, she seemed to belong to a former generation; most of the pupils had finished their education at seventeen or eighteen, and had returned to their homes in Flanders, France, or England. There had been several English pupils, for Louvain and Douai had for a century been the seminaries for English Romanists.

The pupils of to-day were Angela's juniors, with whom she had nothing in common, except to teach English to a class of small Flemings, who were almost unteachable.

She had heard no more from her father, and knew not where or with whom he might have cast in his lot.

She wrote to him under cover to her sister; but of late
Hyacinth's letters had been rare and brief, only long
enough, indeed, to apologise for their brevity. Lady
Fareham had been in London or at Hampton Court
from the beginning of the previous winter. There was
talk of the plague having come to London from Amsterdam, that the Privy Council was sitting at Sion House,
instead of in London, that the judges had removed to
Windsor, and that the Court might speedily remove to
Salisbury or Oxford. "And if the Court goes to Oxford, we shall go to Chilton," wrote Hyacinth; and that
was the last of her communications.

July passed without news from father or sister; and
Angela grew daily more uneasy about both. The great
horror of the plague was in the air. It had been raging
in Amsterdam in the previous summer and autumn, and
a nun had brought the disease to Louvain, where she
might have died in the convent infirmary but for Angela's
devoted attention. She had assisted the over-worked
infirmarian at a time of unusual sickness—for there was
a good deal of illness among the nuns and pupils that
summer—mostly engendered of the fear lest the pestilence in Holland should reach Flanders. Doctor and
infirmarian had alike praised the girl's quiet courage,
and her instinct for doing the right thing.

Remembering all the nun had told of the horrors of
Amsterdam, Angela awaited with fear and trembling for
news from London; and as the summer wore on, every
news-letter that reached the Ursulines brought tidings
of increasing sickness in the great prosperous city, which
was being gradually deserted by all who could afford to
travel. The Court had moved first to Hampton Court,

in June, and later to Salisbury, where again the French Ambassador's people reported strange horrors—corpses found lying in the street hard by their lodgings—the King's servants sickening. The air of the cathedral city was tainted—though deaths had been few as compared with London, which was becoming one vast lazar-house—and it was thought the Court and Ambassadors would remove themselves to Oxford, where Parliament was to assemble in the autumn, instead of at Westminster.

Most alarming of all was the news that the Queen-mother had fled with all her people, and most of her treasures, from her palace at Somerset House—for Henrietta Maria was not a woman to fly before a phantom fear. She had seen too much of the stern realities of life to be scared by shadows; and she had neither establishment nor power in France equal to those she left in England. In Paris the daughter of the great Henry was a dependent. In London she was second only to the King; and her Court was more esteemed than Whitehall.

"If she has fled, there must be reason for it," said the newly elected Superior, who boasted of correspondents at Paris, notably a cousin in that famous convent, the Visitandines de Chaillot, founded by Queen Henrietta, and which had ever been a centre of political and religious intrigue, the most fashionable, patrician, exalted, and altogether worldly establishment.

Alarmed at this dismal news, Angela wrote urgently to her sister, but with no effect; and the passage of every day, with occasional rumours of an increasing death-rate in London, strengthened her fears, until terror nerved her to a desperate resolve. She would go to London to see her sister; to nurse her if she were sick; to mourn for her if she were dead.

The Superior did all she could to oppose this decision, and even asserted authority over the pupil who, since her eighteenth year had been released from discipline, subject but to the lightest laws of the convent. As the great-niece and beloved child of the late Superior she had enjoyed all possible privileges; while the liberal sum annually remitted for her maintenance gave her a certain importance in the house.

And now on being told she must not go, her spirit rose against the Superior's authority.

"I recognise no earthly power that can keep me from those I love in their time of peril!" she said.

"You do not know that they are in sickness or danger. My last letters from Paris stated that it was only the low people whom the contagion in London was attacking."

"If it was only the low people, why did the Queen-mother leave? If it was safe for my sister to be in London it would have been safe for the Queen."

"Lady Fareham is doubtless in Oxfordshire."

"I have written to Chilton Abbey as well as to Fareham House, and I can get no answer. Indeed, reverend mother, it is time for me to go to those to whom I belong. I never meant to stay in this house after my aunt's death. I have only been waiting my father's orders. If all be well with my sister I shall go to the Manor Moat, and wait his commands quietly there. I am home-sick for England."

"You have chosen an ill time for home-sickness, when a pestilence is raging."

Argument could not touch the girl, whose mind was braced for battle. The reverend mother ceded with as good a grace as she could assume, on the top of a very arbitrary temper. An English priest was heard of who was about to travel to London on his return to a noble friend and patron in the north of England, in whose house he had lived before the troubles; and in this good man's charge Angela was permitted to depart, on a long and weary journey by way of Antwerp and the Scheldt. They were five days at sea, the voyage lengthened by the almost unprecedented calm which had prevailed all that fatal summer—a weary voyage in a small trading vessel, on board which Angela had to suffer every hardship that a delicate woman can be subjected to on board ship: a wretched berth in a floating cellar called a cabin, want of fresh water, of female attendance, and of any food but the coarsest. These deprivations she bore without a murmur. It was only the slowness of the passage that troubled her.

The great city came in view at last, the long roof of St. Paul's dominating the thickly clustered gables and chimneys, and the vessel dropped anchor opposite the dark walls of the Tower, whose form had been made familiar to Angela by a print in a History of London, which she had hung over many an evening in Mother Anastasia's parlour. A row-boat conveyed her and her fellow-traveller to the Tower stairs, where they landed, the priest being duly provided with an efficient voucher that they came from a city free of the plague. Yes, this was London. Her foot touched her native soil for

the first time after fifteen years of absence. The good-
natured priest would not leave her till he had seen her
in charge of an elderly and most reputable waterman,
recommended by the custodian of the stairs. Then he
bade her an affectionate adieu, and fared on his way
to a house in the city, where one of his kinsfolk, a devout Catholic, dwelt quietly hidden from the public eye,
and where he would rest for the night before setting
out on his journey to the north.

After the impetuous passage through the deep, dark
arch of the bridge, the boat moved slowly up the river
in the peaceful eventide, and Angela's eyes opened wide
with wonder as she looked on the splendours of that
silent highway, this evening verily silent, for the traffic
of business and pleasure had stopped in the terror of
the pestilence, like a clock that had run down. It was
said by one who had seen the fairest cities of Europe
that "the most glorious sight in the world', take land
and water together, was to come upon a high tide from
Gravesend, and shoot the bridge to Westminster;" and
to the convent-bred maiden how much more astonishing
was that prospect!

The boat passed in front of Lord Arundel's sumptuous
mansion, with its spacious garden, where marble statues
showed white in the midst of quincunxes, and prim
hedges of cypress and yew; past the Palace of the
Savoy, with its massive towers, battlemented roof, and
double line of mullioned windows fronting the river;
past Worcester House, where Lord Chancellor Hyde had
been living in a sober splendour, while his princely
mansion was building 'yonder on the Hounslow Road,
or that portion thereof lately known as Piccadilly. That

was the ambitious pile of which Hyacinth had written, a house of clouded memories and briefest tenure; fore-doomed to vanish like a palace seen in a dream; a transient magnificence, indescribable; known for a little while opprobriously as Dunkirk House, the supposed re-sult of the Chancellor's too facile assistance in the sur-render of that last rag of French territory. The boat passed before Rutland House and Cecil House, some portion of which had lately been converted into the Middle Exchange, the haunt of fine ladies and Golconda of gentlewomen milliners, favourite scene for assignations and intrigues; and so by Durham House, where in the Protector Seymour's time the Royal Mint had been established; a house whose stately rooms were haunted by tragic associations, shadows of Northumberland's niece and victim, hapless Jane Grey, and of fated Raleigh. Here, too, commerce shouldered aristocracy, and the New Exchange of King James's time competed with the Middle Exchange of later date, providing more milliners, perfumers, glovers, barbers, and toymen, and more opportunity for illicit loves and secret meetings.

Before Angela's eyes those splendid mansions passed like phantom pictures. The westering sunlight showed golden above the dark Abbey, while she sat silent, with awe-stricken gaze, looking out upon the widespread city that lay chastened and afflicted under the hand of an angry God. The beautiful, gay, proud, and splendid London of the West, the new London of Covent Garden, St. James's Street, and Piccadilly, whose glories her sister's pen had depicted with such fond enthusiasm, was now deserted by the rabble of quality who had peopled its palaces, while the old London of the East,

the historic city, was sitting in sackcloth and ashes, a
place of lamentations, a city where men and women
rose up in the morning hale and healthy, and at nightfall were carried away in the dead-cart, to be flung
into the pit where the dead lay shroudless and un-
honoured.

How still and sweet the summer air seemed in that
sunset hour; how placid the light ripple of the incom-
ing tide; how soothing even the silence of the city!
And yet it all meant death. It was but a few months
since the fatal infection had been brought from Holland
in a bundle of merchandise: and, behold, through city
and suburbs, the pestilence had crept with slow and
stealthy foot, now on this side of a street, now on another. The history of the plague was like a game at
draughts, where man after man vanishes off the board,
and the game can only end by exhaustion.

"See, mistress, yonder is Somerset House," said the
boatman, pointing to one of the most commanding
façades in that highway of palaces. "That is the
palace which the Queen-mother has raised from the
ashes of the ruins her folly made, for the husband who
loved her too well. She came back to us no wiser for
years of exile—came back with her priests and her
Italian singing-boys, her incense-bearers and golden
candlesticks and gaudy rags of Rome. She fled from
England with the roar of cannon in her ears, and the
fear of death in her heart. She came back in pride
and vain-glory, and boasted that had she known the
English people better, she would never have gone away;
and she has squandered thousands in yonder palace,
upon floors of coloured woods, and Italian marbles—

the people's money, mark you, money that should have built ships and fed sailors; and she meant to end her days among us. But a worse enemy than Cromwell has driven her out of the house that she made beautiful for herself; and who knows if she will ever see London again?"

"Then those were right who told me that it was for fear of the plague her Majesty left London?" said Angela.

"For what else should she flee? She was loth enough to leave, you may be sure, for she had seated herself in her pride yonder, and her Court was as splendid, and more looked up to than Queen Catherine's. The Queen-mother is the prouder woman, and held her head higher than her son's wife has ever dared to hold hers; yet there are those who say King Charles's widow has fallen so low as to marry Lord St. Albans, a son of Belial, who would hazard his immortal soul on a cast of the dice, and lose it as freely as he has squandered his royal mistress's money. She paid for Jermyn's feasting and wine-bibbing in Paris, 'tis said, when her son and his friends were on short commons."

"You do wrong to slander that royal lady," remonstrated Angela. "She is of all widows the saddest and most desolate—ever the mark of evil fortune. Even in the glorious year of her son's restoration sorrow pursued her, and she had to mourn a daughter and a son. She is a most unhappy lady."

"You would scarcely say as much, young madam, had you seen her in her pomp and power yonder. And as for Lord St. Albans, if he is not her husband——! Well, thou art a young innocent thing—so

I had best hold my peace. Both palaces are empty and forsaken, both Whitehall and Somerset House. The rats and the spiders can take their own pleasure in the rooms that were full of music and dancing, card-playing and feasting, two or three months ago. Why, there was no better sight in London, after the dead-cart, than to watch the train of carriages and horse-men, carts and wagons, upon any of the great high-roads, carrying the people of London away to the country, as if the whole city had been moving in one mass like a routed army."

"But in palaces and noblemen's houses surely there would be little danger?" said Angela. "Plagues and fevers are the outcome of hunger and uncleanliness, and all such evils as the poor have to suffer."

"Nay, but the pestilence that walketh in darkness is no respecter of persons," answered the grim boat-man. "I grant you that death has dealt hardest with the poor who dwell in crowded lanes and alleys. But now the very air reeks with poison. It may be carried in the folds of a woman's gown, or among the feathers of a courtier's hat. They are wise to go who can go. It is only such as I, who have to work for my grand-children's bread, that must needs stay."

"You speak like one who has seen better days," said Angela.

"I was a sergeant in Hampden's regiment, madam, and went all through the war. When the King came back I had friends who stood by me, and bought me this boat. I was used to handle an oar in my boy-hood, when I lived on a little bit of a farm that be-longed to my father, between Reading and Henley. I

was oftener on the water than on the land in those
days. There are some who have treated me roughly
because I fought against the late King; but folks are
beginning to find out that the Brewer's disbanded red-
coats can be honest and serviceable in time of peace."

After passing the Queen-mother's desolate palace
the boat crept along near the Middlesex shore, till it
stopped at the bottom of a flight of stone steps, against
which the tide washed with a pleasant rippling sound,
and above which there rose the walls of a stately building facing south-west; small as compared with Somerset
and Northumberland houses, midway between which it
stood, yet a spacious and noble mansion, with a richly
decorated river-front, lofty windows with sculptured
pediments, floriated cornice, and two side towers topped
with leaded cupolas, the whole edifice gilded by the
low sun, and very beautiful to look upon, the windows
gleaming as if there were a thousand candles burning
within, a light that gave a false idea of life and festivity,
since that brilliant illumination was only a reflected
glory.

"This, madam, is Fareham House," said the boatman, holding out his hand for his fee.

He charged treble the sum he would have asked half
a year ago. In this time of evil those intrepid spirits
who still plied their trades in the tainted city demanded
a heavy fee for their labour; and it would have been
hard to dispute their claim, since each man knew that
he risked his life, and that the limbs which toiled to-day
might be lifeless clay to-night. There was an awfulness
about the time, a taste and odour of death mixed with
all the common things of daily life, a morbid dwelling

6*

upon thoughts of corruption, a feverish expectancy of the end of all things, which no man can rightly conceive who has not passed through the Valley of the Shadow of Death.

Angela paid the man his price without question. She stepped lightly from the boat, while he deposited her two small leather-covered trunks on the stone landing-place in front of the Italian terrace which occupied the whole length of the façade. She went up a flight of marble steps, to a door facing the river. Here she rang a bell which pealed long and loud over the quiet water, a bell that must have been heard upon the Surrey shore. Yet no one opened the great oak door; and Angela had a sudden sinking at the heart as the slow minutes passed and brought no sound of footsteps within, no scrooping of a bolt to betoken the opening of the door.

"Belike the house is deserted, madam," said the boatman, who had moored his wherry to the landing-stage, and had carried the two trunks to the doorstep. "You had best try if the door be fastened or no. Stay!" he cried suddenly, pointing upwards, "Go not in, madam, for your life! Look at the red cross on the door, the sign of a plague-stricken house."

Angela looked up with awe and horror. A great cross was smeared upon the door with red paint, and above it someone had scrawled the words, "Lord, have mercy upon us!"

And the sister she loved, and the children whose faces she had never seen, were within that house, sick and in peril of death, perhaps dying—or dead! She did not hesitate for an instant, but took hold of the heavy iron ring which served as a handle for the door and tried to open it.

"I have no fear for myself," she said to the boatman; "I have nursed the sick and the fever-stricken, and am not afraid of contagion—and there are those within whom I love. Good night, friend."

The handle of the door turned somewhat stiffly in her hand, but it did turn, and the door opened, and she stood upon the threshold looking into a vast hall that was wrapped in shadow, save for a shaft of golden light that streamed from an oval window on the staircase. Other windows there were on each side of the door, shuttered and barred.

Seeing her enter the house, the old Cromwellian shrugged his shoulders, shook his head despondently, shoved the two trunks hastily over the threshold, ran back to his boat, and pushed off.

"God guard thy young life, mistress!" he cried, and the wherry shot out into the stream.

There had been silence on the river, the silence of a deserted city at eventide; but that had seemed as nothing to the stillness of this marble-paved hall, where the sunset was reflected on the dark oak panelling in one lurid splash like blood.

Not a mortal to be seen. Not a sound of voice or footstep. A crowd of gods and goddesses in draperies of azure and crimson, purple and orange, looked down from the ceiling. Curtains of tawny velvet hung beside the shuttered windows. A great brazen candelabrum, filled with half-consumed candles, stood tall and splendid at the foot of a wide oak staircase, the banister-rail whereof was cushioned with tawny velvet. Splendour of fabric, wood and marble, colour and gilding, showed on every side; but of humanity there was no sign.

Angela shuddered at the sight of all that splendour, as if death were playing hide and seek in those voluminous curtains, or were lurking in the deep shadow which the massive staircase cast across the hall. She looked about her, full of fear, then seeing a silver bell upon the table, she took it up and rang it loudly. Upon the same carved ebony table there lay a plumed hat, a cane with an amber handle, and a velvet cloak neatly folded, as if placed ready for the master of the house, when he went abroad; but looking at these things closely, even in that dim light, she saw that cloak and hat were white with dust, and, more even than the silence, that spectacle of the thick dust on the dark velvet impressed her with the idea of a deserted house.

She had no lack of courage, this pupil of the Flemish nuns, and her footstep did not falter as she went quickly up the broad staircase until she found herself in a spacious gallery, and amidst a flood of light, for the windows on this upper or noble floor were all unshuttered, and the sunset streamed in through the lofty Italian casements. Fareham House was built upon the plan of the Hôtel de Rambouillet, of which the illustrious Catherine de Vivonne was herself at once owner and architect. The staircase, instead of being a central feature, was at the western end of the house, allowing space for an unbroken suite of rooms communicating one with the other, and terminating in an apartment with a fine oriel window looking east.

The folding doors of a spacious saloon stood wide open, and Angela entered a room whose splendour was a surprise to her who had been accustomed to the sober simplicity of a convent parlour and the cold grey walls of the refectory, where the only picture was a pinched and angular Virgin by Memling, and the only ornament a crucifix of ebony and brass.

Here for the first time she beheld a saloon for whose decoration palaces had been ransacked and churches desecrated—the stolen treasures of many an ancestral mansion, spoil of rough soldiery or city rabble, things that had been slyly stowed away by their possessors during the stern simplicity of the Commonwealth, and had been brought out of their hiding-places and sold to the highest bidder. Gold and silver had been melted down in the Great Rebellion; but art treasures would not serve to pay soldiers or to buy ammunition; so these had escaped the melting-pot. At home and abroad the storehouses of curiosity merchants had been explored to beautify Lady Fareham's reception-rooms; and in the fading light Angela gazed upon hangings that were worthy of a royal palace, upon Italian crystals and Indian carvings, upon ivory and amber and jade and jasper, upon tables of Florentine mosaic, and ebony cabinets incrusted with rare agates, and upon pictures in frames of massive and elaborate carving, Venetian mirrors which gave back the dying light from a thousand facets, curtains and portières of sumptuous brocade, gold-embroidered, gorgeous with the silken semblance of peacock plumage, done with the needle, from the royal manufactory of the Crown Furniture at the Gobelins.

She passed into an ante-room, with tapestried walls, and a divan covered with raised velvet, a music desk

of gilded wood, and a spinet, on which was painted the
story of Orpheus and Eurydice. Beyond this there was
the dining-room, more soberly though no less richly
furnished than the saloon. Here the hangings were of
Cordovan leather, stamped and gilded with *fleur-de-lys,*
suggesting a French origin, and indeed these very hangings had been bought by a Dutch Jew dealer in the
time of the Fronde, had belonged to the hated minister
Mazarin, and had been sold among other of his effects
when he fled from Paris: to vanish for a brief season
behind the clouds of public animosity, and to blaze out
again, an elderly phœnix, in a new palace, adorned with
new treasures of art and industry that made royal
princes envious.

Angela gazed on all this splendour as one bewildered.
In front of that gilded wall, quivering in mid-air, as if it
had been painted upon the shaft of light that streamed
in from the tall window, her fancy pictured the blood-
red cross and the piteous legend, "Lord, have mercy on
us!" written in the same blood colour. For herself she
had neither horror of the pestilence nor fear of death.
Religion had familiarised her mind with the image of
the destroyer. From her childhood she had been
acquainted with the grave, and with visions of a world
beyond the grave. It was not for herself she trembled,
but for her sister, and her sister's children; for Lord
Fareham, whose likeness she recalled even at this
moment, the grave dark face which Hyacinth had shown
her on the locket she wore upon her neck, the face
which Sir John said reminded him of Strafford.

"He has just that fatal look," her father had told her
afterwards when they talked of Fareham, "the look that

men saw in Wentworth's face when he came from Ireland, and in his Majesty's countenance, after Wentworth's
murder."

While she stood in the dying light, wavering for a
moment, doubtful which way to turn—since the room
had no less than three tall oak doors, two of them ajar
—there came a pattering upon the polished floor, a
scampering of feet that were lighter and quicker than
those of the smallest child, and the first living creature
Angela saw in that silent house came running towards
her. It was only a little black-and-tan spaniel, with long
silky hair and drooping ears, and great brown eyes, fond
and gentle, a very toy and trifle in the canine kingdom;
yet the sight of that living thing thrilled her awe-stricken
heart, and her tears came thick and fast as she knelt
and took the little dog in her arms and pressed him
against her bosom, and kissed the cold muzzle, and
looked, half laughing, half crying, into the pathetic brown
eyes.

"At least there is life near. This dog would not be
left in a deserted house," she thought, as the creature
trembled against her bosom and licked the hand that
held him.

The pattering was repeated in the adjoining room,
and another spaniel, which might have been twin brother
of the one she held, came through the half open door,
and ran to her, and set up a jealous barking which
reverberated in the lofty room, and from within that
unseen chamber on the other side of the door there
came a groan, a deep and hollow sound, as of mortal
agony.

She set down the dog in an instant, and was on

her feet again, trembling but alert. She pushed the
door a little wider and went into the next apartment, a
bedroom more splendid than any bed-chamber her fancy
had ever depicted when she read of royal palaces.

The walls were hung with Mortlake tapestries, representing in four great panels the story of Perseus and
Andromeda, and the Rape of Proserpine. To her who
knew not the old Greek fables those figures looked
strangely diabolical. Naked maiden and fiery dragon,
flying horse and Greek hero, Demeter and Persephone,
hell-god and chariot, seemed alike demoniac and unholy,
seen in the dim light of expiring day. The high chimney-
piece, with its Oriental jars, blood-red and amber, faced
her as she entered the room, and opposite the three tall
windows stood the state bed, of carved ebony, the posts
adorned with massive bouquets of chased silver flowers,
the curtains of wine coloured velvet, heavy with bullion
fringes. One curtain had been looped back, showing
the amber satin lining, and on this bed of state lay a
man, writhing in agony, with one bloodless hand pluck-
ing at the cambric upon his bosom, while with the
other he grasped the ebony bed-post in a paroxysm
of pain.

Angela knew that dark and powerful face at the first
glance, though the features were distorted by suffering.
This sick man, the sole occupant of a deserted mansion,
was her brother-in-law, Lord Fareham. A large high-
backed armchair stood beside the bed, and on this
Angela seated herself. She recollected the Superior's
injunction just in time to put one of the anti-pestilential
lozenges into her mouth before she bent over the sufferer, and took his clammy hand in hers, and endured

the acrimony of his poisonous breath. That anxious gaze, the dark yellow complexion, and those great beads of sweat that poured down the pinched countenance too plainly indicated the disease which had desolated London. The Moslem's invisible plague-angel had entered this palace, and had touched the master with his deadly lance. That terrible Presence, which for the most part had been found among the dwellings of the poor, was here amidst purple and fine linen, here on this bed of state, enthroned in ebony and silver, hung round with velvet and bullion. She needed not to discover the pestilential spots beneath that semi-diaphanous cambric which hung loose upon the muscular frame, to be convinced of the cruel fact. Here, abandoned and alone, lay the master of the house, with nothing better than a pair of spaniels for his companions, and neither nurse nor watcher, wife nor friend, to help him towards recovery, or to comfort his passing soul.

One of the little dogs leapt on the bed, and licked his master's face again and again, whining piteously between whiles.

The sick man looked at Angela with awful, unseeing eyes, and then burst into a wild laugh—

"See them run, the crop-headed clod-hoppers!" he cried. "Ride after them—mow them down—scatter the rebel clot-pols! The day is ours!" And then, passing from English to French, from visions of Lindsey and Rupert and the pursuit at Edgehill to memories of Condé and Turenne, he shouted with the voice that was like the sound of a trumpet, "*Boutte-selle! boutte-selle! Monte à cheval! monte à cheval! à l'arme, à l'arme!*"

He was in the field of battle again. His wandering

wits had carried him back to his first fight, when he was a lad in his father's company of horse, following the King's fortunes, breathing gunpowder, and splashed with human blood for the first time—when it was not so long since he had been blooded at the death of his first fox. He was a young man again, with the Prince, that Bourbon prince and hero whom he loved and honoured far above any of his own countrymen.

"*O, la folle entreprise du Prince de Condé,*" he sang, waving his hand above his head, while the spaniels barked loud and shrill, adding their clamour to his. He raved of battles and sieges. He was lying in the trenches, in cold and rain and wind—in the tempestuous darkness. He was mounting the breach at Dunkirk against the Spaniard; at Charenton in a hand-to-hand fight with Frondeurs. He raved of Châtillon and Chanleu, and the slaughter of that fatal day when Condé mourned a friend and each side lost a leader. Fever gave force to gesture and voice; but in the midst of his ravings he fell back, half fainting, upon the pillow, his heart beating in a tumult which fluttered the lace upon the bosom of his shirt, while the acrid drops upon his brow gathered thicker than poisonous dew. Angela remembered how last year in Holland these death-like sweats had not always pointed to a fatal result, but in some cases had afforded an outlet to the pestilential influences, though in too many instances they had served only to enfeeble the patient, the fire of disease still burning, while the damps of approaching dissolution oozed from the fevered body—flame within and ice without.

CHAPTER V.

A MINISTERING ANGEL.

ANGELA flung off hood and mantle, and looked anxiously round the room. There were some empty phials and ointment boxes, some soiled linen rags and wet sponges, upon a table near the bed, and the chamber reeked with the odour of drugs, hartshorn and elder vinegar, cantharides, and aloes; enough to show that a doctor had been there, and that there had been some attempt at nursing the patient. But she had heard how in Holland the nurses had sometimes robbed and abandoned their charges, taking advantage of the confusions and uncertainties of that period of despair, quick and skilful to profit by sudden death, and the fears and agonies of relatives and friends, whose grief made plunder easy. She deemed it likely that one of those devilish women had first pretended to succour, and had then abandoned Lord Fareham to his fate, after robbing his house. Indeed, the open doors of a stately inlaid wardrobe between two windows over against the bed, and the confused appearance of the clothes and linen on the shelves, indicated that it had been ransacked by hasty hands; while, doubtless, there had been many valuables lying loose about a house where there was every indication of a careless profusion.

"Alas! poor gentleman, to be left by some mercenary wretch—left to die like the camel in the desert!"

She bent over him, and laid her hand with gentle firmness upon his death-cold forehead.

"What! are there saints and angels in hell as well as felons and devils?" he cried, clutching her by the wrist, and looking up at her with distended eyes, in which the natural colour of the eye-ball was tarnished almost to blackness with injected blood.

For long and lonely hours, that seemed an eternity, he had been tossing in a burning fever upon that disordered bed, until he verily believed himself in a place of everlasting torment. He had that strange, double sense which goes with delirium—the consciousness of his real surroundings, the tapestry and furniture of his own chamber, and yet the conviction that this was hell, and had always been hell, and that he had descended to this terrible under-world through infinite abysses of darkness. The glow of sunset had been to him the fierce light of everlasting flames; the burning of fever was the fire that is never quenched; the pain that racked his limbs was the worm that dieth not. And now in his torment there came the vision of a seraphic face bending over him in gentle solicitude; a face that brought comfort with it, even in the midst of his agony. After that one wild question he sank slowly back upon the pillows, and lay faint and weak, his breathing scarce audible. Angela laid her fingers on his wrist. The pulse was fluttering and intermittent.

She remembered every detail of her aunt's treatment of the plague-patient in the convent infirmary, and how the turning-point of the malady and beginning of cure

had seemed to be brought about by a draught of strong
wine which the reverend mother had made her give the
poor fainting creature at a crisis of extreme weakness.
She looked about the room for any flask which might
contain wine; but there was nothing there except the
apothecary's phials and medicaments.

It was dusk already, and she was alone in a strange
house. It would seem no easy task to find what she
wanted, but the case was desperate, and she knew
enough of this mysterious disease to know that if the
patient could not rally speedily from his prostrate condition the end must be near. With steady brain she set
herself to face the difficulty—first to administer something which should sustain the sick man's strength, and
then, without loss of time, to seek a physician, and bring
him to that deserted bed. Wine was the one thing
she could trust to in this crisis; for of the doses and
lotions on yonder table she knew nothing, nor had her
experience made her a believer in the happy influence
of drugs.

Her first search must be for light with which to
explore the lower part of the house, where in pantry or
stillroom, or, if not above ground, in the cellars, she
must find what she wanted. Surely somewhere in that
spacious bedchamber there would be tinder-box and
matches. There were a pair of silver candlesticks on
the dressing-table, with thick wax candles burnt nearly
to the sockets.

A careful search at last discovered a tinder-box and
matches in a dark angle of the fireless hearth, hidden
behind the heavy iron dog. She struck a light, kindled
her match, and lighted a candle, the sick man's eyes

following all her movements, but his lips mute.   As she
went out of the door he called after her—

"Leave me not, thou holy visitant—leave not my
soul in hell!"

"I will return!" she cried.   "Have no fear, sir; I go
to fetch some wine."

Her errand was not done quickly.   Amidst all the
magnificence she had noted on her journey through the
long suite of reception-rooms—the littered treasures of
amber and gold, and ivory and porcelain and silver—
she had seen only an empty wine-flask; so with quick
footfall she ran down the wide, shallow stairs to the lower
floor, and here she found herself in a labyrinth of
passages opening into small rooms and servants' offices.
Here there were darkness and gloom rather than
splendour; though in many of those smaller rooms there
was a sober and substantial luxury which became the
inferior apartments of a palace.   She came at last to
a room which she took to be the butler's office, where
there were dressers with a great array of costly Venetian
glass, and a great many pieces of silver—cups, tankards,
salvers, and other ornamental plate—in presses behind
glazed door.   One of the glass panels had been broken,
and the shelves in that press were empty.

Wine there was none to be found in any part of the
room; but a small army of empty bottles in a corner
of the floor, and a confusion of greasy plates, knives,
chicken bones, and other scraps, indicated that there
had been carousing here at no remote time.

The cellars were doubtless below these offices; but
the wine-cellars would assuredly be locked, and she had
to search for the keys.   She opened drawer after drawer

in the lower part of the presses, and at last, in an inner and secret drawer, found a multitude of keys, some of which were provided with parchment labels, and among these happily were two labelled "Ye great wine cellar, S." and "Ye smaller wine cellar, W."

This was a point gained; but the search had occupied a considerable time. She had yet enough candle to last for about half an hour, and her next business was to find one of those cellars which those keys opened. She was intensely anxious to return to her patient, having heard how in some cases unhappy wretches had leapt from the bed of death and rushed out-of-doors, delirious, half naked, to anticipate their end by a fatal chill.

On her way to the butler's office she had seen a stone archway at the head of a flight of stairs leading down into darkness. By this staircase she hoped to find the wine-cellars, and presently descended, her candlestick in one hand, and the two great keys in the other. As she went down into the stone basement, which was built with the solidity of a dungeon, she heard the plash of the tide, and felt that she was now on a level with the river. Here she found herself again in a labyrinth of passages, with many doors standing ajar. At the end of one passage she came to a locked door, and on trying her keys, found one of them to fit the lock; it was "Ye great wine cellar, S.," and she understood by the initial "S." that the cellar looked south and faced the river.

She turned the heavy key with an effort that strained the slender fingers which held it; but she was unconscious of the pain, and wondered afterwards to see her hand dented and bruised where the iron had wrung it.

The clumsy door revolved on massive hinges, and she entered a cellar so large that the light of her candle did not reach the furthermost corners and recesses.

This cellar was built in a series of arches, fitted with stone bins, and in the upper part of one southward-fronting arch there was a narrow grating, through which came the cool breath of evening air and the sound of water lapping against stone. A patch of faint light showed pale against the iron bars, and as Angela looked that way, a great grey rat leapt through the grating, and ran along the topmost bin, making the bottles shiver as he cuttled across them. Then came a thud on the sawdust-covered stones, and she knew that the loathsome thing was on the floor upon which she was standing. She lowered her light shudderingly, and, for the first time since she entered that house of dread, the young brave heart sank with the sickness of fear.

The cellar might swarm with such creatures; the darkness of the fast-coming night might be alive with them! And if yonder dungeon-like door were to swing to and shut with a spring lock, she might perish there in the darkness. She might die the most hideous of deaths, and her fate remain for ever unknown.

In a sudden panic she rushed back to the door, and pushed it wider—pushed it to its extremest opening. It seemed too heavy to be likely to swing back upon its hinges; yet the mere idea of such a contingency appalled her. Remembering her labour in unlocking the door from the outside, she doubted if she could open it from within were it once to close upon that awful vault. And all this time the lapping of the tide against the stone

sounded louder, and she saw little spirts of spray flashing
against the bars in the lessening light.

She collected herself with an effort, and began her
search for the wine. Sack was the wine she had given
to the sick nun, and it was that wine for which she
looked. Of Burgundy, and claret, labelled "Clary Wine,"
she found several full bins, and more that were nearly
empty. Tokay and other rarer wines were denoted by
the parchment labels which hung above each bin; but
it was some minutes before she came to a bin labelled
"Sherris," which she knew was another name for sack.
The bottles had evidently been undisturbed for a long
time, for the bin was full of cobweb, and the thick
coating of dust upon the glass betokened a respectable
age in the wine. She carried off two bottles, one under
each arm, and then, with even quicker steps than had
brought her to that darksome place, she hastened back
to the upper floor, leaving the key in the cellar door,
and the door unlocked. There would be time enough
to look after Lord Fareham's wine when she had cared
for Lord Fareham himself.

His eyes were fixed upon the doorway as she entered.
They shone upon her in the dusk with an awful glassi-
ness, as if life's last look had become fixed in death.
He did not speak as she drew near the bed, and set the
wine bottles down upon the table among the drugs and
cataplasms.

She had found a silver-handled corkscrew in the
buttler's room among the relics of the feast, and with
this she opened one of the bottles, Fareham watching
her all the time.

"Is that some new alexipharmic?" he asked with a

7*

sudden rational air, which was almost as startling as
if a dead man had spoken. "I will have no more of
their loathsome drugs. They have made an apothecary's
shop of my body. I would rather they let me rot by
the plague than that they should poison me with their
antidotes, or dissolve me to death with their sudorifics."

"This is not a medicine, Lord Fareham, but your own
wine; and I want you to drink a long draught of it, and
then, who knows but you may sleep off your malady?"

"Ay, sleep in the grave, sweet friend! I have seen
the tokens on my breast that mean death. There is
but one inevitable end for all who are so marked.
'Tis like the forester's notch upon the tree. It means
doom. He was king of the forest once, perhaps; but
no matter. His time has come. Oh, Lord, thou hast
tormented me with hot burning coals!" he cried, in
a sudden access of pain; and in the next minute he was
raving.

Angela filled a beaker with the bright golden wine,
and offered it to the sick man's lips. It was not without
infinite pains and coaxing that she induced him to
drink; but, when once his parched lips had tasted the
cold liquor, he drank eagerly, as if that strong wine
had been a draught of water. He gave a deep sigh
of solace when the beaker was empty, for he had been
enduring an agony of thirst through all the glare and
heat of the afternoon, and there was unspeakable comfort in that first long drink. He would have drunk foul
water with almost as keen a relish.

He talked fast and furiously, in the disjointed sentences of delirium, for some little time; and then, little
by little, he grew more tranquil; and Angela, sitting be-

side the bed, with her fingers laid gently on his wrist, marked the quieter beat of the pulse, which no longer fluttered like the wing of a frightened bird. Then with deep thankfulness she saw the eyelids droop over the bloodshot eyeballs, while the breathing grew slower and heavier as sleep clouded the wearied brain. The spaniels crept nearer him, and nestled close to his pillow, so that the man's dark locks were mixed with the silken curls of the dogs.

Would he die in that sleep? she wondered.

It was only now for the first time since she entered this unpeopled house that she had leisure to speculate on the circumstances which had brought about such loneliness and neglect, here where rank and state, and wealth almost without limit should have secured the patient every care and comfort that devoted service could lavish upon a sufferer. How was it that she found her sister's husband abandoned to the care of hirelings, left to the chances of paid service?

To the cloister-reared maiden the idea of wifely duty was elevated almost to a religion. To father or to husband she would have given a boundless devotion, in sickness most of all devoted. To leave husband or father in a plague-stricken city would have seemed to her a crime as abominable as Tullia's, a treachery base as Goneril's or Regan's. Could it be that her sister, that bright and lovely creature, whose face she remembered as a sunbeam incarnate, could she have been swept away by the pestilence which spared neither youth nor beauty, neither the strong man nor the weakling child? Her heart grew heavy as lead at the thought that this stranger, by whose pillow she was watching,

might be the sole survivor in that forsaken palace, and
that in a few more hours he, too, would be numbered
with the dead, in that dreadful city where Death reigned
omnipotent, and where the living seemed but a vanishing minority, pale shadows of living creatures passing
silently along one inevitable pathway to the pest-house
or pit.

That calm sleep of the plague-stricken might mean
recovery, or it might mean death. Angela examined
the potions and unguents on the table near the bed,
and read the instructions on jars and phials. One was
an alexipharmic draught, to be taken the last thing at
night, another a sudorific, to be administered once in
every hour.

"I would not wake him to give him the finest
medicine that ever physician prescribed," Angela said to
herself. "I remember what a happy change one hour
of quiet slumber made in Sister Monica, when she was
all but dead of a quartan fever. Sleep is God's physic."

She knelt upon a Prie-Dieu chair remote from the
bed, knowing that contagion lurked amid those voluminous hangings, beneath that stately canopy with its
lustrous satin lining, on which the light of the wax
candles was reflected in shining patches as upon a lake
of golden water. She had no fear of the pestilence; but
an instinctive prudence made her hold herself aloof,
now that there was nothing more to be done for the
sufferer.

She remained long in prayer, repeating one of those
litanies which she had learnt in her infancy, and which
of late had seemed to her to have somewhat too set
and mechanical a rhythm. The earnestness and fervour

seemed to have gone out of them in somewise since she
had come to womanhood. The names of the saints her
lips invoked were dull and cold, and evolved no image
of human or superhuman love and power. What need
of intercessors whose personality was vague and dim,
whose earthly histories were made up of truth so interwoven with fable that she scarce dared believe even
that which might be true? In the One Crucified was
help for all sinners, gospel and creed, the rule of life
here, the promise of immortality hereafter.

The litanies to Virgin and Saints were said as a
duty—a part of implicit obedience which was the
groundwork of her religion; and then all the aspirations
of her heart, her prayers for the sick man yonder, her
fears for her absent sister, for her father in his foreign
wanderings, went up in one stream of invocation to
Christ the Redeemer. To Him, and Him alone, the
strong flame of faith and love rose, like the incense upon
an altar—the altar of a girl's trusting heart.

She was so lost in meditation that she was unconscious of an approaching footstep in the stillness of the
deserted house, till it drew near to the threshold of the
sick-room. The night was close and sultry, so she had
left the door open, and that slow tread had crossed the
threshold by the time she rose from her knees. Her
heart beat fast, startled by the first human presence
which she had known in that melancholy place, save the
presence of the pest-stricken sufferer.

She found herself face to face with a middle-aged
gentleman of medium stature, clad in the sober colouring that suggested one of the learned professions. He
appeared even more startled than Angela at the un-

expected vision which met his gaze, faintly seen in the
dim light.

There was silence for a few moments, and then the
stranger saluted the lady with a formal reverence, as he
laid down, his gold-handled cane.

"Surely, madam, this mansion of my Lord Fareham's
must be enchanted," he said. "I left a crowd of at-
tendants, and the stir of life below and above stairs,
only this forenoon last past. I find silence and vacancy.
That is scarce strange in this dejected and unhappy
time; for it is but too common a trick of hireling nurses
to abandon their patients, and for servants to plunder
and then desert a sick house. But to find an angel
where I left a hag! That is the miracle! And an angel
who has brought healing, if I mistake not," he added,
in a lower voice, bending over the speaker.

"I am no angel, sir, but a weak, erring mortal,"
answered the girl, gravely. "For pity's sake, kind
doctor—since I doubt not you are my lord's physician—
tell me where are my dearest sister, Lady Fareham, and
her children. Tell me the worst, I entreat you!"

"Sweet lady, there is no ill news to tell. Her ladyship and the little ones are safe at my lord's house in
Oxfordshire, and it is only his lordship yonder who has
fallen a victim to the contagion. Lady Fareham and
her girl and boy have not been in London since the
plague began to rage. My lord had business in the
city, and came hither alone. He and the young Lord
Rochester, who is the most audacious infidel this town
can show, have been bidding defiance to the pestilence,
deeming their nobility safe from a sickness which has for
the most part chosen its victims among the vulgar."

"His lordship is very ill, I fear, sir?" said Angela interrogatively.

"I left him at eleven o'clock this morning with but scanty hope of finding him alive after sundown. The woman I left to nurse him was his house-steward's wife, and far above the common kind of plague-nurse. I did not think she would turn traitor."

"Her husband has proved a false steward. The house has been robbed of plate and valuables, as I believe, from signs I saw below stairs; and I suppose husband and wife went off together."

"Alack! madam, this pestilence has brought into play some of the worst attributes of human nature. The tokens and loathly boils which break out upon the flesh of the plague-stricken are less revolting to humanity than the cruelty of those who minister to the sick, and whose only desire is to profit by the miseries that surround them; wretches so vile that they have been known wilfully to convey the seeds of death from house to house, in order to infect the sound, and so enlarge their area of gains. It was an artful device of those plunderers to paint the red cross on the door, and thus scare away any visitor who might have discovered their depredations. But you, madam, a being so young and fragile, have you no fear of the contagion?"

"Nay, sir, I know that I am in God's hand. Yonder poor gentleman is not the first plague-patient I have nursed. There was a nun came from Holland to our convent at Louvain last year, and had scarce been one night in the house before tokens of the pestilence were discovered upon her. I helped the infirmarian to nurse her, and with God's help we brought her round. My

aunt, the reverend mother, bade me give her the best
wine there was in the house—strong Spanish wine that
a rich merchant had given to the convent for the use
of the sick—and it was as though that good wine drove
the poison from her blood. She recovered by the grace
of God after only a few days' careful nursing. Finding
his lordship stricken with such great weakness, I ventured to give him a draught of the best sack I could
find in his cellar."

"Dear lady, thou art a miracle of good sense and
compassionate bounty. I doubt thou hast saved thy
sister from widow's weeds," said Dr. Hodgkin, seated by
the bed, with his fingers on the patient's wrist, and his
massive gold watch in the other hand. "This sound
sleep promises well, and the pulse beats somewhat slower
and steadier than it did this morning. Then the case
seemed hopeless, and I feared to give wine—though
a free use of generous wine is my particular treatment—
lest it should fly to his brain, and disturb his intellectuals
at a time when he should need all his senses for the
final disposition of his affairs. Great estates sometimes
hang upon the breath of a dying man."

"Oh, sir, but your patient! To save his life, that
would sure be your first and chiefest thought?"

"Ay, ay, my pretty miss; but I had other measures.
Apollo twangs not ever on the same bowstring. Did
my sudorific work well, think you?"

"He was bathed in perspiration when first I found
him; but the sweat-drops seemed cold and deadly, as if
life itself were being dissolved out of him."

"Ay, there are cases in which that copious sweat is
the forerunner of dissolution; but in others it augurs

cure. The pent-up poison which is corrupting the patient's blood finds a sudden vent, its virulence is diluted, and if the end prove fatal, it is that the patient lacks power to rally after the ravages of the disease, rather than that the poison kills. Was it instantly after that profuse sweat you gave him the wine, I wonder?"

"It was as speedily as I could procure it from the cellar below."

"And that strong wine, given in the nick of time, reassembled Nature's scattered forces, and rekindled the flame of life. Upon my soul, sweet young lady, I believe thou hast saved him! All the drugs in Bucklersbury could do no more. And now tell me what symptoms you have noted since you have watched by his bed; and tell me further if you have strength to continue his nurse, with such precautions as I shall dictate, and such help as I can send you in the shape of a stout, honest, serving-wench of mine, and a man to guard the lower part of your house, and fetch and carry for you?"

"I will do everything you bid me, with all my heart, and with such skill as I can command."

"Those delicate fingers were formed to minister to the sick. And you will not shrink from loathsome offices —from the application of cataplasms, from cleansing foul sores? Those blains and boils upon that poor body will need care for many days to come."

"I will shrink from nothing that may be needful for his benefit. I should love to go on nursing him, were it only for my sister's sake. How sorry she would feel to be so far from him, could she but know of his sickness!"

"Yes, I believe Lady Fareham would be sorry,"

answered the physician, with a dry little laugh; "though there are not many married ladies about Rowley's court of whom I would diagnose as much. Not Lady Denham, for instance, that handsome, unprincipled houri, married to a septuagenarian poet, who would rather lock her up in a garret than see her shine at Whitehall; or Lady Castlemaine, whose husband has been uncivil enough to show discontent at a peerage that was not of his own earning; or a dozen others I could name, were not such scandals as these Hebrew to thine innocent ear."

"Nay, sir, my sister has written of Court scandals in many of her letters, and it has grieved me to think her lot should be cast among people of whose reckless doings she tells me with a lively wit that makes sin seem something less than sin."

"There is no such word as 'sin' in Charles Stuart's Court, my dear young lady. It is harder to achieve bad repute nowadays than it was once to be thought a saint. Existence in this town is a succession of bagatelles. Men's lives and women's reputations drift down to the bottomless pit upon a rivulet of epigrams and chansons. You have heard of that Dance of Death, which was one of the nervous diseases of the fifteenth century—a malady which, after beginning with one lively caperer, would infect a whole townspeople, and send an entire population curvetting and prancing, until death stopped them. I sometimes think, when I watch the follies at Whitehall, that those graceful dancers, sliding upon pointed toe through a coranto, amid a blaze of candles and starshine of diamonds, are capering along the same fatal road by which St. Vitus lured his votaries to the grave.

And then I look at Rowley's licentious eye and cynical lip, and think to myself, 'This man's father perished on the scaffold; this man's lovely ancestress paid the penalty of her manifold treacheries after sixteen years imprisonment; this man has passed through the jaws of death, has left his country a fugitive and a pauper, has returned, as if by a miracle, carried back to a throne upon the hearts of his people; and behold him now— saunterer, sybarite, sensualist—strolling through life without one noble aim or one virtuous instinct; a King who traffics in the pride and honour of his country, and would sell her most precious possessions, level her strongest defences, if his cousin and patron t'other side the Channel would but bid high enough.' But a plague on my tongue, dear lady, that it must always be wagging. Not one word more, save for instructions."

Dr. Hodgkin loved talking even better than he loved a fee, and he allowed himself a physician's licence to be prosy; but he now proceeded to give minute directions for the treatment of the patient—the poultices and stoups and lotions which were to reduce the external indications of the contagion, the medicines which were to be given at intervals during the night. Medicine in those days left very little to Nature, and if patients perished it was seldom for want of drugs and medicaments.

"The servant I send you will bring meat and all needful herbs for making a strong broth, with which you will feed the patient once an hour. There are many who hold with the boiling of gold in such a broth, but I will not enter upon the merits of aurum potabile as a fortifiant. I take it that in this case you will find beef and mutton serve your turn. I shall send you from my

own larder as much beef as will suffice for to-night's
use; and to-morrow your servant must go to the place
where the country people sell their goods, butchers'
meat, poultry, and garden-stuff; for the butchers' shops
of London are nearly all closed, and people scent contagion in any intercourse with their fellow-citizens. You
will have, therefore, to look to the country people for
your supplies; but of all this my own man will give you
information. So now, good night, sweet young lady. It
is on the stroke of nine. Before eleven you shall have
those who will help and protect you. Meanwhile you
had best go downstairs with me, and lock and bolt
the great door leading into the garden, which I found
ajar."

"There is the door facing the river, too, by which I
entered."

"Ay, that should be barred also. Keep a good
heart, madam. Before eleven you shall have a sturdy
watchman on the premises."

Angela took a lighted candle and followed the physician through the great empty rooms, and down the
echoing staircase; under the ceiling where Jove, with
upraised goblet, drank to his queen, while all the galaxy
of the Greek pantheon circled his imperial throne. Upon
how many a festal procession had those Olympians
looked down since that famous house-warming, when the
colours were fresh from the painter's brush, and when
the third Lord Fareham's friend and gossip, King James,
deigned to witness the representation of Jonson's "Time
Vindicated," enacted by ladies and gentlemen of quality,
in the great saloon, a performance which—with the
banquet and confectionery brought from Paris, and "the

sweet waters which came down the room like a shower from heaven," as one wrote who was present at that splendid entertainment, and the *feux d'artifice* on the river—cost his lordship a year's income, but stamped him at once a fine gentleman. Had he been a trifle handsomer, and somewhat softer of speech, that masque and banquet might have placed Richard Revel, Baron Fareham, in the front rank of royal favourites; but the Revels were always a black-visaged race, with more force than comeliness in their countenances, and more gall than honey upon their tongues.

It was past eleven before the expected succour arrived, and in the interval Lord Fareham had awakened once, and had swallowed a composing draught, having apparently but little consciousness of the hand that administered it. At twenty minutes past eleven Angela heard the bell ring, and ran blithely down the now familiar staircase to open the garden door, outside which she found a middle-aged woman and a tall, sturdy young man, each carrying a bundle. These were the nurse and the watchman sent by Dr. Hodgkin. The woman gave Angela a slip of paper from the doctor, by way of introduction.

"You will find Bridget Basset a worthy woman, and able to turn her hand to anything; and Thomas Stokes is an honest, serviceable youth, whom you may trust upon the premises, till some of his lordship's servants can be sent from Chilton Abbey, where I take it there is a large staff."

It was with an unspeakable relief that Angela welcomed these humble friends. The silence of the great empty house had been weighing upon her spirits, until

the sense of solitude and helplessness had grown almost
unbearable. Again and again she had watched Lord
Fareham turn his feverish head upon his pillow, while
the parched lips moved in inarticulate mutterings;
and she had thought of what she should do if a
stronger delirium were to possess him, and he were
to try and do himself some mischief If he were to
start up from his bed and rush through the empty
rooms, or burst open one of yonder lofty casements and
fling himself headlong to the terrace below! She had
been told of the terrible things that plague-patients had
done to themselves in their agony; how they had run
naked into the streets to perish on the stones of the
highway; how they had gashed themselves with knives;
or set fire to their bed-clothes, seeking any escape from
the torments of that foul disease. She knew that those
burning plague-spots, which her hands had dressed, must
cause a continual anguish that might wear out the
patience of a saint; and as the dark face turned on the
tumbled pillow, she saw by the clenched teeth and
writhing lips, and the convulsive frown of the strongly
marked brows, that even in delirium the sufferer was
struggling to restrain all unmanly expressions of his
agony. But now, at least, there would be this strong,
capable woman to share in the long night watch; and
if the patient grew desperate there would be three pair
of hands to protect him from his own fury.

She made her arrangements promptly and decisively.
Mrs. Basset was to stay all night with her in the
patient's chamber, with such needful intervals of rest as
each might take without leaving the sick-room; and
Stokes was first to see to the fastening of the various

basement doors, and to assure himself that there was
no one hidden either in the cellars or on the ground
floor; also to examine all upper chambers, and lock all
doors; and was then to make himself a bed in a dress-
ing closet adjoining Lord Fareham's chamber, and was
to lie there in his clothes, ready to help at any hour of
the night, should help be wanted.

CHAPTER VI.

BETWEEN LONDON AND OXFORD.

THREE nights and days had gone since Angela first
set her foot upon the threshold of Fareham House, and
in all that time she had not once gone out into the
great city, where dismal silence reigned by day and
night, save for the hideous cries of the men with the
dead-carts, calling to the inhabitants of the infected
houses to bring out their dead, and roaring their awful
summons with as automatic a monotony as if they had
been hawking some common necessary of life—a dismal
cry that was but occasionally varied by the hollow tones
of a Puritan fanatic, stalking, gaunt and half clad, along
the Strand, and shouting some sentence of fatal bode-
ment from the Hebrew prophets; just as before the siege
of Titus there walked through the streets of Jerusalem
one who cried, "Woe to the wicked city!" and whose
voice could not be stopped but by death.

 In those three days and nights the worst symptoms
of the contagion were subjugated. But the ravages of
the disease had left the patient in a state of weakness

which bordered on death; and his nurses were full of
apprehension lest the shattered forces of his constitution
should fail even in the hour of recovery. The violence
of the fever was abated, and the delirium had become
intermittent, while there were hours in which the sufferer
was conscious and reasonable, in which calmer intervals
he would fain have talked with Angela more than her
anxiety would allow.

He was full of wonder at her presence in that
house; and when he had been told who she was, he
wanted to know how and why she had come there.
By what happy accident, by what interposition of Pro-
vidence, had she been sent to save him from a hideous
death?

"I should have died but for you," he said. "I
should have lain here till the cart fetched my putrid
carcase. I should be rotting in one of their plague-pits
yonder, behind the old Abbey."

"Nay, indeed, my lord, your good doctor would have
discovered your desolate condition, and would have
brought Mrs. Basset to nurse you."

"He would have been too late. I was drifting out
to the dark sea of death. I felt as if the river were
bearing me so much nearer to that unknown sea with
every ripple of the hurrying tide. 'Twas your draught
of strong wine snatched me back from the cruel river,
drew me on to *terra firma* again, renewed my consciousness of manhood, and that I was not a weed to be
washed away. Oh, that wine! Ye gods! what elixir
to this parched, burning throat! Did ever drunkard in
all Alsatia snatch such fierce joy from a brimmer?"

Angela put her finger on her lip, and with the other

hand drew the silken coverlet over the sick man's shoulders.

"You are not to talk," she said, "you are to sleep. Slumber is to be your diet and medicine after that good soup at which you make such a wry face."

"I would swallow the stuff were it Locusta's hell-broth, for your sake."

"You will take it for wisdom's sake, that you may mend speedily, and go home to my sister," said Angela.

"Home, yes! It will be bliss ineffable to see flowery pastures and wooded hills after this pest-haunted town; but oh, Angela, mine angel, why dost thou linger in this poisonous chamber where every breath of mine exhales infection? Why do you not fly while you are still un-stricken? Truly the plague-fiend cometh as a thief in the night. To-day you are safe. To-night you may be doomed.

"I have no fear, sir. You are not the first plague-patient I have nursed."

"And thou fanciest thyself pestilence-proof! Sweet girl, it may be that the divine lymph which fills those azure veins has no affinity with poisons that slay rude mortals like myself."

"Will you ever be talking?" she said with grave reproach, and left him to the care of Mrs. Basset, whose comfortable and stolid personality did not stimulate his imagination.

She had a strong desire to explore that city of which she had yet seen so little, and her patient being now arrived at a state of his disorder when it was best for him to be tempted to prolonged slumbers by silence and solitude, she put on her hood and gloves and went

8*

out alone to see the horrors of the deserted streets, of
which nurse Basset had given her so appalling a picture.

It was four o'clock, and the afternoon was at its
hottest; the blue of a cloudless sky was reflected in the
blue of the silent river, where, instead of the flotilla of
gaily painted wherries, the procession of gilded barges,
the music and song, the ceaseless traffic of Court and
City, there was only the faint ripple of the stream, or
here and there a solitary barge creeping slowly down
the tide with ineffectual sail flapping in the sultry atmosphere.

That unusual calm which had marked this never-to
be-forgotten year, from the beginning of spring, was yet
unbroken, and the silent city lay like a great ship be-
calmed on a tropical ocean; the same dead silence; the
same cruel, smiling sky above; the same hopeless submission to fate in every soul on board that death-ship.
How would those poor dying creatures, panting out their
latest breath in sultry, airless chambers, have welcomed
the rush of rain, the cool freshness of a strong wind
blowing along those sun-baked streets, sweeping away
the polluted dust, dispersing noxious odours, bringing
the pure scents of far-off woodlands, of hillside heather
and autumn gorse, the sweetness of the country across
the corruption of the town. But at this dreadful season,
when storm and rain would have been welcomed with
passionate thanksgiving, the skies were brass, and the
ground was arid and fiery as the sands of the Arabian
desert, while even the grass that grew in the streets,
where last year multitudinous feet had trodden, sickened
as it grew, and faded speedily from green to yellow.

Pausing on the garden terrace to survey the prospect before she descended to the street, Angela thought of that river as her imagination had depicted it, after reading a letter of Hyacinth's, written so late as last May; the gay processions, the gaudy liveries of watermen and servants, the gilded barges, the sound of viol and guitar, the harmony of voices in part songs, "Go, lovely rose," or "Why so pale and wan, fond lover?" the beauty and the splendour; fair faces under vast plumed hats, those picturesque hats which the maids of honour snatched from each other's heads with giddy laughter, exchanging head-gear here on the royal barge, as they did sometimes walking about the great rooms at Whitehall; the King with his boon companions clustered round him on the richly carpeted daïs in the stern, his courtiers and his favoured mistresses; haughty Castlemaine, empres, regnant over the royal heart, false, dissolute, impudent, glorious as Cleopatra when her purple sails bore her down the swift-flowing Cydnus; the wit and folly and gladness. All had vanished like the visions of a dreamer; and there remained but this mourning city, with its closed windows and doors, its watchmen guarding the marked houses, lest disease and death should hold communion with that poor remnant of health and life left in the infected town. Would that fantastic vision of careless, pleasure-loving monarch and butterfly Court ever be realised again? Angela thought not. It seemed to her serious mind that the glory of those wild years since his Majesty's restoration was a delusive and pernicious brightness which could never shine again. That extravagant splendour, that reckless gaiety had borne beneath their glittering surface the seeds of ruin and death. An

angry God had stretched out His hand against the
wicked city where sin and profaneness sat in the high
places.   If Charles Stuart and his courtiers ever came
back to London they would return sobered and chastened, taught wisdom by adversity.   The Puritan spirit
would reign once more in the land, and an age of
penitence and Lenten self-abasement would succeed the
orgies of the Restoration; while the light loves of Whitehall, the noble ladies, the impudent actresses, would
vanish into obscurity.   Angela's loyal young heart was
full of faith in the King.   She was ready to believe that
his sins were the sins of a man whose head had been
turned by the sudden change from exile to a throne,
from poverty to wealth, from dependence upon his
Bourbon cousin and his friends in Holland to the lavish
subsidies of a too-indulgent Commons.

No words could paint the desolation which reigned
between the Strand and the City in that fatal summer,
now drawing to its melancholy close.   More than once
in her brief pilgrimage Angela drew back, shuddering,
from the embrasure of a door, or the inlet to some
narrow alley, at sight of death lying on the threshold,
stiff, stark, unheeded; more than once in her progress
from the New Exchange to St. Paul's she heard the
shrill wail of women lamenting for a soul just departed.
Death was about and around her.   The great bell of
the cathedral tolled with an inexorable stroke in the
summer stillness, as it had tolled every day through
those long months of heat, and drought, and ever-grow-
ing fear, and ever-thickening graves.

Eastward there rose the red glare of a great fire,
and she feared that some of those old wooden houses

in the narrower streets were blazing, but on inquiry of a
solitary foot passenger, she learnt that this fire was one
of many which had been burning for three days, at
street corners and in open spaces, at a great expense of
sea-coal, with the hope of purifying the atmosphere and
dispersing poisonous gases—but that so far no ameliora-
tion had followed upon this outlay and labour. She
came presently to a junction of roads near the Fleet
ditch, and saw the huge coal-fire flaming with a sickly
glare in the sunshine, tended by a spectral figure, half-
clad and hungry-looking, to whom she gave an alms;
and at this juncture of ways a great peril awaited her,
for there sprang, as it were, out of the very ground, so
quickly did they assemble from neighbouring courts and
alleys, a throng of mendicants, who clustered round her,
with filthy hands outstretched, and shrill voices implor-
ing charity. So wasted were their half-naked limbs, so
ghastly and livid their countenances, that they might
have all been plague-patients, and Angela recoiled from
them in horror.

"Keep your distance, for pity's sake, good friends, and
I will give you all the money I carry," she exclaimed,
and there was something of command in her voice and
aspect, as she stood before them, straight and tall, with
pale, earnest face.

They fell off a little way, and waited till she scattered
the contents of her purse—small Flemish coin—upon
the ground in front of her, where they scrambled for it,
snarling and scuffling with each other like dogs fighting
for a bone.

Hastening her footsteps after the horror of that encounter, she went by Ludgate Hill to the great cathedral,

keeping carefully to the middle of the street, and glancing at the walls and shuttered casements on either side
of her, recalling that appalling story which the Italian
choir-mistress at the Ursulines had told her of the great
plague in Milan—how one morning the walls and doors
of many houses in the city had been found smeared with
some foul substance, in broad streaks of white and yellow,
which was believed to be a poisonous compost carrying
contagion to every creature who touched or went within
the influence of its mephitic odour; how this thing had
happened not once, but many times; until the Milanese
believed that Satan himself was the prime mover in this
horror, and that there were a company of wretches who
had sold themselves to the devil, and were his servants
and agents, spreading disease and death through the
city. Strange tales were told of those who had seen
the foul fiend face to face, and had refused his proffered
gold. Innocent men were denounced, and but narrowly
escaped being torn limb from limb, or trampled to death,
under the suspicion of being concerned in this anointing
of the walls, and even the cathedral benches, with
plague-poison; yet no death, that the nun could remember, had ever been traced directly to the compost.
It was a mysterious terror which struck deep into the
hearts of a frightened people, so that at last, against his
better reason, and at the repeated prayer of his flock,
the good Archbishop allowed the crystal coffin of
St. Carlo Borromeo to be carried in solemn procession,
upon the shoulders of Cardinals, from end to end of the
city—on which occasion all Milan crowded into the
streets, and clustered thick on either side of the pompous
train of monks and incense-bearers, priests and acolytes.

But soon there fell a deeper despair upon the inhabitants of the doomed city; for within two days after this solemn carrying of the saintly remains the death-rate had tripled and there was scarce a house in which the contagion had not entered. Then it was said that the anointers had been in active work in the midst of the crowd, and had been busiest in the public squares where the bearers of the crystal coffin halted for a space with their sacred load, and where the people clustered thickest. The Archbishop had foreseen the danger of this gathering of the people, many but just recovering from the disease, many infected and unconscious of their state; but his flock saw only the handiwork of the fiend in this increase of evil.

In Protestant London there had been less inclination to superstition; yet even here a comet which, under ordinary circumstances, would have appeared but as other comets, was thought to wear the shape of a fiery sword stretched over the city in awful threatening.

Full of pity and of gravest, saddest thoughts, the lonely girl walked through the lonely town to that part of the city where the streets were narrowest, a labyrinth of lanes and alleys, with a church-tower or steeple rising up amidst the crowded dwellings at almost every point to which the eye looked. Angela wondered at the sight of so many fine churches in this heretical land. Many of these city churches were left open in this day of wrath, so that unhappy souls who had a mind to pray might go in at will, and kneel there. Angela peered in at an old church in a narrow court, holding the door a little way ajar, and looking along the cold grey nave. All was gloom and silence, save for a monotonous and suppressed

murmur of one invisible worshipper in a pew near the
altar, who varied his supplicatory mutterings with long-
drawn sighs.

Angela turned with a shudder from the cold empti-
ness of the great grey church, with its sombre woodwork,
and lack of all those beautiful forms which appeal to the
heart and imagination in a Romanist temple. She
thought how in Flanders there would have been tapers
burning, and censors swinging, and the rolling thunder
of the organ pealing along the vaulted roof in the solemn
strains of a *Dies Irae,* lifting the soul of the worshipper
into the far-off heaven of the world beyond death, soothing the sorrowful heart with visions of eternal bliss.

She wandered through the maze of streets and lanes,
sometimes coming back unawares to a street she had
lately traversed, till at last she came to a church that
was not silent, for through the open door she heard a
voice within, preaching or praying. She hesitated for a
few minutes on the threshold, having been taught that
it was a sin to enter a Protestant church; and then
something within her, some new sense of independence
and revolt against old traditions, moved her to enter,
and take her place quietly in one of the curious wooden
boxes where the sparse congregation were seated, listening to a man in a Geneva gown, who was preaching in
a tall oaken pulpit, surmounted by a massive sounding-
board, and furnished with a crimson velvet cushion,
which the preacher used with great effect during his
discourse, now folding his arms upon it and leaning for-
ward to argue familiarly with his flock, now stretching a
long, lean arm above it to point a denouncing finger at

the sinners below, anon belabouring it severely in the passion of his eloquence.

The flock was small, but devout, consisting for the most part of middle-aged and elderly persons in sombre attire and of Puritanical aspect; for the preacher was one of those Calvinistic clergy of Cromwell's time who had been lately evicted from their pulpits, and prosecuted for assembling congregations under the roofs of private citizens, and had shown a noble perseverance in serving God in circumstances of peculiar difficulty. And now, though the Primate had remained at his post, unfaltering and unafraid, many of the orthodox shepherds had fled and left their sheep, being too careful of their own tender persons to remain in the plague-stricken town and minister to the sick and dying; whereupon the evicted clergy had in some cases taken possession of the deserted pulpits and the silent churches, and were preaching Christ's Gospel to that remnant of the faithful which feared not to assemble in the House of God.

Angela listened to a sermon marked by a rough eloquence which enchained her attention and moved her heart. It was not difficult to utter heart-stirring words or move the tender breast to pity when the Preacher's theme was death; with all its train of attendant agonies; its partings and farewells; its awful suddenness, as shown in this pestilence, where a young man rejoicing in his health and strength at noontide sees, as the sun slopes westward, the death-tokens on his bosom, and is lying dumb and stark at nightfall; where the joyous maiden is surprised in the midst of her mirth by the apparition of the plague-spot, and in a few hours is lifeless clay. The Preacher dwelt upon the sins and follies and vanities of the inhabitants of that great city; their alacrity in the pursuit of pleasure; their slackness in the service of God.

"A man who will give twenty shillings for a pair of laced gloves to a pretty shopwoman at the New Exchange, will grudge a crown for the maintenance of God's people that are in distress; and one who is not hardy enough to walk half a mile to church, will stand for a whole afternoon in the pit of a theatre, to see painted women-actors defile a stage that was evil enough in the late King's time, but which has in these latter days sunk to a depth of infamy that it befits not me to speak of in this holy place. Oh, my Brethren, out of that glittering dream which you have dreamt since his Majesty's return, out of the groves of Baal, where you have sung and danced, and feasted, worshipping false gods, steeping your benighted souls in the vices of pagans and image-worshippers, it has pleased the God of Israel to give you a rough waking. Can you doubt that this plague, which has desolated a city, and filled many a yawning pit with the promiscuous dead, has been God's way of chastening a profligate people, a people caring only for fleshly pleasures, for rich meats and strong wines, for fine clothing and jovial company, and despising the spiritual blessings that the Almighty Father has reserved for them that love Him? Oh, my afflicted Brethren, bethink you that this pestilence is a chastisement upon a blind and foolish people; and if it strikes the innocent as well as the guilty, if it falls as heavily upon the spotless virgin as upon the hoary sinner, remember that it is not for us to measure the workings of Omnipotence with the fathom-line of our earthly intellects; or to say this fair girl should be spared, and that hoary sinner taken. Has not the Angel of Death ever chosen the fairest blossoms? His business is to people the skies rather than to depopulate the earth. The innocent are taken, but the warning is for the guilty; for the sinners whose debaucheries have made this world so polluted a place that God's greatest mercy to the pure is an early death. The call is loud and instant, a call to repentance and sacrifice. Let each bear his portion of suffering with patience, as under that wise rule of a score years past each family forewent a weekly meal to help those who needed bread. Let each acknowledge his debt to God, and be content to have paid it in a season of universal sorrow."

And then the Preacher turned from that awful image of an angry and avenging God to contemplate Divine compassion in the Redeemer of mankind—godlike power joined with human love. He preached of Christ the Saviour with a fulness and a force which were new to Angela. He held up that commanding, that touching image, unobscured by any other personality. All those surrounding figures which Angela had seen crowded around the godlike form, all those sufferings and virtues of the spotless Mother of God were ignored in that impassioned oration. The preacher held up Christ crucified, Him only, as the fountain of pity and pardon. He reduced Christianity to its simplest elements, primitive as when the memory of the God-man was yet fresh in the minds of those who had seen the Divine countenance and listened to the Divine voice; and Angela felt as she had never felt before the singleness and purity of the Christian's faith.

It was the day of long sermons, when a preacher who measured his discourse by the sands of an hour-glass was deemed moderate. Among the Nonconformists there were those who turned the glass, and let the flood of eloquence flow on far into the second hour. The old man had been preaching a long time when Angela awoke as from a dream, and remembered that sick-chamber where duty called her. She left the church quietly and hurried westward, guided chiefly by the sun, till she found herself once more in the Strand; and very soon afterwards she was ringing the bell at the chief entrance of Fareham House. She returned far more depressed in spirits than she went out, for all the horror of the plague-stricken city was upon her; and, fresh from the spectacle of death, she felt less hopeful of Lord Fareham's recovery.

Thomas Stokes opened the great door to admit that one modest figure, a door which looked as if it should open only to noble visitors, to a procession of courtiers and court beauties, in the fitful light of wind-blown torches. Thomas, when interrogated, was not cheerful in his account of the patient's health during Angela's absence. My lord had been strangely disordered; Mrs. Basset had found the fever increasing, and was "afeared the gentleman was relapsing."

Angela's heart sickened at the thought. The Preacher had dwelt on the sudden alternations of the disease, how apparent recovery was sometimes the precursor of death. She hurried up the stairs, and through the seemingly endless suite of rooms which nobody wanted, which never might be inhabited again perhaps, except by bats and owls, to his lordship's chamber, and found him sitting up in bed, with his eyes fixed on the door by which she entered.

"At last!" he cried. "Why did you inflict such torturing apprehensions upon me? This woman has been telling me of the horrors of the streets where you have been; and I figured you stricken suddenly with this foul malady, creeping into some deserted alley to expire uncared for, dying with your head upon a stone, lying there to be carried off by the dead-cart. You must not leave this house again, save for the coach that shall fetch you to Oxfordshire to join Hyacinth and her children—and that coach shall start to-morrow. I am a madman to have let you stay so long in this infected house."

"You forget that I am plague-proof," she answered, throwing off hood and cloak, and going to his bedside, to the chair in which she had spent many hours watching by him and praying for him.

No, there was no relapse. He had only been restless and uneasy because of her absence. The disease was conquered, the pest-spots were healing fairly, and his nurses had only to contend against the weakness and depression which seemed but the natural sequence of the malady.

Dr. Hodgkin was satisfied with his patient's progress. He had written to Lady Fareham, advising her to send some of her servants with horses for his lordship's coach, and to provide for relays of post-horses between London and Oxfordshire, a matter of easier accomplishment than it would have been in the earlier summer, when the quality were flying to the country, and post-horses were at a premium. Now there were but few

people of rank or standing who had the courage to stay
in town, like the Archbishop, who had not left Lambeth,
or the stout old Duke of Albemarle, at the Cockpit, who
feared the pestilence no more than he feared sword or
cannon.

Two of his lordship's lackeys, and his Oxfordshire
major-domo and clerk of the kitchen, arrived a week
after Angela's landing, bringing loving letters from
Hyacinth to her husband and sister. The physician had
so written as not to scare the wife. She had been told
that her husband had been ill, but was in a fair way to
recovery, and would post to Oxfordshire as soon as he
was strong enough for the journey, carrying his sister-in-
law with him, and lying at the accustomed inn at High
Wycombe, or perchance resting two nights and spending
three days upon the road.

That was a happy day for Angela when her patient
was well enough to start on his journey. She had been
longing to see her sister and the children, longing still
more intensely to escape from the horror of that house,
where death had seemed to lie in ambush behind the
tapestry hangings, and where few of her hours had been
free from a great fear. Even while Fareham was on the
high-road to recovery there had been in her mind the
ever-present dread of a relapse. She rejoiced with fear
and trembling, and was almost afraid to believe physician and nurse when they assured her that all danger
was over.

The pestilence had passed by, and they went out in
the sunshine, in the freshness of a September morning,
balmy, yet cool, with a scent of flowers from the gardens
of Lambeth and Bankside blowing across the river.

Even this terrible London, the forsaken city, looked fair
in the morning light; her palaces and churches, her
streets of heavily timbered houses, their projecting windows enriched with carved wood and wrought iron—
streets that recalled the days of the Tudors and even
suggested an earlier and rougher age, when the French
King rode in all honour, albeit a prisoner, at his con-
queror's side; or later, when fallen Richard, shorn of all
royal dignity, rode abject and forlorn through the city,
and caps were flung up for his usurping cousin.   But
oh, the horror of closed shops and deserted houses, and
pestiferous wretches running by the coach door in their
poisonous rags, begging alms, whenever the horses went
slowly, in those narrow streets that lay between Fareham
House and Westminster!

To Angela's wondering eyes Westminster Hall and
the Abbey offered a new idea of magnificence, so grandly
placed, so dignified in their antiquity.   Fareham watched
her eager countenance as the great family coach, which
had been sent up from Oxfordshire for his accommoda-
tion, moved ponderously westward, past the Chancellor's
new palace, and other new mansions, to the Hercules
Pillars Inn, past Knightsbridge and Kensington, and
then northward by rustic lanes, and through the village
of Ealing to the Oxford road.

The family coach was as big as a small parlour, and
afforded ample room for the convalescent to recline at
his ease on one seat, while Angela and the steward, a
confidential servant with the manners of a courtier, sat
side by side upon the other.

They had the two spaniels with them, Puck and
Ganymede, silky-haired little beasts, black and tan, with

bulging foreheads, crowded with intellect, pug noses so
short as hardly to count for noses, goggle eyes that
expressed shrewdness, greediness, and affection. Puck
snuggled cosily in the soft lace of his lordship's shirt;
Ganymede sat and blinked at the sunshine from Angela's
lap. Both snarled at Mr. Manningtree, the steward, and
resented the slightest familiarity on his part.

Lord Fareham's thoughtful face brightened with its
rare smile—half amused, half cynical—as he watched
Angela's eager looks, devouring every object on the
road.

"Those grave eyes look at our London grandeurs
with a meek wonder, something as thy namesake an
angel might look upon the splendours of Babylon. You
can remember nothing of yonder palace, or senate house,
or Abbey, I think, child?"

"Yes, I remember the Abbey, though it looked
different then. I saw it through a cloud of falling snow.
It was all faint and dim there. There were soldiers in
the streets, and it was bitter cold; and my father sat in
the coach with his elbows on his knees and his face
hidden in his hands. And when I spoke to him, and
tried to pull his hands away—for I was afraid of that
hidden face—he shook me off and groaned aloud. Oh,
such a harrowing groan! I should have thought him
mad had I known what madness meant; but I know
not what I thought. I remember only that I was
frightened. And later, when I asked him why he was
sorry, he said it was for the King."

"Ay, poor King! We have all supped full of sorrow
for his sake. We have cursed and hated his enemies,
and drawn and quartered their vile carcases, and have

dug them out of the darkness where the worms were eating them. We have been distraught with indignation, cruel in our fury; and I look back to-day, after fifteen years, and see but too clearly now that Charles Stuart's death lies at one man's door."

"At Cromwell's? At Bradshaw's?"

"No, child; at his own. Cromwell would have never been heard of, save in Huntingdon Market-place, as a God-fearing yeoman, had Charles been strong and true. The King's weakness was Cromwell's opportunity. He dug his own grave with false promises, with shilly-shally, with an inimitable talent for always doing the wrong thing and choosing the wrong road. Open not so wide those reproachful eyes. Oh, I grant you, he was a noble king, a king of kings to walk in a royal procession, to sit upon a daïs under a velvet and gold canopy, to receive ambassadors, and patronise foreign painters, and fulfil all that is splendid and stately in ideal kingship. He was an adoring husband—confiding to simplicity—a kind father, a fond friend, though never a firm one."

"Oh, surely, surely you loved him?"

"Not as your father loved him, for I never suffered with him. It was those who sacrificed the most who loved him best, those who were with him to the end, long after common sense told them his cause was hopeless; indeed, I believe my father knew as much at Nottingham, when that luckless standard was blown down in the tempest. Those who starved for him, and lay out on barren moors through the cold English nights for him, and wore their clothes threadbare and their shoes into holes for him, and left wife and children, and

melted their silver and squandered their gold for him—
those are the men who love his memory dearest, and
for whose poor sakes we of the younger generation must
make believe to think him a saint and a martyr."

"Oh, my lord, say not that you think him a bad
man!"

"Bad! Nay, I believe that all his instincts were
virtuous and honourable, and that—until the whirlwind
of those latter days in which he scarce knew what he
was doing—he meant fairly by his people, and had
their welfare at heart. He might have done far better
for himself and others had he been a brave bad man
like Wentworth—audacious, unscrupulous, driving straight
to a fixed goal. No, Angela, he was that which is worse
for mankind—an obstinate, weak man. A bundle of
impulses, some good and some evil; a man who had
many chances, and lost them all; who loved foolishly
and too well, and let himself be ruled by a wife who
could not rule herself. Blind impulse, passionate folly
were sailing the State ship through that sea of troubles
which could be crossed but by a navigator as politic,
profound, and crafty as Richelieu or Mazarin. Who
can wonder that the Royal Charles went down?"

"It must seem strange to you, looking back from the
Court, as Hyacinth's letters have painted it—to that time
of trouble?"

"Strange! I stand in the crowd at Whitehall sometimes, amidst their masking and folly, their frolic schemes,
their malice, their jeering wit and riotous merriment,
and wonder whether it is all a dream, and I shall wake
and see the England of '44, the year Henrietta Maria
vanished—a discrowned fugitive, from the scene where

she had lived to do harm. I look along the perspective of painted faces and flowing hair, jewels, and gay colours, towards that window through which Charles I. walked to his bloody death, suffered with a kingly grandeur that made the world forget all that was poor and petty in his life; and I wonder does anyone else recall that suffering or reflect upon that doom. Not one! Each has his jest, and his mistress—the eyes he worships, the lips he adores. It is only the rural Put that feels himself lost in the crowd whose thoughts turn sadly to the sad past."

"Yet whatever your lordship may say——"

"Tush, child, I am no lordship to you! Call me brother, or Fareham; and never talk to me as if I were anything else than your brother in affection."

"It is sweet to hear you say so much, sir," she answered gently. "I have often envied my companions at the Ursulines when they talked of their brothers. It was so strange to hear them tell of bickering and ill-will between brother and sister. Had God given me a brother, I would not quarrel with him."

"Nor shalt thou quarrel with me, sweetheart; but we will be fast friends always. Do I not owe thee my life?"

"I will not hear you say so; it is blasphemy against your Creator, who relented and spared you."

"What! you think that Omnipotence, in the inaccessible mystery of Heaven, keeps the muster-roll of earth open before Him, and reckons each little life as it drops off the list? That is hardly my notion of Divinity. I see the Almighty rather as the Roman poet saw Him—an inexorable Father, hurling the thunderbolt our folly has deserved from His red right hand, yet merciful to stay that hand when we have taken our punishment meekly. That, Angela, is the nearest my mind can reach to the idea of a personal God. But do not bend those pencilled brows with such a sad perplexity. You know, doubtless, that I come of a Catholic family, and was bred in the old faith. Alas! I have conformed ill to Church discipline. I am no theologian, nor quite an infidel, and should be as much at sea in an argument with Hobbes as with Bossuet. Trouble not thy gentle spirit for my sins of thought or deed. Your tender care has given me time to repent all my errors. You were going to tell my lordship something, when I chid you for excess of ceremony——"

"Nay, sir—brother, I had but to say that this wicked Court, of which my father and you have spoken so ill, can scarcely fail to be turned from its sins by so terrible a visitation. Those who have looked upon the city as I saw it a week ago can scarce return with unchastened hearts to feasting and dancing and idle company."

"But the beaux and belles of Whitehall have not seen the city as my brave girl saw it," cried Fareham. "They have not met the dead-cart, nor heard the groans of the dying, nor seen the red cross upon the doors. They made off with the first rumour of peril. The roads were crowded with their coaches, their saddle-horses, their furniture and finery; one could scarce command a post-horse for love or money. 'A thousand less this week,' says one. 'We may be going back to town and have the theatres open again in the cold weather.'"

They dined at the Crown, at Uxbridge, which was that "fair house at the end of the town" provided for the meeting of the late King's Commissioners with the representatives of the Parliament in the year '44. Fareham showed his sister-in-law a spacious panelled parlour, which was that "fair room in the middle of the house" that had been handsomely dressed up for the Commissioners to sit in.

They pushed on to High Wycombe before nightfall, and supped *tête-à-tête* in the best room of the inn, with Fareham's faithful Manningtree to bring in the chief dish, and the people of the house to wait upon them. They were very friendly and happy together, Fareham telling his companion much of his adventurous life in France, and how in the first Fronde war he had been on the side of Queen and Minister, and afterwards, for love and admiration of Condé, had joined the party of the Princes.

"Well, it was a time worth living in—a good education for the boy-king, Louis, for it showed him that the hereditary ruler of a great nation has something more to do than to be born, and to exist, and to spend money."

Lord Fareham described the shining lights of that brilliant court with a caustic tongue; but he was more indulgent to the follies of the Palais Royal and the Louvre than he had been to the debaucheries of Whitehall.

"There is a grace even in their vices," he said. "Their wit is lighter, and there is more mind in their follies. Our mirth is vulgar even when it is not bestial. I know of no Parisian adventure so degrading as certain

pranks of Buckhurst's, which I would not dare mention
in your hearing. We imitate them, and out-herod Herod,
but we are never like them. We send to Paris for our
clothes, and borrow their newest words—for they are
ever inventing some cant phrase to startle dulness—and
we make our language a foreign farrago. Why, here is
even plain John Evelyn, that most pious of pedants,
pleading for the enlistment of a troop of Gallic sub-
stantives and adjectives to eke out our native English!"

Fareham told Angela much of his past life during
the freedom of that long *tête-à-tête*, talking to her as if
she had indeed been a young sister from whom he had
been separated since her childhood. That mild, pensive
manner promised sympathy and understanding, and he
unconsciously inclined to confide his thoughts and opinions
to her, as well as the history of his youth.

He had fought at Edgehill as a lad of thirteen, had
been with the King at Beverley, York, and Nottingham,
and had only left the Court to accompany the Prince of
Wales to Jersey, and afterwards to Paris.

"I soon sickened of a Court life and its petty plots
and parlour intrigues," he told Angela, "and was glad
to join Condé's army, where my father's influence got
me a captaincy before I was eighteen. To fight under
such a leader as that was to serve under the god of
war. I can imagine Mars himself no grander soldier.
Oh, my dear, what a man! Nay, I will not call him by
that common name. He was something more or less
than man—of another species. In the thick of the fight
a lion; in his dominion over armies, in his calmness
amidst danger, a god. Shall I ever see it again, I wonder

—that vulture face, those eyes that flashed Jove's red lightning?"

"Your own face changes when you speak of him," said Angela, awestricken at that fierce energy which heroic memories evoked in Fareham's wasted countenance.

"Nay, you should have seen the change in *his* face when he flung off the courtier for the captain. His whole being was transformed. Those who knew Condé at St. Germain, at the Hôtel de Rambouillet, at the Palais Royal, knew not the measure or the might of that great nature. He was born to conquer. But you must not think that with him victory meant brute force. It meant thought and patience, the power to foresee and to combine, the rapid apprehension of opposing circumstances, the just measure of his own materials. A strict disciplinarian, a severe master, but willing to work at the lowest details, the humblest offices of war. A soldier, did I say? He was the Genius of modern warfare."

"You talk as if you loved him dearly."

"I loved him as I shall never love any other man. He was my friend as well as my General. But I claim no merit in loving one whom all the world honoured. Could you have seen princes and nobles, as I saw them when I was a boy at Paris, standing on chairs, on tables, kneeling, to drink his health! A demi-god could have received no more fervent adulation. Alas! sister, I look back at those years of foreign service and know they were the best of my life!"

They started early next morning, and were within half a dozen miles of Oxford before the sun was low.

They drove by a level road that skirted the river; and now, for the first time, Angela saw that river flowing placidly through a rural landscape, the rich green of marshy meadows in the foreground, and low wooded hills on the opposite bank, while midway across the stream an islet covered with reed and willow cast a shadow over the rosy water painted by the western sun.

"Are we near them now?" she asked eagerly, knowing that her brother-in-law's mansion lay within a few miles of Oxford.

"We are very near," answered Fareham; "I can see the chimneys, and the white stone pillars of the great gate."

He had his head out of the carriage, looking sunward, shading his eyes with his big doe-skin gauntlet as he looked. Those two days on the road, the fresh autumn air, the generous diet, the variety and movement of the journey, had made a new man of him. Lean and gaunt he must needs be for some time to come; but the dark face was no longer bloodless; the eyes had the fire of health.

"I see the gate—and there is more than that in view!" he cried excitedly. "Your sister is coming in a troop to meet us, with her children, and visitors, and servants. Stop the coach, Manningtree, and let us out."

The postboys pulled up their horses, and the steward opened the coach door and assisted his master to alight. Fareham's footsteps were somewhat uncertain as he walked slowly along the waste grass by the roadside, leaning a little upon Angela's shoulder.

Lady Fareham came running towards them in advance of children and friends, an airy figure in blue and white, her fair hair flying in the wind, her arms stretched out as if to greet them from afar. She clasped her sister to her breast even before she saluted her husband, clasped her and kissed her, laughing between the kisses.

"Welcome, my escaped nun!" she cried. "I never thought they would let thee out of thy prison, or that thou wouldst muster courage to break thy bonds. Welcome, and a hundred times, welcome. And that thou shouldst have nursed and tended my ailing lord! Oh, the wonder of it! While I, within a hundred miles of him, knew not that he was ill, here didst thou come across seas to save him! Why, 'tis a modern fairy tale."

"And she is the good fairy," said Fareham, taking his wife's face between his two hands and bending down to kiss the white forehead under its cloud of pale golden curls, "and you must cherish her for all the rest of your life. But for her I should have died alone in that great gaudy house, and the rats would have eaten me, and then perhaps you would have cared no longer for the mansion, and would have had to build another further west, by my Lord Clarendon's, where all the fine folks are going—and that would have been a pity."

"Oh, Fareham, do not begin with thy irony-stop! I know all your organ tones, from the tenor of your kindness to the bourdon of your displeasure. Do you think I am not glad to have you here safe and sound? Do you think I have not been miserable about you since I knew of your sickness? Monsieur de Malfort will tell you whether I have been unhappy or not."

"Why, Malfort! What wind blew you hither at this

perilous season, when Englishmen are going abroad for
fear of the pestilence, and when your friend St. Evremond has fled from the beauties of Oxford to the malo-
dorous sewers and fusty fraus of the Netherlands?"

"I had no fear of the contagion, and I wanted to
see my friends. I am in lodgings in Oxford, where
there is almost as much good company as there ever
was at Whitehall."

The Comte de Malfort and Fareham clasped hands
with a cordiality which bespoke old friendship; and it
was only an instinctive recoil on the part of the English-
man which spared him his friend's kisses. They had
lived in camps and in courts together, these two, and
had much in common, and much that was antagonistic,
in temperament and habits, Malfort being lazy and
luxurious, when no fighting was on hand; a man whose
one business, when not under canvas, was to surpass
everybody else in the fashion and folly of the hour, to
be quite the finest gentleman in whatever company he
found himself.

He was a godson and favourite of Madame de Montrond, who had numbered his father among the army
of her devoted admirers. He had been Hyacinth's
play-fellow and slave in her early girlhood, and had
been *l'ami de la maison* in those brilliant years of the
young King's reign, when the Farehams were living in
the Marais. To him had been permitted all privileges
that a being as harmless and innocent as he was
polished and elegant might be allowed, by a husband
who had too much confidence in his wife's virtue, and
too good an opinion of his own merits to be easily

jealous. Nor was Henri de Malfort a man to provoke jealousy by any superior gifts of mind or person. Nature had not been especially kind to him. His features were insignificant, his eyes pale, and he had not escaped that scourge of the seventeenth century, the small-pox. His pale and clear complexion was but slightly pitted, however, and his eyelids had not suffered. Men were inclined to call him ugly; women thought him interesting. His frame was badly built from the athlete's point of view; but it had the suppleness which makes the graceful dancer, and was an elegant scaffolding on which to hang the picturesque costume of the day. For the rest, all that he was he had made himself, during those eighteen years of intelligent self-culture, which had been his engrossing occupation since his fifteenth birthday, when he determined to be one of the finest gentlemen of his epoch.

A fine gentleman at the Court of Louis had to be something more than a figure steeped in perfumes and hung with ribbons. His red-heeled shoes, his periwig and cannon sleeves, were indispensable to fashion, but not enough for fame. The favoured guest of the Hôtel de Rambouillet, and of Mademoiselle de Scudéry's "Saturdays," must have wit and learning, or at least that capacity for smart speech and pedantic allusion which might pass current for both in a society where the critics were chiefly feminine. Henri de Malfort had graduated in a college of blue-stockings. He had grown up in an atmosphere of gunpowder and *bouts rimés*. He had stormed the breach at sieges where the assault was led off by a company of violins, in the Spanish fashion. He had fought with distinction under the

finest soldiers in Europe, and had seen some of his
dearest friends expire at his side.

Unlike Gramont and St. Évremond, he was still in
the floodtide of royal favour in his own country; and it
seemed a curious caprice that had led him to follow
those gentlemen to England, to shine in a duller society,
and sparkle at a less magnificent court.

The children hung upon their father, Papillon on one
side, Cupid on the other, and it was in them rather
than in her sister's friend that Angela was interested.
The girl resembled her mother only in the grace and
flexibility of her slender form, the quickness of her
movements, and the vivacity of her speech. Her hair
and eyes were dark, like her father's, and her colouring
was that of a brunette, with something of a pale bronze
under the delicate carmine of her cheeks. The boy
favoured his mother, and was worthy of the sobriquet
Rochester had bestowed upon him. His blue eyes,
chubby cheeks, cherry lips, and golden hair were like
the typical Cupid of Rubens, and might be seen repeated *ad libitum* on the ceiling of the Banqueting
House.

"I'll warrant this is all flummery," said Fareham,
looking down at the girl as she hung upon him. "Thou
art not glad to see me."

"I am so glad that I could eat you, as the Giant
would have eaten Jack," answered the girl, leaping up
to kiss him, her hair flying back like a dark cloud, her
nimble legs struggling for freedom in her long brocade
petticoat.

"And you are not afraid of the contagion?"

"Afraid! Why, I wanted mother to take me to you as soon as I heard you were ill."

"Well, I have been smoke-dried and pickled in strong waters, until Dr. Hodgkin accounts me safe, or I would not come nigh thee. See, sweetheart, this is your aunt, whom you are to love next best to your mother."

"But not so well as you, sir. You are first," said the child, and then turned to Angela and held up her rosebud mouth to be kissed. "You saved my father's life," she said. "If you ever want anybody to die for you let it be me."

"Gud! what a delicate wit! The sweet child is positively *tuant,*" exclaimed a young lady, who was strolling beside them, and whom Lady Fareham had not taken the trouble to introduce by name to anyone, but who was now accounted for as a country neighbour, Mrs. Dorothy Lettsome.

Angela was watching her brother-in-law as they sauntered along, and she saw that the fatigue and agitation of this meeting were beginning to affect him. He was carrying his hat in one hand, while the other caressed Papillon. There were beads of perspiration on his forehead, and his footsteps began to drag a little. Happily the coach had kept a few paces in their rear, and Manningtree was walking beside it; so Angela proposed that his lordship should resume his seat in the vehicle and drive on to his house, while she went on foot with her sister.

"I must go with his lordship," cried Papillon, and leapt into the coach before her father.

Hyacinth put her arm through Angela's, and led

her slowly along the grassy walk to the great gates, the
Frenchman and Mrs. Lettsome following; and unversed
as the convent-bred girl was in the ways of this particular world, she could nevertheless perceive that in the
conversation between these two, M. de Malfort was
amusing himself at the expense of his fair companion.
His own English was by no means despicable, as he
had spent more than a year at the Embassy immediately after the Restoration, to say nothing of his
constant intercourse with the Farehams and other
English exiles in France; but he was encouraging the
young lady to talk to him in French, which was spoken
with an affected drawl, that was even more ridiculous
than its errors in grammar.

CHAPTER VII.

AT THE TOP OF THE FASHION.

NOTHING could have been more cordial than Lady
Fareham's welcome to her sister, nor were it easy to
imagine a life more delightful than that at Chilton
Abbey in that autumnal season, when every stage of
the decaying year clothed itself with a variety and
brilliancy of colouring which made ruin beautiful, and
disguised the approach of winter, as a court harridan
might hide age and wrinkles under a yellow satin mask
and flame-coloured domino. The Abbey was one of
those capacious, irregular buildings in which all that a
house was in the past and all that it is in the present

are composed into a harmonious whole, and in which past and present are so cunningly interwoven that it would have been difficult for anyone but an architect to distinguish where the improvements and additions of yesterday were grafted on to the masonry of the fourteenth century. Here, where the spacious plate-room and pantry began, there were walls massive enough for the immuring of refractory nuns; and this corkscrew Jacobean staircase, which wound with carved balusters up to the garret story, had its foundations in a flight of Cyclopean stone steps that descended to the cellars, where the monks kept their strong liquors and brewed their beer. Half of my lady's drawing-room had been the refectory, and the long dining-parlour still showed the groined roof of an ancient cloister; while the music-room, into which it opened, had been designed by Inigo Jones, and built by the last Lord Fareham. All that there is of the romantic in this kind of architectural patchwork had been enhanced by the collection of old furniture that the present possessors of the Abbey had imported from Lady Fareham's *château* in Normandy, and which was more interesting though less splendid than the furniture of Fareham's town mansion, as it was the result of gradual accumulation in the Montrond family, or of purchase from the wreck of noble houses, ruined in the civil war which had distracted France before the reign of the Bearnais.

To Angela the change from an enclosed convent to such a house as Chilton Abbey, was a change that filled all her days with wonder. The splendour, the air of careless luxury that pervaded her sister's house, and suggested costliness and waste in every detail, could but be distressing to the pupil of Flemish nuns, who had seen even the trenchers scraped to make soup for the poor, and every morsel of bread garnered as if it were gold dust. From that sparse fare of the convent to this Rabelaisian plenty, this plethora of meat and poultry, huge game pies and elaborate confectionery, this perpetual too much of everything, was a transition that startled and shocked her. She heard with wonder of the numerous dinner tables that were spread every day at Chilton. Mr. Manningtree's table, at which the Roman Priest from Oxford dined, except on those rare occasions when he was invited to sit down with the quality; and Mrs. Hubbock's table, where the superior servants dined, and at which Henriette's dancing-master considered it a privilege to over-eat himself; and the two great tables in the servants' hall, twenty at each table; and the *gouvernante*, Mrs. Priscilla Goodman's table in the blue parlour upstairs, at which my lady's English and French waiting-women, and my lord's gentlemen ate, and at which Henriette and her brother were supposed to take their meals, but where they seldom appeared, usually claiming the right to eat with their parents. She wondered as she heard of the fine-drawn distinctions among that rabble of servants, the upper ranks of whom were supplied by the small gentry—of servants who waited upon servants, and again other servants who waited on those, down to that lowest stratum of kitchen sluts and turnspits, who actually made their own beds and scraped their own trenchers. Everywhere there was lavish expenditure—everywhere the abundance which, among that uneducated and unthoughtful class, ever degenerates into wanton waste.

It sickened Angela to see the long dining-table loaded, day after day, with dishes that were many of them left untouched amidst the superabundance, while the massive Cromwellian sideboard seemed to need all the thickness of its gouty legs to sustain the "regalia" of hams and tongues, pasties, salads and jellies. And all this time *The Weekly Gazette* from London told of the unexampled distress in that afflicted city, which was but the natural result of an epidemic that had driven all the well-to-do away, and left neither trade nor employment for the lower classes.

"What becomes of that mountain of food?" Angela asked her sister, after her second dinner at Chilton, by which time she and Hyacinth had become familiar and at ease with each other. "Is it given to the poor?"

"Some of it, perhaps, love; but I'll warrant that most of it is eaten in the offices—with many a handsome sirloin and haunch to boot."

"Oh, sister, it is dreadful to think of such a troop! I am always meeting strange faces. How many servants have you?"

"I have never reckoned them. Manningtree knows, no doubt; for his wages book would tell him. I take it there may be more than fifty, and less than a hundred. Anyhow, we could not exist were they fewer."

"More than fifty people to wait upon four!"

"For our state and importance, *chérie*. We are very ill-waited upon. I nearly died last week before I could get anyone to bring me my afternoon chocolate. The men had all rushed off to a bull-baiting, and the women were romping or fighting in the laundry, except my own women, who are too genteel to play with the under-

10*

servants, and had taken a holiday to go and see a tragedy at Oxford. I found myself in a deserted house. I might have been burnt alive, or have expired in a fit, for aught any of those over-fed devils cared."

"But could they not be better regulated?"

"They are, when Manningtree is at home. He has them all under his thumb."

"And he is an honest, conscientious man?"

"Who knows? I dare say he robs us, and takes a *pot de vin* wherever 'tis offered. But it is better to be robbed by one than by an army; and if Manningtree keeps others from cheating he is worth his wages."

"And you, dear Hyacinth. Do you keep no accounts?"

"Keep accounts! Why, my dearest simpleton, did you ever hear of a woman of quality keeping accounts—unless it were some lunatic universal genius like her Grace of Newcastle, who rises in the middle of the night to scribble verses, and who might do anything preposterous. Keep accounts! Why, if you was to tell me that two and two make five I couldn't contróvert you, from my own knowledge."

"It all seems so strange to me," murmured Angela. "My aunt supervised all the expenditure of the convent, and was unhappy if she discovered waste in the smallest item."

"Unhappy! Yes, my dear innocent. And do you think if I was to investigate the cost of kitchen and cellar, and calculate how many pounds of meat each of our tall lackeys consumes per diem, I should not speedily be plagued into grey hairs and wrinkles? I hope we are rich enough to support their wastefulness. And if we are not—why, *vogue la galère*—when we are ruined the King must do something for Fareham—make him Lord Chancellor. His Majesty is mighty sick of poor old Clarendon and his lectures. Fareham has a long head, and would do as well as anybody else for Chancellor if he would but show himself at Court oftener, and conform to the fashion of the time, instead of holding himself aloof, with a Puritanical disdain for amusements and people that please his betters. He has taken a leaf out of Lord Southampton's book, and would not allow me to return a visit Lady Castlemaine paid me the other day, in the utmost friendliness: and to slight her is the quickest way to offend his Majesty."

"But, sister, you would not consort with an infamous woman?"

"Infamous! Who told you she is infamous? Your innocency should be ignorant of such trumpery tittle-tattle. And one can be civil without consorting, as you call it."

Angela took her sister's reckless speech for mere sportiveness. Hyacinth might be careless and ignorant of business, but his lordship doubtless knew the extent of his income, and was too grave and experienced a personage to be a spendthrift. He had confessed to seven and thirty, which to the girl of twenty seemed serious middle-age.

'There were musicians in her ladyship's household—youths who played lute and viol, and sang the dainty, meaningless songs of the latest ballad-mongers very prettily. The warm weather, which had a bad effect upon the bills of mortality, was so far advantageous that it allowed these gentlemen to sing in the garden while the family were at supper, or on the river while the family were taking their evening airing. Their newest performance was an arrangement of Lord Dorset's lines —"To all you ladies now on land," set as a round. There could scarcely be anything prettier than the dying fall of the refrain that ended every verse:—

> "With a fa, la, la,
> Perhaps permit some happier man
> To kiss your hand or flirt your fan,
> With a fa, la, la."

The last lines died away in the distance of the moonlit garden, as the singers slowly retired, while Henri de Malfort illustrated that final couplet with Hyacinth's fan, as he sat beside her.

"Music, and moonlight, and a garden. You might fancy yourself amidst the grottoes and terraces of St. Germain."

"I note that whenever there is anything meritorious in our English life Malfort is reminded of France, and when he discovers any obnoxious feature in our manners or habits he expatiates on the vast difference between the two nations," said his lordship.

"Dear Fareham, I am a human being. When I am in England I remember all I loved in my own country. I must return to it before I shall understand the worth of all I leave here—and the understanding may be bitter. Call your singers back, and let us have those two last verses again. 'Tis a fine tune, and your fellows perform it with sweetness and brio."

The song was new. The victory which it celebrated was fresh in the minds of men. The disgrace of later Dutch experiences—the ships in the Nore ravaging and insulting—was yet to come. England still believed her floating castles invincible.

To Angela's mind the life at Chilton was full of change and joyous expectancy. No hour of the day but offered some variety of recreation, from battledore and shuttlecock in the *plaisance* to long days with the hounds or the hawks. Angela learnt to ride in less than a month, instructed by the stud-groom, a gentleman of considerable importance in the household; an old campaigner, who had groomed Fareham's horses after many a battle, and many a skirmish, and had suffered scant food and rough quarters without murmuring; and also with considerable assistance and counsel from Lord Fareham, and occasional lectures from Papillon, who was a Diana at ten years old, and rode with her father in the first flight. Angela was soon equal to accompanying her sister in the hunting-field, for Hyacinth liked following the chase after the French rather than the English fashion, affecting no ruder sport than to wait at an opening of the wood, or on the crest of a common, to see hounds and riders sweep by; or, favoured by chance now and then, to signal the villain's whereabouts by a lace handkerchief waved high above her head. This was how a beautiful lady who had hunted in the forests of St. Germain and Fontainebleau understood sport; and such performances as this Angela found easy and agreeable. They had many cavaliers who came to talk with them for a few minutes, to tell them what was doing or not doing yonder where the hounds were hidden in thicket or coppice; but Henri de Malfort was their most constant attendant. He rarely left them, and dawdled through the earlier half of an October day,

walking his horse from point to point, or dismounting at
sheltered corners to stand and talk at Lady Fareham's
side, with a patience that made Angela wonder at the
contrast between English headlong eagerness, crashing
and splashing through hedge and brook, and French
indifference.

"I have not Fareham's passion for mud," he ex-
plained to her, when she remarked upon his lack of
interest in the chase, even when the music of the hounds
was ringing through wood and valley, now close beside
them, anon diminishing in the distance, thin in the thin
air. "If he comes not home at dark plastered with mire
from boots to eyebrows he will cry, like Alexander, 'I
have lost a day.'"

Partridge-hawking in the wide fields between Chilton
and Nettlebed was more to Malfort's taste, and it was
a sport for which Lady Fareham expressed a certain
enthusiasm, and for which she attired herself to the
perfection of picturesque costume. Her hunting-coats
were marvels of embroidery on atlas and smooth cloth;
but her smartest velvet and brocade she kept for the
sunny mornings, when, with hooded peregrine on wrist,
she sallied forth intent on slaughter, Angela, Papillon,
and De Malfort for her *cortége,* an easy-paced horse to
amble over the grass with her, and the Dutch falconer
to tell her the right moment at which to slip her falcon's
hood.

The nuns at the Ursuline Convent would scarcely
have recognised their quondam pupil in the girl on the
grey palfrey, whose hair flew loose under a beaver hat,
mingling its tresses with the long ostrich plume, whose
trimly fitting jacket had a masculine air which only

accentuated the womanliness of the fair face above it,
and whose complexion, somewhat too colourless within
the convent walls, now glowed with a carnation that
brightened and darkened the large grey eyes into new
beauty.

That open-air life was a revelation to the cloister-
bred girl. Could this earth hold greater bliss than to
roam at large over spacious gardens, to cross the river,
sculling her boat with strong hands, with her niece
Henriette, otherwise Papillon, sitting in the stern to steer,
and scream instructions to the novice in navigation; and
then to lose themselves in the woods on the further
shore, to wander in a labyrinth of reddening beeches,
and oaks on which the thick foliage still kept its dusky
green; to emerge upon open lawns where the pale gold
birches looked like fairy trees, and where amber and
crimson toadstools shone like jewels on the skirts of the
dense undergrowth of holly and hawthorn? The liberty
of it all, the delicious feeling of freedom, the release
from convent rules and convent hours, bells ringing for
chapel, bells ringing for meals, bells ringing to mark the
end of the brief recreation—a perpetual ringing and
drilling which had made conventual life a dull machine,
working always in the same grooves.

Oh, this liberty, this variety, this beauty in all things
around and about her! How the young glad soul, newly
escaped from prison, revelled and expatiated in its
freedom! Papillon, who at ten years old, had skimmed
the cream off all the simple pleasures, appointed herself
her aunt's instructress in most things, and taught her to
row, with some help from Lord Fareham, who was an
expert waterman; and, at the same time, tried to teach

her to despise the country, and all rustic pleasures,
except hunting—although in her inmost heart the minx
preferred the liberty of Oxfordshire woods to the
splendour of Fareham House, where she was cooped in
a nursery with her *gouvernante* for the greater part of her
time, and was only exhibited like a doll to her mother's
fine company, or seated upon a cushion to tinkle a
saraband and display her precocious talent on the guitar,
which she played almost as badly as Lady Fareham
herself, at whose feeble endeavours even the courteous
De Malfort laughed.

Never was sister kinder than Hyacinth, impelled by
that impulsive sweetness which was her chief charac-
teristic, and also, it might be, moved to lavish generosity
by some scruples of conscience with regard to her grandmother's will. Her first business was to send for the
best milliner in Oxford, a London Madam who had
followed her court customers to the university town, and
to order everything that was beautiful and seemly for a
young person of quality.

"I implore you not to make me too fine, dearest,"
pleaded Angela, who was more horrified at the milliner's
painted face and exuberant figure than charmed by the
contents of the baskets which she had brought with her
in the spacious leather coach—velvets and brocades,
hoods and gloves, silk stockings, fans, perfumes and
pulvilios, sweet-bags and scented boxes—all of which the
woman spread out upon Lady Fareham's embroidered
satin bed, for the young lady's admiration. "I pray you
remember that I am accustomed to have only two gowns
—a black and a grey. You will make me afraid of my
image in the glass if you dress me like—like——"

She glanced from her sister's *décolleté* bodice to the far more appalling charms of the milliner, which a gauze kerchief rather emphasised than concealed, and could find no proper conclusion for her sentence.

"Nay, sweetheart, let not thy modesty take fright. Thou shalt be clad as demurely as the nun thou·hast escaped being—

> 'And sable stole of Cyprus lawn
> Over thy decent shoulders drawn.'

We will have no blacks, but as much decency as you choose. You will mark the distinction between my sister and your maids of honour, Mrs. Lewin. She is but a *débutante* in our modish world, and must be dressed as modestly as you can contrive, to be consistent with the fashion."

"Oh, my lady, I catch your ladyship's meaning, and your ladyship's instructions shall be carried out as far as can be without making a savage of the young lady. I know what some young ladies are when they first come to Court. I had fuss enough with Miss Hamilton before I could persuade her to have her bodice cut like a Christian. And even the beautiful Miss Brooks were all for high tuckers and modesty-pieces when I began to make for them; but they soon came round. And now with my Lady Denham it is always, 'Gud, Lewin, do you call that the right cut for a bosom? Udsbud, woman, you haven't made the curve half deep enough.' And with my Lady Chesterfield it is, 'Sure, if they say my legs are thick and ugly, I'll let them know my shoulders are worth looking at. Give me your scissors, creature,' and then with her own delicate hand she will scoop me a good inch off the satin, till I am fit to swoon at seeing the cold steel against her milk-white flesh."

Mrs. Lewin talked with but little interruption for the best part of an hour while measuring her new customer, showing her pattern-book, and exhibiting the ready-made wares she had brought, the greater number of which Hyacinth insisted on buying for Angela—who was horrified at the slanderous innuendoes that dropped in casual abundance from the painted lips of the milliner; horrified, too, that her sister could loll back in her armchair and laugh at the woman's coarse and malignant talk.

"Indeed, sister, you are far too generous, and you have overpowered me with gifts," she said, when the milliner had curtsied herself out of the room; "for I fear my own income will never pay for all these costly things. Three pounds, I think she said, was the price of the Mazarine hood alone—and there are stockings and gloves innumerable."

"Mon Ange, while you are with me your own income is but for charities and vails. I will have it spent for nothing else. You know how rich the Marquise has made me—while I believe Fareham is a kind of modern Crœsus, though we do not boast of his wealth, for all that is most substantial in his fortune comes from his mother, whose father was a great merchant trading with Spain and the Indies, all through James's reign, and luckier in the hunt for gold than poor Raleigh. Never must you talk to me of obligation. Are we not sisters, and was it not a mere accident that made me the elder, and Madame de Montrond's *protégée!*"

"I have no words to thank you for so much kindness. I will only say I am so happy here that I could never have believed there was such full content on this sinful earth."

"Wait till we are in London, Angélique. Here we endure existence. It is only in London that we live."

"Nay, I believe the country will always please me better than the town. But, sister, do you not hate that Mrs. Lewin—that horrid painted face and evil tongue?"

"My dearest child, one hates a milliner for the spoiling of a bodice or the ill cut of a sleeve—not for her character. I believe Mrs. Lewin's is among the worst, and that she has had as many intrigues as Lady Castlemaine. As for her painting, doubtless she does that to remind her customers that she sells alabaster powder and ceruse."

"Nay, if she wants to disgust them with painted faces she has but to show her own."

"I grant she lays the stuff on badly. I hope, if I live to have as many wrinkles, I shall fill them better than she does. Yet who can tell what a hideous toad she might be in her natural skin? It may be Christian charity that induces her to paint, and so to spare us the sight of a monster. She will make thee a beauty, Ange, be sure of that. For satin or velvet, birthday or gala gowns, nobody can beat her. The wretch has had thousands of my money, so I ought to know. But for thy riding-habit and hawking-jacket we want the firmer grip of a man's hand. Those must be made by Roget."

"A Frenchman?"

"Yes, child. One only accepts British workmanship when a Parisian artist is not to be had. Clever as Lewin is, if I want to eclipse my dearest enemy on any special

occasion I send Manningtree across the Channel, or ask
De Malfort to let his valet—who spends his life in transit
like a king's messenger—bring me the latest confection
from the Rue de Richelieu."

"What infinite trouble about a gown—and for you
who would look lovely in anything!"

"Tush, child! You have never seen me in 'anything.' If ever you should surprise me in an ill gown
you will see how much the feathers make the bird.
Poets and playwrights may pretend to believe that we
need no embellishment from art; but the very men who
write all that romantic nonsense are the first to court a
well-dressed woman. And there are few of them who
could calculate with any exactness the relation of beauty
to its surroundings. That is why women go deep into
debt to their milliners, and would sooner be dead in
well-made graveclothes than alive in an old-fashioned
mantua."

Angela could not be in her sister's company for a
month without discovering that Lady Fareham's whole
life was given up to the worship of the trivial. She was
kind, she was amiable, generous, even to recklessness.
She was not irreligious, heard Mass and went to confession as often as the hard conditions of an alien and
jealously treated Church would allow, had never disputed
the truth of any tenet that was taught her—but of
serious views, of an earnest consideration of life and
death, husband and children, Hyacinth Fareham was as
incapable as her ten-year-old daughter. Indeed, it sometimes seemed to Angela that the child had broader and
deeper thoughts than the mother, and saw her surroundings with a shrewder and clearer eye, despite the

natural frivolity of childhood, and the exuberance of a
fine physique.

It was not for the younger sister to teach the elder,
nor did Angela deem herself capable of teaching. Her
nature was thoughtful and earnest; but she lacked that
experience of life which can alone give the thinker a
broad and philosophic view of other people's conduct.
She was still far from the stage of existence in which to
understand all is to pardon all.

She beheld the life about her with wonder and
bewilderment. It was so pleasant, so full of beauty and
variety; yet things were said and done that shocked her.
There was nothing in her sister's own behaviour to alarm
her modesty; but to hear her sister talk of other women's
conduct outraged all her ideas of decency and virtue. If
there were really such wickedness in the world, women
so shameless and vile, was it right that good women
should know of them, that pure lips should speak of
their iniquity?

She was still more shocked when Hyacinth talked
of Lady Castlemaine with a good-humoured indulgence.

"There is something fine about her," Lady Fareham
said one day, "in spite of her tempers and pranks."

"What!" cried Angela, aghast, having thought these
creatures unrecognised by any honest woman, "do you
know her—that Lady Castlemaine of whom you have
told me such dreadful things?"

"C'est vrai. J'en ai dit des raides. Mon Ange, in
town one must needs know everybody, though I doubt
that after not returning her visit t'other day, I shall be
in her black books, and in somebody else's. She has
never been one of my intimates. If I were often at

Whitehall, I should have to be friends with her. But
Fareham is jealous of Court influences; and I am only
allowed to appear on gala nights—perhaps not a half-
dozen times in a season. There is a distinction in not
showing oneself often: but it is provoking to hear of
the frolics and jollities which go on every day and every
night, and from which I am banished. It mattered little
while the Queen-mother was at Somerset House, for her
Court ranked higher—and was certainly more refined
in its splendour—than her son's ragamuffin herd. But
now she is gone, I shall miss our intellectual *milieu,* and
wish myself in the Rue St. Thomas du Louvre, where
the Hôtel du Rambouillet, even in its decline, offers a
finer style of company than anything you will see in
England."

"Sister, I fear you left half your heart in France."

"Nay, sweet; perhaps some of it has followed me,"
answered Hyacinth, with a blush and an enigmatic
smile. *"Peste!* I am not a woman to make a fuss
about hearts! There is not a grain of tragedy in my
composition. I am like that girl in the play we saw at
Oxford t'other day. Fletcher's was it, or Shakespeare's?
'A star danced, and under that was I born.' Yes, I
was born under a dancing star; and I shall never break
my heart—for love."

"But you regret Paris?"

"Hélas! Paris means my girlhood; and were you
to take me back there to-morrow you could not make
me seventeen again—and so where's the use? I should
see wrinkles in the faces of my friends; and should
know that they were seeing the same ugly lines in mine.
Indeed, Ange, I think it is my youth I sigh for rather

than the friends I lived with. They were such merry days: battles and sieges in the provinces, parliaments disputing here and there; Condé in and out of prison— now the King's loyal servant, now in arms against him; swords clashing, cannon roaring under our very windows; alarm bells pealing, cries of fire, barricades in the streets; and amidst it all, lute and theorbo, *bouts rimés* and madrigals, dancing and play-acting, and foolish practical jests! One could not take the smallest step in life but one of the wits would make a song about it. Oh, it was a boisterous time! And we were all mad, I think; so lightly did we reckon life and death, even when the cannon slew some of our noblest, and the finest saloons were hung with black. You have done less than live, Angélique, not to have lived in that time."

Hyacinth loved to ring the changes on her sister's name. Angela was too English, and sounded too much like the name of a nun; but Angélique suggested one of the most enchanting personalities in that brilliant circle on which Lady Fareham so often rhapsodised. This was the beautiful Angélique Paulet, whose father invented the tax called by this name, La Paulette—a financial measure, which was the main cause of the first Fronde war.

"I only knew her when she was between fifty and sixty," said Lady Fareham, "but she hardly looked forty; and she was still handsome, in spite of her red hair. *Trop doré,* her admirers called it; but, my love, it was as red as that scullion's we saw in the poultry yard yesterday. She was a reigning beauty at three Courts, and had a crowd of adorers when she was only fourteen. Ah, Papillon, you may open your eyes! What will you be at fourteen? Still playing with your babies, or mad about your shock dogs, I dare swear!"

"I gave my babies to the housekeeper's granddaughter last year," said Papillon, much offended, "when father gave me the peregrine. I only care for live things now I am old."

"And at fourteen thou wilt be an awkward, long-legged wench that will frighten away all my admirers, yet not be worth the trouble of a compliment on thine own account."

"I want no such stuff!" cried Papillon. "Do you think I would like a French fop always at my elbow as Monsieur de Malfort is ever at yours? I love hunting and hawking, and a man that can ride, and shoot, and row, and fight, like father or Sir Denzil Warner—not a man who thinks more of his ribbons and periwig and cannon-sleeves than of killing his fox or flying his falcon."

"Oh, you are beginning to have opinions!" sighed Hyacinth. "I am indeed an old woman! Go and find yourself something to play with, alive or dead. You are vastly too clever for my company."

"I'll go and saddle Brownie. Will you come for a ride, Aunt Angy?"

"Yes, dear, if her ladyship does not want me at home."

"Her ladyship knows your heart is in the fields and woods. Yes, sweetheart, saddle your pony, and order your aunt's horse and a pair of grooms to take care of you."

The child ran off rejoicing.

"Precocious little devil! She will pick up all our jargon before she is in her teens,"

"Dear sister, if you talk so indiscreetly before her——"

"Indiscreet! Am I really so indiscreet? That is Fareham's word. I believe I was born so. But I was telling you about your namesake, Mademoiselle Paulet. She began to reign when Henri was king, and no doubt he was one of her most ardent admirers. Don't look frightened! She was always a model of virtue. Mademoiselle Scudèry has devoted pages to painting her perfections under an Oriental alias. She sang, she danced, she talked divinely. She did everything better than everybody else. Priests and Bishops praised her. And after changes and losses and troubles, she died far from Paris, a spinster, nearly sixty years old. It was a paltry finish to a life that began in a blaze of glory."

CHAPTER VIII.

SUPERIOR TO FASHION.

At Oxford Angela was so happy as to be presented to Catharine of Braganza, a little dark woman, whose attire still bore some traces of its original Portuguese heaviness; such a dress—clumsy, ugly, infinitely rich and expensive—as one sees in old portraits of Spanish and Netherlandish matrons, in which every elaborate detail of the costly fabric seems to have been devised in the research of ugliness. She saw the King also; met him casually—she walking with her brother-in-law, while Lady Fareham and her friends ran from shop to shop in the High Street—in Magdalen College grounds, a group of beauties and a family of spaniels fawning upon him as he sauntered slowly, or stopped to feed the swans that swam close by the bank, keeping pace with him, and stretching long necks in greedy solicitation.

The loveliest woman Angela had ever seen—tall, built like a goddess—walked on the King's right hand. She carried a heap of broken bread in the satin petticoat which she held up over one white arm, while with her other hand she gave the pieces one by one to the King. Angela saw that as each hunch changed hands the royal fingers touched the lady's tapering fingertips and tried to detain them.

Fareham took off his hat, bowed low in a grave and stately salutation, and passed on; but Charles called him back.

"Nay, Fareham, has the world grown so dull that you have nothing to tell us this November morning?"

"Indeed, sir, I fear that my riverside hermitage can afford very little news that could interest your Majesty or these ladies."

"A fox gone to ground, an otter killed among your reeds, or a hawk in the sulks, is an event in the country. Anything would be a relief from the weekly total of London deaths, which is our chief subject of conversation, or the General's complaints that there is no one in town but himself to transact business, or dismal prophecies of a Nonconformist rebellion that is to follow the Five Mile Act."

The group of ladies stared at Angela in a smiling silence, one haughtier than the rest standing a little aloof. She was older, and of a more audacious love-liness than the lady who carried broken bread in her petticoat; but she too was splendidly beautiful as a goddess on a painted ceiling, and as much painted perhaps.

Angela contemplated her with the reverence youth gives to consummate beauty, unaware that she was ad-miring the notorious Barbara Palmer.

Fareham waited, hat in hand, grave almost to sullenness. It was not for him to do more than reply to his Majesty's remarks, nor could he retire till dis-missed.

"You have a strange face at your side, man. Pray introduce the lady," said the King, smiling at Angela, whose vivid blush was as fresh as Miss Stewart's had been a year or two ago, before she had her first quarrel with Lady Castlemaine, or rode in Gramont's glass coach, or gave her classic profile to embellish the coin of the realm—the "common drudge 'tween man and man."

I have the honour to present my sister-in-law, Mis-tress Kirkland, to your Majesty."

The King shook hands with Angela in the easiest way, as if he had been mortal.

"Welcome to our poor court, Mistress Kirkland. Your father was my father's friend and companion in the evil days. They starved together at Beverley, and rode side by side through the Warwickshire lanes to suffer the insolence of Coventry. I have not forgotten. If I had I have a monitor yonder to remind me," glancing in the direction of a middle-aged gentleman, stately, and sober of attire, who was walking slowly towards them. "The

Chancellor is a living chronicle, and his conversation chiefly consists in reminiscences of events I would rather forget."

"Memory is an invention of Old Nick," said Lady Castlemaine. "Who the deuce wants to remember anything, except what cards are out and what are in?"

"Not you, Fairest. You should be the last to cultivate mnemonics for yourself or for your friends. Is your father in England, sweet mistress?"

Angela faltered a negative, as if with somebody else's voice—or so it seemed to her. A swarthy, heavy-browed man, wearing a dark-blue ribbon and a star—a man with whom his intimates jested in shameless freedom— a man whom the town called Rowley, after some ignominious quadruped—a man who had distinguished himself neither in the field nor in the drawing-room by any excellence above the majority, since the wit men praised has resolved itself for posterity into half a dozen happy repartees. Only this! But he was a King, a crowned and anointed King, and even Angela, who was less frivolous and shallow than most women, stood before him abashed and dazzled.

His Majesty bowed a gracious adieu, yawned, flung another crust to the swans, and sauntered on, the Stewart whispering in his ear, the Castlemaine talking loud to her neighbour, Lady Chesterfield, this latter lady very pretty, very bold and mischievous, newly restored to the Court after exile with her jealous husband at his mansion in Wales.

They were gone; Charles to be button-holed by Lord Clarendon, who waited for him at the end of the walk; the ladies to wander as they pleased till the two-o'clock dinner. They were gone, like a dream of beauty and splendour, and Fareham and Angela pursued their walk by the river, grey in the sunless November.

"Well, sister, you have seen the man whom we brought back in a whirlwind of loyalty five years ago, and for whose sake we rebuilt the fabric of monarchical government. Do you think we are much the gainers by that tempest of enthusiasm which blew us home Charles the Second? We had suffered all the trouble of the change to a Republic; a life that should have been sacred had been sacrificed to the principles of liberty. While abhorring the regicides, we might have profited by their crime. We might have been a free state to-day, like the United Provinces. Do you think we are better off with a King like Rowley, to amuse himself at the expense of the nation?"

"I detest the idea of a Republic."

"Youth worships the supernatural in anointed kings. Think not that I am opposed to a constitutional monarchy, so long as it works well for the majority. But when England had with such terrible convulsions shaken off all those shackles and trappings of royalty, and when the ship, so lightened, had sailed so steadily with no ballast but common sense, does it not seem almost a pity to undo what has been done—to begin again the long procession of good kings and bad kings, foolish or wise—for the sake of such a man as yonder saunterer?" with a glance towards the British Sultan and his harem.

"England was never better governed than by Cromwell," he continued. "She was tranquil at home and victorious abroad, admired and feared. Mazarin, while pretending to be the faithful friend of Charles, was the obsequious courtier of Oliver. The finest form of government is a limited despotism. See how France prospered under the sagacious tyrant, Louis the Eleventh, under the soldier-statesman, Sully, under pure reason incarnate in Richelieu. Whether you call your tyrant king or protector, minister or president, matters nothing. It is the man and not the institution, the mind and not the machinery that is wanted."

"I did not know you were a Republican, like Sir Denzil Warner."

"I am nothing now I have left off being a soldier. I have no strong opinions about anything. I am a looker on; and life seems little more real to me than a stage play. Warner is of a different stamp. He is an enthusiastic in politics—godson of Hollis—a disciple of Milton's, the son of a Puritan, and a Puritan himself. A fine nature, Angela, allied to a handsome presence."

Sir Denzil Warner was their neighbour at Chilton, and Angela had met him often enough for them to become friends. He had ridden by her side with hawk and hound, had been one of her instructors in English sport, and had sometimes, by an accident, joined her and Henriette in their boating expeditions, and helped her to perfect herself in the management of a pair of sculls.

"Hyacinth has her fancies about Warner," Fareham said presently, as they strolled along.

There was a significance in his tone that the girl could not mistake; more especially as her sister had not been reticent about those notions to which Fareham alluded.

"Hyacinth has fancies about many things," she said, blushing a little.

Fareham noted the slightness of the blush.

"I verily believe that handsome youth has found you adamant," he said, after a thoughtful silence. "Yet you might easily choose a worse suitor. Your sister has often the strangest whims about marriage-making; but in this fancy I did not oppose her. It would be a very suitable alliance."

"I hope your lordship does not begin to think me a burden on your household," faltered Angela, wounded by his cold-blooded air in disposing of her. "When you and my sister are tired of me I can go back to my convent."

"What! Return to those imprisoning walls; immure your sweet youth in a cloister? Not for the Indies. I would not suffer such a sacrifice. Tired of you! I— so deeply bound! I who owe you my life! I who looked up out of a burning hell of pain and madness and saw an angel standing by my bed! Tired of you! Indeed you know me better than to think so badly of me were it but in one flash of thought. You can need no protestations from me. Only, as a young and beautiful woman, living in an age that is full of peril for women, I should like to see you married to a good and true man—such as Denzil Warner."

"I am sorry to disappoint you," Angela answered coldly; "but Papillon and I have agreed that I am always to be her spinster aunt, and am to keep her house when she is married, and wear a linsey gown and a bunch of keys at my girdle, like Mrs. Hubbuck, at Chilton."

"That's just like Henriette. She takes after her mother, and thinks that this globe and all the people upon it were created principally for her pleasure. The Americas to give her chocolate, the Indian isles to sweeten it for her, the ocean tides to bring her feathers and finery. She is her own centre and circumference, like her mother."

"You should not say such an ill thing of your wife, Fareham," said Angela, deeply shocked. "Hyacinth is not one to look into the heart of things. She has too happy a disposition for grave backward-reaching thoughts; but I will swear that she loves you—ay—almost to reverence."

"Yes, to reverence, to over much reverence, perhaps. She might have given a freer, fonder love to a more amiable man. I have some strain of my unhappy kinsman's temper, perhaps—the disposition that keeps a wife at a distance. He managed to make three wives afraid of him; and it was darkly rumoured that he killed one."

"Strafford—a murderer! No, no."

"Not by intent. An accident—only an accident. They who most hated him pretended that he pushed her from him somewhat roughly when she was least able to bear roughness, and that the after consequences of the blow were fatal. He was one of the doomed always, you see. He knew that himself, and told his bosom friend that he was not long-lived. The brand of misfortune was upon him even at the height of his power. You may read his destiny in his face."

They walked on in silence for some time, Angela depressed and unhappy. It seemed as if Fareham had lifted a mask and shown her his real countenance, with all the lines that tell a life history. She had suspected that he was not happy; that the joyous existence amidst fairest surroundings which seemed so exquisite to her was dull and vapid for him. She could but think that he was like her father, and that action and danger were necessary to him, and that it was only this rustic tranquillity that weighed upon his spirits.

"Do not for a moment believe that I would speak slightingly of your sister," Fareham resumed, after that silent interval. "It were indeed an ill thing in me—most of all to disparage her in your hearing. She is lovely, accomplished, learned even, after the fashion of the Rue St. Thomas du Louvre. She used to shine among the brightest at the Scudèrys' Saturday parties, which were the most wearisome assemblies I ever ran away from. The match was made for us by others, and I was her betrothed husband before I saw her. Yet I loved her at first sight. Who could help loving a face as fair as morning over the eastward hills, a voice as sweet as the nightingales in the Tuileries garden? She was so young—a child almost; so gentle and confiding. And to see her now with Papillon is to question which is the younger, mother or daughter. Love her? Why, of course I love her. I loved her then. I love her now. Her beauty has but ripened with the passing years; and she has walked the furnace of fine company in two cities, and has never been seared by fire. Love her! Could a man help loving beauty, and frankness, and a natural innocence which cannot be spoiled even by the knowledge of things evil, even by daily contact with sin in high places?"

Again there was a silence, and then, in a deeper tone, after a long sigh, Fareham said—

"I love and honour my wife; I adore my children; yet I am alone, Angela, and I shall be alone till death."

"I don't understand."

"Oh yes, you do; you understand as well as I who suffer. My wife and I love each other dearly. If she have a fit of the vapours, or an aching tooth, I am wretched. But we have never been companions. The things that she loves are charmless for me. She is enchanted with people from whom I run away. Is it companionship, do you think, for me to look on while she walks a coranto or tosses shuttlecocks with De Malfort? Roxalana is as much my companion when I admire her on the stage from my seat in the pit. There are times when my wife seems no nearer to me than a beautiful picture. If I sit in a corner, and listen to her pretty babble about the last fan she bought at the Middle Exchange, or the last witless comedy she saw at the King's Theatre, is that companionship, think you? I may be charmed to-day—as I was charmed ten years ago—with the silvery sweetness of her voice, with the graceful turn of her head, the white roundness of her throat. At least I am constant. There is no change in her or in me. We are just as near and just as far apart as when the priest joined our hands at St. Eustache. And it must be so to the end, I suppose; and I think the fault is in me. I am out of joint with the world I live in. I cannot set myself in tune with their new music. I look back, and remember, and regret; yet hardly know why I remember or what I regret."

Again a silence, briefer than the last, and he went on:—

"Do you think it strange that I talk so freely—to you—who are scarce more than a child, less learned than Henriette in worldly knowledge? It is a comfort sometimes to talk of oneself; of what one has missed as well as of what one has. And you have such an air of being wise beyond your years; wise in all thoughts that are not of the world—thoughts of things of which there is no truck at the Exchanges; which no one buys or sells at Abingdon fair. And you are so near allied to me—a sister! I never had a sister of my own blood, Angela. I was an only child. Solitude was my portion. I lived alone with my tutor and *gouvernante*—a poor relation of my mother's—alone in a house that was mostly deserted, for Lord and Lady Fareham were in London with the King, till the troubles brought the Court to Christchurch, and them to Chilton. I have had few in whom to confide. And you—remember what you have been to me, and do not wonder if I trust you more than others. Thou didst go down to the very grave with me, didst pluck me out of the pit. Corruption could not touch a creature so lovely and so innocent. Thou didst walk unharmed through the charnel-house. Remembering this, as I ever must remember, can you wonder that you are nearer to me than all the rest of the world?"

She had seated herself on a bench that commanded a view of the river, and her dreaming eyes were looking far away along the dim perspective of mist and water, bare pollard willows, ragged sedges. Her head drooped a little so that he could not see her face, and one ungloved hand hung listlessly at her side.

He bent down to take the slender hand in his, lifted

it to his lips, and quickly let it go; but not before she had felt his tears upon it. She looked up a few minutes later, and the place was empty. Her tears fell thick and fast. Never before had she suffered this exquisite pain—sadness so intense, yet touching so close on joy. She sat alone in the inexpressible melancholy of the late autumn; pale mists rising from the river; dead leaves falling; and Fareham's tears upon her hand.

CHAPTER IX.

IN A PURITAN HOUSE.

How quickly the days passed in that gay household at Chilton! and yet every day of Angela's life held so much of action and emotion that, looking back at Christmas time to the three months that had slipped by since she had brought Fareham from his sick bed to his country home, she could but experience that common feeling of youth in such circumstances. Surely it was half a lifetime that had lapsed; or else she, by some subtle and supernatural change, had become a new creature.

She thought of her life in the Convent, thought of it much and deeply on those Sunday mornings when she and her sister and De Malfort and a score or so of servants crept quietly to a room in the heart of the house where a Priest, who had been fetched from Oxford in Lady Fareham's coach, said Mass within locked doors. The familiar words of the service, the odour of the incense, brought back the old time—the unforgotten atmosphere, the dull tranquillity of ten years, which had been as one year by reason of their level monotony.

Could she go back to such a life as that? Go back! Leave all she loved? At the mere suggestion her trembling hand was stretched out involuntarily to clasp her niece Henriette, kneeling beside her. Leave them— leave those with whom and for whom she lived? Leave this loving child—her sister—her brother? Fareham had told her to call him "Brother." He had been to her as a brother, with all a brother's kindness, counselling her, confiding in her.

Only with one person at Chilton Abbey had she ever conversed as seriously as with Fareham, and that person was Sir Denzil Warner, who at five and twenty was more serious in his way of looking at serious things than most men of fifty.

"I cannot make a jest of life," he said once, in reply to some flippant speech of De Malfort's; "it is too painful a business for the majority."

"What has that to do with us—the minority? Can we smooth a sick man's pillow by pulling a long face? We shall do him more good by tossing him a crown, if he be poor; or helping to build him a hospital by the sacrifice of a night's winnings at ombre. Long faces help nobody; that is what you Puritans will never consider."

"No; but if the long faces are the faces of men who think, something may come of their thoughts for the good of humanity."

Denzil Warner was the only person who ever spoke to Angela of her religion. With extreme courtesy, and with gentle excuses for his temerity in touching on so

delicate a theme, he ventured to express his abhorrence
of the superstitions interwoven with the Romanist's
creed. He talked as one who had sat at the feet of
the blind poet—talked sometimes in the very words of
John Milton.

There was much in what he said that appealed to
her reason; but there was no charm in that severer form
of worship which he offered in exchange for her own.
He was frank and generous; he had a fine nature, but
was too much given to judging his fellow-men. He had
all the arrogance of Puritanism superadded to the natural
arrogance of youth that has never known humiliating
reverses, that has never been the servant of circum-
stance.

He was Angela's senior by something less than four
years; yet it seemed to her that he was in every attribute infinitely her superior. In education, in depth of
thought, in resolution for good, and scorn of evil. If he
loved her—as Hyacinth insisted upon declaring—there
was nothing of youthful impetuosity in his passion. He
had, indeed, betrayed his sentiments by no direct speech.
He had told her gravely that he was interested in her,
and deeply concerned that one so worthy and so
amiable should have been brought up in the house of
idolaters, should have been taught falsehood instead of
truth.

She stood up boldly for the faith of her maternal
ancestors.

"I cannot continue your friend if you speak evil of
those I love, Sir Denzil," she said. "Could you have
seen the lives of those good ladies of the Ursuline
Convent, their unselfishness, their charity, you must

needs have respected their religion. I cannot think why you love to say hard words of us Catholics; for in all I have ever heard or seen of the lives of the Nonconformists they approach us far more nearly in their principles than the members of the Church of England, who, if my sister does not paint them with too black a brush, practise their religion with a laxity and indifference that would go far to turn religion to a jest."

Whatever Sir Denzil's ideas might be upon the question of creed—and he did not scruple to tell Angela that he thought every Papist foredoomed to everlasting punishment—he showed so much pleasure in her society as to be at Chilton Abbey, and the sharer of her walks and rides, as often as possible. Lady Fareham encouraged his visits, and was always gracious to him. She discovered that he possessed the gift of music, though not in the same remarkable degree as Henri de Malfort, who played the guitar exquisitely, and into whose hands you had but to put a musical instrument for him to extract sweetness from it. Lute or theorbo, viola or viol di gamba, treble or bass, came alike to his hand and ear. Some instruments he had studied; with some his skill came by intuition.

Denzil Warner performed very creditably upon the organ. He had played on John Milton's organ in St. Bride's Church, when he was a boy, and he had played of late in the church at Chalfont St. Giles, where he had visited Milton frequently, since the poet had left his lodgings in Artillery Walk, carrying his family and his books to that sequestered village in the shelter of the hills between Uxbridge and Beaconsfield. Here from the lips of his sometime tutor the Puritan had heard such stories of the Court as made him hourly expectant of exterminating fires. Doubtless the fire would have come, as it came upon Sodom and Gomorrah, but for those righteous lives of the Nonconformists, which redeemed the time; quiet, God-fearing lives in dull old city houses, in streets almost as narrow as those which Milton remembered in his beloved Italy; streets where the sun looked in for an hour, shooting golden arrows down upon the diamond-paned casements, and deepening the shadow of the massive timbers that held up the overlapping stories, looked in and bade "good night" within an hour or so, leaving an atmosphere of sober grey, cool, and quiet, and dull, in those obscure streets and alleys where the great traffic of Cheapside or Ludgate sounded like the murmur of a far-off sea.

Pious men and women worshipped the implacable God of the Puritans in the secret chambers of those narrow streets; and those who gathered together in these days—if they rejected the Liturgy of the Church of England—must indeed be few, and must meet by stealth, as if to pray or preach after their own manner were a crime. Charles, within a year or so of his general amnesty and happy restoration, had made such worship criminal; and now the Five Mile Act, lately passed at Oxford, had rendered the restrictions and penalties of Nonconformity utterly intolerable. Men were lying in prison here and there about merry England for no greater offence than preaching the gospel to a handful of God-fearing people. But that a Puritan tinker should moulder for a dozen years in a damp jail could count for little against the blessed fact of the Maypole reinstated in the Strand, and five playhouses in

London performing ribald comedies, till but recently, when the plague shut their doors.

Milton, old and blind, and somewhat soured by domestic disappointments, had imparted no optimistic philosophy to young Denzil Warner, whose father he had known and loved. The fight at Hopton Heath had made Denzil fatherless; the Colonel of Warner's horse riding to his death in the last fatal charge of that memorable day.

Denzil had grown up under the prosperous rule of the Protector, and his boyhood had been spent in the guardianship of a most watchful and serious-minded mother. He had been somewhat over-cosseted and apron-stringed, it may be, in that tranquil atmosphere of the rich widow's house; but not all Lady Warner's tenderness could make her son a milksop. Except for a period of two years in London, when he had lived under the roof of the great Republican, a docile pupil to a stern but kind master, Denzil had lived mostly under the open sky, was a keen sportsman, and loved the country with almost as sensitive a love as his quondam master and present friend, John Milton; and it was perhaps this appreciation of rural beauty which had made a bond of friendship between the great poet and the Puritan squire.

"You have a knack of painting rural scenes which needs but to be joined with the gift of music to make you a poet," he said, when Denzil had been expatiating upon the landscape amidst which he had enjoyed his last bout of falconry, or his last run with his half-dozen couple of hounds. "You are almost as the power of sight to me when you describe those downs and valleys

12*

whose every shape and shadow I once knew so well.
Alas, that I should be changed so much and they so
little!"

"It is one thing, sir, to feel that this world is beautiful, and another to find golden words and phrases
which to a prisoner in the Tower could conjure up as
fair a landscape as Claude Lorraine ever painted. Those
sonorous and mellifluous lines which you were so gracious
as to repeat to me, forming part of the great epic which
the world is waiting for, bear witness to the power that
can turn words into music, and make pictures out of
the common tongue. That splendid art, sir, is but
given to one man in a century—or in several centuries;
since I know but Dante and Virgil who have ever
equalled your vision of heaven and hell."

"Do not over-praise me, Denzil, in thy charity to
poverty and affliction. It is pleasing to be understood
by a youth who loves hawk and hound better than
books; for it offers the promise of popular appreciation
in years to come. Yet the world is so little athirst for
my epic that I doubt if I shall find a bookseller to give
me a few pounds for the right to print a work that has
cost me years of thought and laborious revision. But
at least it has been my consolation in the long blank
night of my decay, and has saved me many a heartache.
For while I am building up my verses, and engraving
line after line upon the tablets of memory, I can forget
that I am blind, and poor, and neglected, and that the
dear saint I loved was snatched from me in the noontide of our happiness."

Denzil talked much of John Milton in his conversations with Angela, during those rides or rambles, in

which Papillon was their only chaperon. Lady Fareham
sauntered, like her royal master; but she rarely walked
a mile at a stretch; and she was pleased to encourage
the rural wanderings that brought her sister and Warner
into a closer intimacy, and promised well for the success
of her matrimonial scheme.

"I believe they adore each other already," she told
Fareham one morning, standing by his side in the great
stone porch, to watch those three youthful figures ride
away, aunt and niece side by side, on palfrey and pony,
with Denzil for their cavalier.

"You are always over-quick to be sure of anything
that suits your own fancy, dearest," answered Fareham,
watching them to the curve of the avenue; "but I see
no signs of favour to that solemn youth in your sister.
She suffers his attentions out of pure civility. He is an
accomplished horseman, having given all his life to learning how to jump a fence gracefully; and his company is
at least better than a groom's."

"How scornfully you jeer at him!"

"Oh, I have no more scorn than the Cavalier's
natural contempt for the Roundhead. A hereditary
hatred, perhaps."

"You say such hard things of his Majesty that one
might often take you to be of Sir Denzil's way of thinking."

"I never think about the King. I only wonder. I
may sometimes express my wonderment too freely for a
loyal subject."

"I cannot vouch for Angela, but I will wager that he
is deep in love," persisted Hyacinth.

"Have it your own way, sweetheart. He is dull

enough to be deep in debt, or love, or politics, anything dismal and troublesome," answered his lordship, as he strolled off with his spaniels; not those dainty toy dogs which had been his companions at the gate of death, but the fine liver-and-black shooting dogs that lived in the kennels, and thought it doghood's highest privilege to attend their lord in his walks, whether with or without a gun.

His lordship kept open Christmas that year at Chilton Abbey, and there was great festivity, chiefly devised and carried out by the household, as Fareham and his wife were too much of the modern fashion, and too cosmopolitan in their ideas, to appreciate the fuss and feasting of an English Christmas. They submitted, however, to the festival as arranged for them by Mr. Manningtree and Mrs. Hubbuck—the copious feasting for servants and dependents, the mummers and carol-singers, the garlands and greenery which disguised the fine old tapestry, and made a bower of the vaulted hall. Everything was done with a lavish plenteousness, and no doubt the household enjoyed the fun and feasting all the more because of that dismal season of a few years back, when all Christmas ceremonies had been denounced as idolatrous, and when the members of the Anglican Church had assembled for their Christmas service secretly in private houses, and as much under the ban of the law as the Nonconformists were now.

Angela was interested in everything in that bright world where all things were new. The children piping Christmas hymns in the clear cold morning enchanted her. She ran down to kiss and fondle the smaller among them, and finding them thinly clad promised to make them warm cloaks and hoods as fast as her fingers could sew. Denzil found her there in the wide snowy space before the porch, prattling with the children, bareheaded, her soft brown hair blown about in the wind; and he was moved, as a man must needs be moved by the aspect of the woman that he loves caressing a small child, melted almost to tears by the thought that in some blessed time to come she might so caress, only more warmly, a child whose existence should be their bond of union.

And yet, being both shy and somewhat cold of temperament, he restrained himself, and greeted her only as a friend; for his mother's influence was holding him back, urging him not to marry a Papist, were she ever so lovely or lovable.

He had known Angela for nearly three months, and his acquaintance with her had reached this point of intimacy, yet Lady Warner had never seen her. This fact distressed him, and he had tried hard to awaken his mother's interest by praises of the Fareham family and of Angela's exquisite character; but the Scarlet Spectre came between the Puritan lady and the house of Fareham.

"There is nothing you can tell me about this girl, upon whom I fear you have foolishly set your affection, which can make me forget that she has been nursed and swaddled in the bondage of a corrupt Church, taught to worship idols, and to cherish lying traditions, while the light of God's holy word has been made dark for her."

"She is young enough to embrace a purer creed,

and to walk by the clearer light that leads your footsteps, mother. If she were my wife I should not despair of winning her to think as we do."

"And in all the length of England was there no young woman of right principles fit to be thy wife, that thou must needs fall into the snare of the first Popish witch who set her lure for thee?"

"Popish witch! Oh, mother, how ill you can conceive the image of my dear love, who has no witchcraft but beauty, no charm so potent as her truth and innocency!"

"I know them—these children of the Scarlet Woman—and I know their works, and the fate of those who trust them. The late King—weak and stubborn as he was—might have been alive this day, and reigning over a contented people, but for that fair witch who ruled him. It was the Frenchwoman's sorceries that wrought Charles's ruin."

"If thou wouldst but see my Angela," pleaded the son, with a caressing arm about his mother's spare shoulders.

"Thine! What! is she thine—pledged and promised already? Then, indeed, these white hairs will go down with sorrow to the grave."

"Mother, I doubt if thou couldst find so much as a single grey hair in that comely head of thine," said the son; and the mother smiled in the midst of her affliction. "And as for promise—there has been none. I have said no word of love; nor have I been encouraged to speak by any token of liking on the lady's part. I stand aloof and admire, and wonder at so much modesty and intelligence in Lady Fareham's sister. Let me bring her to see you, mother?"

"This is your house, Denzil. Were you to fill it with the sons and daughters of Belial, I could but pray that your eyes might be opened to their iniquity. I could not shut these doors against you or your companions. But I want no Popish women here."

"Ah, you do not know! Wait until you have seen her," urged Denzil, with the lover's confidence in the omnipotence of his mistress's charms.

And now on this Christmas Day there came the opportunity Denzil had been waiting for. The weather was cold and bright, the landscape was blotted out with snow; and the lake in Chilton Park offered a sound surface for the exercise of that novel amusement of skating, an accomplishment which Lord Fareham had acquired while in the Low Countries, and in which he had been Denzil's instructor during the late severe weather. Angela, at her brother-in-law's entreaty, had also adventured herself upon a pair of skates, and had speedily found delight in the swift motion, which seemed to her like the flight of a bird skimming the steely surface of the frozen lake, and incomparable in enjoyment.

"It is even more delightful than a gallop on Zephyr," she told her sister, who stood on the bank with a cluster of gay company, watching the skaters.

"I doubt not that; since there is even more danger of getting your neck broken upon runaway skates than on a runaway horse," answered Hyacinth.

After an hour on the lake, in which Denzil had distinguished himself by his mastery of the new exercise, being always at hand to support his mistress at the slightest indication of peril, she consented to the removal of her skates, at Papillon's earnest entreaty, who wanted her aunt to walk with her before dinner. After dinner there would be the swift-coming December twilight, and Christmas games, snap-dragon and the like, which Papillon, although a little fine lady, reproducing all her mother's likes and dislikes in miniature, could not, as a human child, altogether disregard.

"I don't care about such nonsense as Georgie does," she told her aunt, with condescending reference to her brother; "but I like to see the others amused. Those village children are such funny little savages. They stick their fingers in their mouths and grin at me, and call me 'Your annar,' or 'Your worship,' and say 'Anan' to everything. They are like Audrey in the play you read to me."

Denzil was in attendance upon aunt and niece.

"If you want to come with us, you must invent a pretty walk, Sir Denzil," said Papillon. "I am tired of long lanes and ploughed fields."

"I know of one of the pleasantest rambles in the shire—across the woods to the Grange. And we can rest there for half an hour, if Mrs. Angela will allow us, and take a light refreshment."

"Dear Sir Denzil, that is the very thing," answered Papillon, breathlessly. "I am dying of hunger. And I don't want to go back to the Abbey. Will there be any cakes or mince pies at the Grange?"

"Cakes in plenty, but I fear there will be no mince pies. My mother does not love Christmas dainties."

Henriette wanted to know why. She was always

wanting the reason of things. A bright inquiring little mind, perpetually on the alert for novelty; an imitative brain like a monkey's; hands and feet that know not rest; and there you have the Honourable Henrietta Maria Revel, *alias* Papillon.

They crossed the river, Angela and Denzil each taking an oar, while Papillon pretended to steer, a process which she effected chiefly by screaming.

"Another lump of ice!" she shrieked. "We shall be swamped. I believe the river will be frozen before Twelfth Night, and we shall be able to dance upon it. We must have bonfires and roast an ox for the poor people. Mrs. Hubbuck told me they roasted an ox the year King Charles was beheaded. Horrid brutes—to think that they could eat at such a time! If they had been sorry they could not have relished roast beef."

Hadley Grange, commonly known as the Grange, was in every detail the antithesis of Chilton Abbey. At the Abbey the eye was dazzled, the mind was bewildered, by an excess of splendour—an overmuch of everything gorgeous or beautiful. At the Grange sight and mind were rested by the low tone of colour, the quaker-like precision of form. All the furniture in the house was Elizabethan, plain, ponderous, the conscientious work of Oxfordshire mechanics. On one side of the house there was a bowling green, on the other a physic garden, where odours of medicinal herbs, camomile, fennel, rosemary, rue, hung ever on the surrounding air. There was nothing modern in Lady Warner's house but the spotless cleanliness; the perfume of last summer's roses and lavender; the polished surface of tables and cabinets, oak chests and oak floors, testifying to the inexorable industry of rustic housemaids. In all other respects the Grange was like a house that had just awakened from a century of sleep.

Lady Warner rose from her high-backed chair by the chimney corner in the oak parlour, and laid aside the book she had been reading, to welcome her son, startled at seeing him followed by a tall, fair girl in a black mantle and hood, and a little slip of a thing, with bright dark eyes and small determined face, pert, pointed, interrogative, framed in swansdown—a small aërial figure in a white cloth cloak, and a scarlet brocade frock, under which two little red shoes danced into the room.

"Mother, I have brought Mrs. Angela Kirkland and her niece to visit you this Christmas morning."

"Mrs. Kirkland and her niece are welcome," and Lady Warner made a deep curtsy, not like one of Lady Fareham's sinking curtsys, as of one near swooning in an ecstasy of politeness, but dignified and inflexible, straight down and straight up again.

"But as for Christmas, 'tis one of those superstitious observances which I have ever associated with a Church I abhor."

Denzil reddened furiously. To have brought this upon his beloved!

Angela drew herself up, and paled at the unexpected assault. The brutality of it was startling, though she knew, from Denzil's opinions, that his mother must be an enemy of her faith.

"Indeed, madam, I am sorry that anybody in England should think it an ill thing to celebrate the birthday of our Redeemer and Lord," she said.

"Do you think, young lady, that foolish romping games, and huge chines of beef, and smoking ale made luscious with spices and roasted pippins, and carol-singing and play-acting, can be the proper honouring of Him who was God first and for ever, and Man only for one brief interval in His eternal existence? To keep God's birthday with drunken rioting! What blasphemy! If you can think that there is not more profaneness than piety in such sensual revelries—why, it is that you do not know how to think. You would have learnt to reason better had you known that sweet poet and musician, and true thinker, Mr. John Milton, with whom it was my privilege to converse frequently during my husband's lifetime, and afterwards when he condescended to accept my son for his pupil, and spent three days and nights under this roof."

"Mr. Milton is still at Chalfont, mother. So you may hope to see him again with a less journey than to London," said Denzil, seizing the first chance of a change in the conversation; "and here is a little Miss to whom I have promised a light collation, with some of your Jersey milk."

"Mistress Kirkland and her niece shall have the best I can provide. The larder will furnish something acceptable, I doubt not, although I and my household observe this day as a fast."

"What, madam, are you sorry that Jesus Christ was born to-day?" asked Papillon.

"I am sorry for my sins, little mistress, and for the sins of all mankind, which nothing but His blood could wash away. To remember His birth is to remember that He died for us; and that is why I spend the twenty-fifth of December in fasting and prayer."

"Are you not glad you are to dine at the Abbey to-day, Sir Denzil?" asked Papillon, by way of commentary.

"Nay, I put no restraint on my son. He can serve God after his own manner, and veer with every wind of passion or fancy, if he will. But you shall have your cake and draught of milk, little lady, and you too, Mistress Kirkland, will, I hope, taste our Jersey milk, unless you would prefer a glass of Malmsey wine."

"Mrs. Kirkland is as much an anchorite as yourself, mother. She takes no wine."

Lady Warner was the soul of hospitality, and particularly proud of her dairy. When kept clear of theology and politics she was not an ill-natured woman. But to be a Puritan in the year of the Five Mile Act was not to think kindly of the Government under which she lived; while her sense of her own wrongs was intensified by rumours of over-indulgence shown to Papists, and the broad assertion that King and Duke were Roman Catholic at heart, and waited only the convenient hour to reforge the fetters that had bound England to Rome.

She was fond of children, most of all of little girls, never having had a daughter. She bent down to kiss Henriette, and then turned to Angela with her kindest smile—

"And this is Lady Fareham's daughter? She is as pretty as a picture."

"And I am as good as a picture— sometimes, madam,"

chirped Papillon. "Mother says I am *douce comme une image.*"

"When thou hast been silent or still for five minutes," said Angela, "and that is but seldom."

A loud handbell summoned the butler, and an Arcadian meal was speedily set out on a table in the hall, where a great fire of logs burnt as merrily as if it had been designed to enliven a Christmas-keeping household. Indeed there was nothing miserly or sparing about the housekeeping at the Grange, which harmonised with the sombre richness of Lady Warner's grey brocade gown, from the old-fashioned silk mercer's at the sign of the Flower-de-luce, in Cheapside. There was liberality without waste, and a certain quiet refinement in every detail, which reminded Angela of the convent parlour and her aunt's room—and contrasted curiously with the elegant disorder of her sister's surroundings.

Papillon clapped her hands at sight of the large plum cake, the jug of milk, and bowl of blackberry conserve.

"I was so hungry," she said apologetically, after Denzil had supplied her with generous slices of cake, and large spoonfuls of jam. "I did not know that Nonconformists had such nice things to eat."

"Did you think we all lay in gaol to suffer cold and hunger for the faith that is in us, like that poor preacher at Bedford?" asked Lady Warner, bitterly. "It will come to that some day, perhaps, under the new Act."

"Will you show Mistress Kirkland your house, mother, and your dairy?" Denzil asked hurriedly. "I know she would like to see one of the neatest dairies in Oxfordshire."

No request could be more acceptable to Lady

Warner, who was a housekeeper first and a controversialist afterwards. Inclined as she was to rail against the Church of Rome—partly because she had made up her mind upon hearsay, chiefly Miltonian, that Roman Catholicism was only another name for image-worship and martyr-burning, and partly on account of the favour that had been shown to Papists, as compared with the cruel treatment of Nonconformists—still there was a charm in Angela's gentle beauty against which the daughterless matron could not steel her heart. She melted in the space of a quarter of an hour, while Denzil was encouraging Henriette to over-eat herself, and trying to persuade Angela to taste this or that dainty, or reproaching her for taking so little; and by the time the child had finished her copious meal, Lady Warner was telling herself how dearly she might have loved this girl for a daughter-in-law, were it not for that fatal objection of a corrupt and pernicious creed.

No! Lovely as she was, modest, refined, and in all things worthy to be loved, the question of creed must be a stumbling-block. And then there were other objections. Rural gossip, the loose talk of servants, had brought a highly coloured description of Lady Fareham's household to her neighbour's ears. The extravagant splendour, the waste and idleness, the late hours, the worship of pleasure, the visiting, the singing, and dancing, and junketing, and worst of all, the too-indulgent friendship shown to a Parisian fopling, had formed the subject of conversation in many an assembly of pious ladies, and hands and eyebrows had been uplifted at the iniquities of Chilton Abbey, as second only to the monstrous goings-on of the Court at Oxford.

Almost ever since the Restoration Lady Warner had been living in meek expectancy of fire from heaven; and the chastisement of this memorable year had seemed to her the inevitable realisation of her fears. The fiery rain had come down—impalpable, invisible, leaving its deadly tokens in burning plague spots, the forerunners of death. That the contagion had mostly visited that humbler class of persons who had been strangers to the excesses and pleasures of the Court made nothing against Lady Warner's conviction that this scourge was Heaven's vengeance upon fashionable vice. Her son had brought her stories of the life at Whitehall, terrible pictures of iniquity, conveyed in the scathing words of one who sat apart, in a humble lodging, where for him the light of day came not, and heard with disgust and horror of that wave of debauchery which had swept over the city he loved, since the triumph of the Royalists. And Lady Warner had heard the words of Milton, and had listened with a reverence as profound as if the blind poet had been the prophet of Israel, alone in his place of hiding, holding himself aloof from an idolatrous monarch and a wicked people.

And now her son had brought her this fair girl, upon whom he had set his foolish hopes, a Papist, and the sister of a woman whose ways were the ways of——! A favourite scriptural substantive closed the sentence in Lady Warner's mind.

No; it might not be. Whatever power she had over her son must be used against his Papistical syren. She would treat her with courtesy, show her house and dairy, and there an end. And so they repaired to the offices, with Papillon running backwards and forwards as they went along, exclaiming and questioning, delighted with the shining oak floors and great oak chests in the corridor, and the armour in the hall, where, as the sacred and central object, hung the breastplate Sir George Warner wore when he fell at Hopton Heath, dinted by sword and pike, as the enemy's horse rode him down in the *melée*. His orange scarf, soiled and torn, was looped across the steel cuirass. Papillon admired everything, most of all the great cool dairy, which had once been a chapel, and where the piscina was converted to a niche for a polished brass milk-can, to the horror of Angela, who could say no word in praise of a place that had been created by the profanation of holy things. A chapel turned into a storehouse for milk and butter! Was this how Protestants valued consecrated places? An awe-stricken silence came upon her, and she was glad when Denzil remembered that they would have barely time to walk back to the Abbey before the two o'clock dinner.

"You keep Court hours even in the country," said Lady Warner. "I dined half an hour before you came."

"I don't care if I have no dinner to-day," said Papillon; "but I hope I shall be able to eat a mince pie. Why don't you love mince pies, madam? He"—pointing to Denzil—"says you do not."

CHAPTER X.

THE PRIEST'S HOLE.

DENZIL dined at the Abbey, where he was always made welcome. Lady Fareham had been warmly insistent upon his presence at their Christmas gaieties.

"We want to show you a Cavalier's Christmas," she told him at dinner, he seated at her side in the place of honour, while Angela sat at the other end of the table between Fareham and De Malfort. "For ourselves we care little for such simple sports: but for the poor folk and the children Yule should be a season to be remembered for good cheer and merriment through all their slow, dull year. Poor wretches! I think of their hard life sometimes, and wonder they don't either drown themselves or massacre us."

"They are like the beasts of the field, Lady Fareham. They have learnt patience from the habit of suffering. They are born poor, and they die poor. It is happy for us that they are not learned enough to consider the inequalities of fortune, or we should have the rising of want against abundance, a bitterer strife, perhaps, than the strife of adverse creeds, which made Ireland so bloody a spectacle for the world's wonder thirty years ago."

"Well, we shall make them all happy this afternoon; and there will be a supper in the great stone barn which

13 *

will acquaint them with abundance for this one evening
at least," answered Hyacinth, gaily.

"We are going to play games after dinner!" cried
Henriette, from her place at her father's elbow.

His lordship was the only person who ever reproved
her seriously, yet she loved him best of all her kindred
or friends.

"Aunt Angy is going to play hide-and-seek with us.
Will you play, Sir Denzil?"

"I shall think myself privileged if I may join in your
amusements.

"What a courteous speech! You will be cutting off
your pretty curly hair, and putting on a French perruque,
like his"—pointing to De Malfort. "Please do not. You
would be like everybody else in London—and now you
are only like yourself—and vastly handsome."

"Hush, Henriette! you are much too pert," remonstrated Fareham.

"But 'tis the very truth, father. All the women who
visit mother paint their faces, so that they are all alike;
and all the men talk alike, so that I don't know one
from t'other, except Lord Rochester, who is impudenter
and younger than the others, and gives me more sugar-
plums and pays me prettier compliments than anybody
else."

"Hold your tongue, mistress! A dinner-table is no
place for pert children. Thy brother there has better
manners," said her father, pointing to the cherubic son
and heir, whose ideas were concentrated upon a loaded
plate of red-deer pasty.

"You mean that he is greedier than I," retorted
Papillon. "He will eat till he won't be able to run

about with us after dinner; and then he will sprawl upon mother's satin train by the fire, with Ganymede and Phosphor, and she will tell everybody how good and gentle he is, and how much better bred than his sister. And now, if people are *ever* going to leave off eating, we may as well begin our games before it is quite dark. Perhaps *you* are ready, auntie, if nobody else is."

Dinner may have ended a little quicker for this speech, although Papillon was sternly suppressed, and bade to keep silence or leave the table. She obeyed so far as to make no further remarks, but expressed her contempt for the gluttony of her elders by several loud yawns, and bounced up out of her seat, like a ball from a racket, directly the little gentleman in black sitting near his lordship had murmured a discreet thanksgiving. This gentleman was the Roman Catholic priest from Oxford, who had said Mass early that morning in the muniment room, and had been invited to his lordship's table in honour of the festival.

Papillon led all the games, and ordered everybody about. Mrs. Dorothy Lettsome, the young lady who was sorry she had not had the honour to be born in France, was of the party, with her brother, honest Dan Lettsome, an Oxfordshire squire, who had been in London only once in his life, to see the Coronation, and had nearly lost his life, as well as his purse and jewellery, in a tavern, after that august ceremonial. This bitter experience had given him a distaste for the pleasures of the town which his poor sister deplored exceedingly; since she was dependent upon his coffers, and subject to his authority, and had no hope of leaving

Oxfordshire unless she were fortunate enough to find a town-bred husband.

These two joined in the sports with ardour, Squire Dan glad to be moving about, rather than to sit still and listen to music which he hated, or to conversation to which he could contribute neither wit nor sense, unless the kennel or the gun-room were the topic under discussion. The talk of a lady and gentleman who had graduated in the salons of the Hôtel de Rambouillet was a foreign language to him; and he told his sister that it was all one to him whether Lady Fareham and the Mounseer talked French or English, since it was quite as hard to understand 'em in one language as in t'other.

Papillon, this rustic youth adored. He knew no greater pleasure than to break and train a pony for her, to teach her the true knack of clearing a hedge, to explain the habits and nature of those vermin in whose lawless lives she was deeply interested—rats, weasels, badgers, and such-like—to attend her when she hunted, or flew her peregrine.

"If you will marry me, sweetheart, when you are of the marrying age, I would rather wait half a dozen years for you than have the best woman in Oxfordshire that I know of at this present."

"Marry you!" cried Lord Fareham's daughter. "Why, I shall marry no one under an earl; and I hope it will be a duke or a marquis. Marchioness is a pretty title: it sounds better than duchess, because it is in three syllables—mar-chion-ess," with an affected drawl. "I am going to be very beautiful. Mrs. Hubbuck says so, and mother's own woman; and I heard that painted old wretch, Mrs. Lewin, tell mother so. 'Eh, gud, your la'ship, the young miss will be almost as great a beauty as your la'ship's self!' Mrs. Lewin always begins her speeches with 'Eh, gud!' or 'What devil!' But I hope I shall be handsomer than *mother*," concluded Papillon, in a tone which implied a poor opinion of the maternal charms.

And now on this Christmas evening, in the thickening twilight of the rambling old house, through long galleries, crooked passages, queer little turns at right angles, rooms opening out of rooms, half a dozen in succession, Squire Dan led the games, ordered about all the time by Papillon, whom he talked of admiringly as a high-mettled filly, declaring that she had more tricks than the running-horse he was training for Abingdon races.

De Malfort, after assisting in their sports for a quarter of an hour with considerable spirit, had deserted them, and sneaked off to the great saloon, where he sat on the Turkey carpet at Lady Fareham's feet, singing chansonettes to his guitar, while George and the spaniels sprawled beside him, the whole group making a picture of indolent enjoyment, fitfully lighted by the blaze of a yule log that filled the width of the chimney. Fareham and the Priest were playing chess at the other end of the long low room, by the light of a single candle.

Papillon ran in at the door and ejaculated her disgust at De Malfort's desertion.

"Was there ever such laziness? It's bad enough in Georgie to be so idle; but then, *he* has over-eaten himself."

"And how do you know that I haven't over-eaten myself, mistress!" asked De Malfort.

"You never do that; but you often drink too much —much, much, much too much!"

"That's a slanderous thing to say of your mother's most devoted servant," laughed De Malfort. "And pray how does a baby-girl like you know when a gentleman has been more thirsty than discreet?"

"By the way you talk—always French. Jarni! ch'dame, n'savons joui d' n'belle s'rée—n'fam-partie d'ombre. Moi j'ai p'du n'belle f'tune, p'rol'd'nneur! You clip your words to nothing. Aren't you coming to play hide-and-seek?"

"Not I, fair slanderer. I am a salamander, and love the fire."

"Is that a kind of Turk? Good-bye. I'm going to hide."

"Beware of the chests in the gallery, sweetheart," said her father, who heard only this last sentence, as his daughter ran past him towards the door. "When I was in Italy I was told of a bride who hid herself in an old dower-chest, on her wedding-day—and the lid clapped to with a spring and kept her there for half a century."

"There's no spring that ever locksmith wrought that will keep down Papillon," cried De Malfort, sounding a light accompaniment to his words on the guitar strings, with delicatest touch, like fairy music.

"I know of better hiding-places," answered the child, and vanished, banging the great door behind her.

She found her aunt with Dorothy Lettsome and her brother and Denzil in the gallery above stairs, walking up and down, and listening with every indication of weariness to the Squire's discourse about his hunters and running-horses.

"Now we are going to have real good sport!" cried Papillon. "Aunt Angy and I are to hide, and you three are to look for us. You must stop in this gallery for ten minutes by the French clock yonder—with the door shut. You must give us ten minutes' law, Mr. Lettsome, as you did the hare the other day, when I was out with you—and then you may begin to look for us. Promise."

"Stay, little miss, you will be outside the house belike, roaming lord knows where; in the shrubberies, or the barns, or halfway to Oxford—while we are made fools of here."

"No, no. We will be inside the house."

"Do you promise that, pretty lady?'

"Yes, I promise."

Mrs. Dorothy suggested that there had been enough of childish play, and that it would be pleasanter to sit in the saloon with her ladyship, and hear Monsieur de Malfort sing.

"I'll wager he was singing when you saw him just now."

"Yes, he is always singing foolish French songs—and I'm sure you can't understand 'em."

"I've learnt the French ever since I was as old as you, Mistress Henriette."

"Ah! that was too late to begin. People who learn French out of books know what it looks like, but not what it sounds like."

"I should be very sorry if I could not understand a French ballad, little miss."

"Would you—would you, really?" cried Papillon, her face alight with impish mirth. "Then, of course, you understand this—

> "Oh, la d'moiselle, comme elle est sot-te,
>   Eh, je me moque de sa sot-ti-se!
>   Eh, la d'moiselle comme elle est bê-te,
>   Eh, je m'ris de sa bê-ti-se!"

She sang this impromptu nonsense *prestissimo* as she danced out of the room, leaving the accomplished Dorothy vexed and perplexed at not having understood a single word.

It was nearly an hour later when Denzil entered the saloon hurriedly, pale and perturbed of aspect, with Dorothy and her brother following him.

"We have been hunting all over the house for Mrs. Angela and Henriette," Denzil said, and Fareham started up from the chess-table, scared at the young man's agitated tone and pallid countenance. "We have looked in every room——"

"In every closet," interrupted Dorothy.

"In every corner of the staircases and passages," said Squire Dan.

"Can your lordship help us? There may be places you know of which we do not know?" said Denzil, his voice trembling a little. "It is alarming that they should be so long in concealment. We have called to them in every part of the house."

Fareham hurried to the door, taking instant alarm—anxious, pale, alert.

"Come!" he said to the others. "The oak chests

in the music-room—the great Florentine coffer in the gallery? Have you looked in those?"

"Yes; we have opened every chest."

"Faith, to see Sir Denzil turn over piles of tapestries, you would have thought he was looking for a fairy that could hide in the folds of a curtain!" said Lettsome.

"It is no theme for jesting. I hate these tricks of hiding in strange corners," said Fareham. "Now, show me where they left you."

"In the long gallery."

"They have gone up to the roof, perhaps."

"We have been in the roof," said Denzil.

"I have scarcely recovered my senses after the cracked skull I got from one of your tie-beams," added Lettsome; and Fareham saw that both men had their doublets coated with dust and cobwebs, in a manner which indicated a remorseless searching of places unvisited by housemaids and brooms.

Mrs. Dorothy, with a due regard for her dainty lace kerchief and ruffles, and her cherry silk petticoat, had avoided these loathly places, the abode of darkness, haunted by the fear of rats.

Fareham tramped the house from cellar to garret, Denzil alone accompanying him.

"We want no posse comitatus," he had said, somewhat discourteously. "You, Squire, had best go and mend your cracked head in the eating-parlour with a brimmer or two of clary wine; and you, Mrs. Dorothy, can go and keep her ladyship company. But not a word of our fright. Swoons and screaming would only hinder us."

He took Mrs. Lettsome's arm, and led her to the

staircase, pushing the Squire after her, and then turned his anxious countenance to Denzil.

"If they are not to be found in the house, they must be found outside the house. Oh, the folly, the madness of it! A December night—snow on the ground—a rising wind—another fall of snow, perhaps—and those two afoot and alone!"

"I do not believe they are out-of-doors," Denzil answered. "Your daughter promised that they would not leave the house."

"My daughter tells the truth. It is her chief virtue."

"And yet we have hunted in every hole and corner," said Denzil, dejectedly.

"Hole!" cried Fareham, almost in a shout. "Thou hast hit it, man! That one word is a flash of lightning. The Priest's Hole! Come this way. Bring your candle!" snatching up that which he had himself set down on a table, when he stood still to deliberate. "The Priest's Hole? The child knew the secret of it—fool that I was ever to show her. God! what a place to hide in on a winter night!"

He was halfway up the staircase to the second story before he had uttered the last of these exclamations, Denzil following him.

Suddenly, through the stillness of the house, there sounded a faint far-off cry, the shrill thin sound of a child's voice. Fareham and Warner would hardly have heard it had they not been sportsmen, with ears trained to listen for distant sounds. No view-hallo sounding across miles of wood and valley was ever fainter or more ethereal.

"You hear them?" cried Fareham. "Quick, quick!"

He led the way along a narrow gallery, about eight feet high, where people had danced in Elizabeth's time, when the house was newly converted to secular uses; and then into a room in which there were several iron chests, the muniment room, where a sliding panel, of which the master of the house knew the trick, revealed an opening in the wall. Fareham squeezed himself through the gap, still carrying the tall iron candlestick, with flaring candle, and vanished. Denzil followed, and found himself descending a narrow stone staircase, very steep, built into an angle of the great chimney, while as if from the bowels of the earth there came, louder at every step, that shrill cry of distress, in a voice he could not doubt was Henriette's.

"The other is mute," groaned Fareham; "scared to death, perhaps, like a frightened bird." And then he called, "I am coming. You are safe, love; safe, safe!" And then he groaned aloud, "Oh, the madness, the folly of it!"

Halfway down the staircase there was a sudden gap of six feet, down which Fareham dropped with his hands on the lowest stair, Denzil following; a break in the continuity of the descent planned for the discomfiture of strangers and the protection of the family hiding-place.

Fareham and Denzil were on a narrow stone landing at the bottom of the house; and the child's wail of anguish changed to a joyous shriek, "Father, father!" close in their ears. Fareham set his shoulder against the heavy oak door, and it burst inwards. There had been no question of secret spring or complicated machinery; but the great, clumsy door dragged upon its rusty hinges, and the united strength of the two girls had not served to pull it open, though Papillon, in her eagerness for concealment in the first fever of hiding, had been strong enough to push the door till she had jammed it, and thus made all after efforts vain.

"Father!" she cried, leaping into his arms, as he came into the room, large enough to hold six men standing upright; but a hideous den in which to perish alone in the dark. "Oh, father! I thought no one would ever find us. I was afraid we should have died like the Italian lady—and people would have found our skeletons and wondered about us. I never was afraid before. Not when the great horse reared as high as a house—and her ladyship screamed. I only laughed then—but to-night I have been afraid."

Fareham put her aside without looking at her.

"Angela! Great God! She is dead!"

No, she was not dead, only in a half swoon, leaning against the angle of the wall, ghastly white in the flare of the candles. She was not quite unconscious. She knew whose strong arms were holding her, whose lips were so near her own, whose head bent suddenly upon her breast, leaning against the lace kerchief, to listen for the beating of her heart.

She made a great effort to relieve his fear, understanding dimly that he thought her dead; but could only murmur broken syllables, till he carried her up three or four stairs, to a secret door that opened into the garden. There in the wintry air, under the steely light of wintry stars, her senses came back to her. She opened her eyes and looked at him.

"I am sorry I have not Papillon's courage," she said.

"Tu m'as donné une affreuse peur—je te croyais morte," muttered Fareham, letting his arms drop like lead as she released herself from their support.

Denzil and Henriette were close to them. They had come to the open door for fresh air, after the charnel-like chill and closeness of the small underground chamber.

"Father is angry with me," said the girl; "he won't speak to me."

"Angry! no, no;" and he bent to kiss her. "But oh, child, the folly of it! She might have died—you too—found just an hour too late."

"It would have taken a long time to kill me," said Papillon; "but I was very cold, and my teeth were chattering, and I should soon have been hungry. Have you had supper yet?"

"Nobody has even thought of supper."

"I am glad of that. And I may have supper with you, mayn't I, and eat what I like, because it's Christmas, and because I might have been starved to death in the Priest's Hole. But it was a good hiding-place, *tout de même*. Who guessed at last?"

"The only person who knew of the place, child. And now, remember, the secret is to be kept. Your dungeon may some day save an honest man's life. You must tell nobody where you were hid."

"But what shall I say when they ask me? I must not tell them a story."

"Say you were hidden in the great chimney—which is truth; for the Priest's Hole is but a recess at the back of the chimney. And you, Warner," turning to Denzil, who had not spoken since the opening of the door, "I know you'll keep the secret."

"Yes. I will keep your secret," Denzil answered, cold as ice; and said no word more.

They walked slowly round the house by the terrace, where the clipped yews stood out like obelisks against the bleak bright sky. Papillon ran and skipped at her father's side, clinging to him, expatiating upon her sufferings in the dust and darkness. Denzil followed with Angela, in a dead silence.

CHAPTER XI.

LIGHTER THAN VANITY.

"I THINK father must be a witch," Henriette said at dinner next day, "or why did he tell me of the Italian lady who was shut in the dower-chest, just before Angela and I were lost in"—she checked herself at a look from his lordship—"in the chimney?"

"It wants no witch to tell that little girls are foolish and mischievous," answered Fareham.

"You ladies must have been vastly black when you came out of your hiding-place," said De Malford. "I should have been sorry to see so much beauty disguised in soot. Perhaps Mrs. Kirkland means to appear in the character of a chimney at our next Court masquerade. She would cause as great a stir as Lady Muskerry, in all her Babylonian splendour; but for other reasons. Nothing could mitigate the Muskerry's ugliness; and no disguise could hide Mrs. Angela's beauty."

"What would the costume be?" asked Papillon.

"Oh, something simple. A long black satin gown, and a brick-dust velvet hat, tall and curiously twisted, like your Tudor chimney; and a cluster of grey feathers on the top, to represent smoke."

"Monsieur le Comte makes a joke of everything. But what would father have said if we had never been found?"

"I should have said that they are right who swear there is a curse upon all property taken from the Church, and that the ban fell black and bitter upon Chilton Abbey," answered his lordship's grave deep voice from the end of the table, where he sat somewhat apart from the rest, gloomy and silent, save when directly addressed.

Her ladyship and De Malfort had always plenty to talk about. They had the past as well as the present for their discourse, and were always sighing for the vanished glories of their youth—at Paris, at Fontainebleau, at St. Germain. Nor were they restricted to the realities of the present and the memories of the past; they had that wider world of unreality in which to circulate; they had the Scudéry language at the tips of their tongues, the fantastic sentimentalism of that marvellous old maid who invented the seventeenth-century hero and heroine; or who crystallised the vanishing figures of that brilliant age and made them immortal. All that little language of toyshop platonics had become a natural form of speech with these two, bred and educated in the Marais, while it was still the select and aristocratic quarter of Paris.

To-day Hyacinth and her old playfellow had been chattering like children, or birds in an aviary, and with little more sense in their conversation; but at this talk of the Church's ban, Hyacinth stopped in her prattle and was almost serious.

"I sometimes think we shall have bad luck in this house," she said, "or that we shall see the ghosts of the wicked monks who were turned out to make room for Fareham's great-grandfather."

"Tush, child! what do you know of their wickedness, after a century?"

"They were very wicked, I believe, for it was one of those quiet little monasteries where the monks could do all manner of evil things, and raise the devil, if they liked, without anybody knowing. And when Henry the Eighth sent his Commissioners, they were taken by surprise; and the altar at which they worshipped Beelzebub was found in a side chapel, and a wax figure of the King stuck with arrows, like St. Sebastian. The Abbot pretended it *was* St. Sebastian; but nobody believed him."

"Nobody wanted to believe him," said Fareham. "King Henry made an example of Chilton Abbey, and gave it to my worthy ancestor, who was a fourth cousin of Jane Seymour's, and had turned Protestant to please his royal master. He went back to the Church of Rome on his death-bed, and we Revels have been Papists ever since. I wish the Church joy of us!"

"The Church has neither profit nor honour from you," said his wife, shaking her fan at him. "You seldom go to Mass; you never go to confession."

"I would rather keep my sins to myself, and atone for them by the pangs of a wounded conscience. That is too easy a religion which shifts the burden of guilt on to the shoulders of a stipendiary priest, and walks away from the confessional absolved by the payment of a few extra prayers."

"I believe you are either an infidel or a Puritan."

"A cross between the two, perhaps—a mongrel in religion, as I am a mongrel in politics."

Angela looked up at him with sad eyes—reproachful, yet full of pity. She remembered his wild talk, semi-delirious some of it, all feverish and excited, during his illness, and how she had listened with aching heart to the ravings of one so near death, and so unfit to die. And now that the pestilence had passed him by, now that he was a strong man again, with half a lifetime before him, her heart was still heavy for him. She who sat in the theatre of life as a spectator had discovered that her sister's husband was not happy. The trifles that delighted Hyacinth left Fareham unamused and discontented; and his wife knew not that there was anything wanting to his felicity. She could go on prattling like a child, could be in a fever about a fan or a bunch of ribbons, could talk for an hour of a new play or the contents of the French *Gazette,* while he sat gloomy and apart.

The sympathy, the companionship that should be in marriage was wanting here. Angela saw and deplored this distance, scarce daring to touch so delicate a theme, fearful lest she, the younger, should seem to sermonise the elder; and yet she could not be silent for ever while duty and religion urged her to speak.

At Chilton Abbey the sisters were rarely alone. Papillon was almost always with them; and De Malfort spent more of his life in attendance upon Lady Fareham

14*

than at Oxford, where he was supposed to be living. Mrs, Lettsome and her brother were frequent guests; and coach-loads of fine people came over from the court almost every day.   Indeed, it was only Fareham's character—austere as Clarendon's or Southampton's—which kept the finest of all company at a distance.   Lady Castlemaine had called at Chilton in her coach-and-four early in July; and her visit had not been returned—a slight which the proud beauty bitterly resented: and from that time she had lost no opportunity of depreciating Lady Fareham.   Happily her jests, not over refined in quality, had not been repeated to Hyacinth's husband.

One January afternoon the longed-for opportunity came.   The sisters were sitting alone in front of the vast mediæval chimney, where the Abbots of old had burnt their surplus timber—Angela busy with her embroidery frame, working a satin coverlet for her niece's bed; Hyacinth yawning over a volume of Cyrus; in whose stately pages she loved to recognise the portraits of her dearest friends, and for which she was a living key.   Angela was now familiar with the famous romance, which she had read with deepest interest, enlightened by her sister.   As an eastern story—a record of battles and sieges evolved from a clever spinster's brain, an account of men and women who had never lived—the book might have seemed passing dull; but the story of actual lives, of living, breathing beauty, and valour that still burnt in warrior breasts, the keen and clever analysis of men and women who were making history, could not fail to interest an intelligent girl, to whom all things in life were new.

Angela read of the siege of Dunkirk, where Fareham had fought; of the tempestuous weather; the camp in the midst of salt marshes and quicksands, and all the sufferings and perils of life in the trenches. He had been in more than one of those battles which mademoiselle's conscientious pen depicted with such graphic power, the *Gazette* at her elbow as she wrote. The names of battles, sieges, Generals, had been on his lips in his delirious ravings. He had talked of the taking of Charenton, the key to Paris, a stronghold dominating Seine and Marne; of Clanleu, the brave defender of the fortress; of Châtillon, who led the charge—both killed there—Châtillon, the friend of Condé, who wept bitterest tears for a loss that poisoned victory. Read by these lights, the "Grand Cyrus" was a book to be pored over, a book to bend over in the grey winter dusk, reading by the broad blaze of the logs that flamed and crackled on wrought-iron standards. Just as merrily the blaze had spread its ruddy light over the room when it was a monkish refectory, and when the droning of a youthful brother reading aloud to the fraternity as they ate their supper was the only sound, except the clattering of knives and grinding of jaws.

Now the room was her ladyship's drawing-room, bright with Gobelin tapestry, dazzling with Venetian mirrors, gaudy with gold and colour, the black oak floor enlivened by many-hued carpets from our new colony of Tangiers. Fareham told his wife that her Moorish carpets had cost the country fifty times the price she had paid for them, and were associated with an irrevocable evil in the existence of a childless Queen; but that piece of malice, Hyacinth told him, had no foundation but his hatred of the Duke, who had always been perfectly civil to him.

"Of two profligate brothers I prefer the bolder sinner," said Fareham. "Bigotry and debauchery are an ill mixture."

"I doubt if his Majesty frets for the want of an heir," remarked De Malfort. "He is not a family man."

"He is not a one family man, Count," answered Fareham.

Fareham and De Malfort were both away on this January evening. Papillon was taking a dancing lesson from a wizened old Frenchman, who brought himself and his fiddle from Oxford twice a week for the damsel's instruction. Mrs. Priscilla, nurse and *gouvernante,* attended these lessons, at which the Honourable Henrietta Maria Revel gave herself prodigious airs, and was indeed so rude to the poor old professor that her aunt had declined to assist at any more performances.

"Has his lordship gone to Oxford?" Angela asked, after a silence broken only by her sister's yawns.

"I doubt he is anywhere rather than in such good company," Hyacinth answered carelessly. "He hates the King, and would like to preach at him, as John Knox did at his great-grandmother. Fareham is riding, or roving with his dogs, I dare say. He has a gloomy taste for solitude."

"Hyacinth, do you not see that he is unhappy?" Angela asked, suddenly, and the pain in her voice startled her sister from the contemplation of the sublime Mandane.

"Unhappy, child! What reason has he to be unhappy?"

"Ah, dearest, it is that I would have you discover. 'Tis a wife's business to know what grieves her husband."

"Unless it be Mrs. Lewin's bill—who is an inexorable harpy—I know of no act of mine that can afflict him."

"I did not mean that his gloom was caused by any act of yours, sister. I only urge you to discover why he is so sad."

"Sad? Sullen, you mean. He has a fine, generous nature. I am sure it is not Lewin's charges that trouble him. But he had always a sullen temper—by fits and starts."

"But of late he has been always silent and gloomy."

"How the child watches him! *Ma très chère*, that silence is natural. There are but two things Fareham loves—the first, war; the second, sport. If he cannot be storming a town, he loves to be killing a fox. This fireside life of ours—our books and music, our idle talk of plays and dances—wearies him. You may see how he avoids us—except out-of-doors."

"Dear Hyacinth, forgive me!" Angela began, falteringly, leaving her embroidery frame and moving to the other side of the hearth, where she dropped on her knees by her ladyship's chair, and was almost swallowed up in the ample folds of her brocade train. "Is it not possible that Lord Fareham is pained to see you so much gayer and more familiar with Monsieur de Malfort than you ever are with him?"

"Gayer! more familiar!" cried Hyacinth. "Can you conceive any creature gay and familiar with Fareham? One could as soon be gay with Don Quixote; indeed, there is much in common between the knight of the

rueful countenance and my husband. Gay and familiar!
And pray, mistress, why should I not take life pleasantly
with a man who understands me, and in whose friendship I have grown up almost as if we were brother and
sister? Do you forget that I have known Henri ever
since I was ten years old—that we played battledore
and shuttlecock together in our dear garden in the Rue
de Touraine, next the bowling-green, when he was at
school with the Jesuit Fathers, and used to spend all
his holiday afternoons with the Marquise? I think I
only learnt to know the saints' days because they brought
me my playfellow. And when I was old enough to
attend the Court—and, indeed, I was but a child when
I first appeared there—it was Henri who sang my
praises, and brought a crowd of admirers about me.
Ah, what a life it was! Love in the city, and war at
the gates: plots, battles, barricades! How happy we all
were! except when there came the news of some great
man killed, and walls were hung with black, where
there had been a thousand wax candles and a crowd of
dancers. Châtillon, Chabot, Laval! *Hélas,* those were
sad losses!"

"Dear sister, I can understand your affection for
an old friend, but I would not have you place him
above your husband; least of all would I have his lordship suspect that you preferred the friend to the husband——"

"Suspect! Fareham! Are you afraid I shall make
Fareham jealous, because I sing duets and cudgel these
poor brains to make *bouts rimés* with De Malfort? Ah,
child, how little those watchful eyes of yours have discovered the man's character! Fareham jealous! Why,

at St. Germain he has seen me surrounded by adorers; the subject of more madrigals than would fill a big book. At the Louvre he has seen me the—what is that Mr. What's-his-name, your friend's old schoolmaster, the Republican poet, calls it—'the cynosure of neighbouring eyes.' Don't think me vain, *ma mie.* I am an old woman now, and I hate my looking-glass ever since it has shown me my first wrinkle; but in those days I had almost as many admirers as Madame Henriette, or the Princess Palatine, or the fair-haired Duchess. I was called *la belle Anglaise.*"

It was difficult to sound a warning-note in ears so obstinately deaf to all serious things. Papillon came bounding in after her dancing-lesson—exuberant, loquacious.

"The little beast has taught me a new step in the coranto. See, mother," and the slim small figure was drawn up to its fullest, and the thin little lithe arms were curved with a studied grace, as Papillon slid and tripped across the room, her dainty little features illumined by a smirk of ineffable conceit.

"Henriette, you are an ill-bred child to call your master so rude a name," remonstrated her mother, languidly.

"'Tis the name you called him last week when his dirty shoes left marks on the stairs. He changes his shoes in my presence," added Papillon, disgustedly. "I saw a hole in his stocking. Monsieur de Malfort calls him Cut-Caper."

CHAPTER XII.

LADY FAREHAM'S DAY.

A MONTH later the *Oxford Gazette* brought Lady Fareham the welcomest news that she had read for ever so long. The London death-rate had decreased, and his Majesty had gone to Hampton Court, attended by the Duke and Prince Rupert, Lord Clarendon, and his other indispensable advisers, and a retinue of servants, to be within easy distance of that sturdy soldier Albemarle; who had remained in London, unafraid of the pestilence, and who declared that while it was essential for him to be in frequent communication with his Majesty, it would be perilous to the interests of the State for him to absent himself from London; for the Dutch war had gone drivelling on ever since the victory in June, and that victory was not to be supposed final. Indeed, according to the General, there was need of speedy action and a considerable increase of our naval strength.

Windsor had been thought of in the first place as a residence for the King; but the law courts had been transferred there, and the judges and their following had overrun the town, while there was a report of an infected house there. So it had been resolved that his Majesty should make a brief residence at Hampton Court, leaving the Queen, the Duchess, and their belongings at Oxford, whither he could return as soon as the business of providing for the setting out of the fleet had been arranged between him and the General, who could travel in a day backwards and forwards between the Cockpit and Wolsey's palace.

When this news came they were snowed up at Chilton. Sport of all kinds had been stopped, and Fareham, who, in his wife's parlance, lived in his boots all the winter, had to amuse himself without the aid of horse and hound; while even walking was made difficult by the snowdrifts that blocked the lanes, and reduced the face of Nature to one muffled and monotonous whiteness, while all the edges of the landscape were outlined vaguely against the misty greyness of the sky.

Hyacinth spent her days half in yawning and sighing, and half in idle laughter and childish games with Henriette and De Malfort. When she was gay she was as much a child as her daughter; when she was fretful and hipped, it was a childish discontent.

They played battledore and shuttlecock in the picture-gallery, and my lady laughed when her volant struck some reverend judge or venerable bishop a rap on the nose. They sat for hours twanging guitars, Hyacinth taking her music-lesson from De Malfort, whose exquisite taste and touch made a guitar seem a different instrument from that on which his pupil's delicate fingers nipped a wiry melody, more suggestive of finger-nails than music.

He taught her, and took all possible pains in the teaching, and laughed at her, and told her plainly that she had no talent for music. He told her that in her hands the finest lute Laux Maler ever made, mellowed by three centuries, would be but wood and catgut.

"It is the prettiest head in the world, and a forehead as white as Queen Anne's," he said one day, with a light touch on the ringletted brow, "but there is nothing inside. I wonder if there is anything here?" and the same light touch fluttered for an instant against her brocade bodice, at the spot where fancy locates the faculty of loving and suffering.

She laughed at his rude speeches, just as she laughed at his flatteries—as if there were safety in that atmosphere of idle mirth. Angela heard and wondered, wondering most perhaps what occupied and interested Lord Fareham in those white winter days, when he lived for the greater part alone in his own rooms, or pacing the long walks from which the gardeners had cleared the snow. He spent some of his time indoors, deep in a book. She knew as much as that. He had allowed Angela to read some of his favourites, though he would not permit any of the new comedies, which everybody at Court was reading, to enter his house, much to Lady Fareham's annoyance.

"I am half a century behind all my friends in intelligence," she said, "because of your Puritanism. One tires of your everlasting gloomy tragedies—your *Broken Hearts* and *Philasters*. I am all for the genius of comedy."

"Then satisfy your inclinations, and read Molière. He is second only to Shakespeare."

"I have him by heart already."

The *Broken Heart* and *Philaster* delighted Angela; indeed, she had read the latter play so often, and with such deep interest, that many passages in it had engraved themselves on her memory, and recurred to her sometimes in the silence of wakeful nights.

That character of Bellario touched her as no heroine of the "Grand Cyrus" had power to move her. How elaborately artificial seemed the Scudèry's polished tirades, her refinements and quintessences of the grand passion, as compared with the fervid simplicity of the woman-page — a love so humble, so intense, so unselfish!

Sir Denzil came to Chilton nearly every day, and was always graciously received by her ladyship. His Puritan gravity fell away from him like a pilgrim's cloak, in the light air of Hyacinth's amusements. He seemed to grow younger; and Henriette's sharp eyes discovered an improvement in his dress.

"This is your second new suit since Christmas," she said, "and I'll swear it is made by the King's tailor. *Regardez donc,* madame! What exquisite embroidery, silver and gold thread intermixed with little sparks of garnets sewn in the pattern! It is better than anything of his lordship's. I wish I had a father who dressed well. I'm sure mine must be the shabbiest lord at Whitehall. You have no right to be more modish than *monsieur mon père,* Sir Denzil."

"Hold that insolent tongue, *p'tit drôle!*" cried the mother. "Sir Denzil is younger by a dozen years than his lordship, and has his reputation to make at Court, and with the ladies he will meet there. I hope you are coming to London, Denzil. You shall have a seat in one of our coaches as soon as the death-rate diminishes, and this odious weather breaks up."

"Your ladyship is all goodness. I shall go where my lode-star leads," answered Denzil, looking at Angela, and blushing at the audacity of his speech.

He was one of those modest lovers who rarely bring a blush to the cheek of the beloved object, but are so poor-spirited as to do most of the blushing themselves.

A week later Lady Fareham could do nothing but praise that severe weather which she had pronounced odious, for her husband, coming in from Oxford after a ride along the road, deep with melting snow, brought the news of a considerable diminution in the London death-rate; and the more startling news that his Majesty had removed to Whitehall for the quicker despatch of business with the Duke of Albemarle, albeit the bills of mortality recorded fifteen hundred deaths from the pestilence in the previous week, and although not a carriage appeared in the deserted streets of the metropolis except those in his Majesty's train.

"How brave, how admirable!" cried Hyacinth, clapping her hands in the exuberance of her joy. "Then we can go to London to-morrow, if horses and coaches can be made ready. Give your orders at once, Fareham, I beseech you. The thaw has set in. There will be no snow to stop us."

"There will be floods which may make fords impassable."

"We can avoid every ford—there is always a *détour* by the lanes."

"Have you any idea what the lanes will be like after two feet deep of snow? Be sure, my love, you are happier twanging your lute by this fireside than you would be stuck in a quagmire, perishing with cold in a windy coach."

"I will risk the quagmires and the windy coach. Oh, my lord, if you ever loved me let us set out to-morrow. I languish for Fareham House—my basset-table, my friends, my watermen to waft me to and fro between

Blackfriars and Westminster, the mercers in St. Paul's Churchyard, the Middle Exchange. I have not bought myself anything pretty since Christmas. Let us go to-morrow."

"And risk spoiling the prettiest thing you own—your face—by a plague-spot."

"The King is there—the plague is ended."

"Do you think he is a God, that the pestilence will flee at his coming?"

"I think his courage is godlike. To be the first to return to that abandoned city."

"What of Monk and the Archbishop, who never left it?"

"A rough old soldier! A Churchman! Such lives were meant to face danger. But his Majesty! A man for whom existence should be one long holiday?"

"He has done his best to make it so; but the pestilence has shown him that there are grim realities in life. Don't fret, dearest. We will go to town as soon as it is prudent to make the move. Kings must brave great hazards; and there is no reason that little people like us should risk our lives because the necessities of State compel his Majesty to imperil his."

"We shall be laughed at if we do not hasten after him."

"Let them laugh who please. I have passed through the ordeal, Hyacinth. I don't want a second attack of the sickness; nor would I for worlds that you or your sister should run into the mouth of danger. Besides, you can lose little pleasure by being absent; for the play-houses are all closed, and the Court is in mourning for the French Queen-mother."

"Poor Queen Anne!" sighed Hyacinth. "She was always kind to me. And to die of a cancer—after outliving those she most loved! King Louis would scarcely believe she was seriously ill, till she was at the point of death. But we know what mourning means at Whitehall—Lady Castlemaine in black velvet, with forty thousand pounds in diamonds to enliven it; a concert instead of a play, perhaps; and the King sitting in a corner whispering with Mrs. Stewart. But as for the contagion, you will see that everybody will rush back to London, and that you and I will be laughing-stocks."

The next week justified Lady Fareham's assertion. As soon as it was known that the King had established himself at Whitehall, the great people came back to their London houses, and the town began to fill. It was as if a God had smiled upon the smitten city, and that healing and happiness radiated from the golden halo round that anointed head. Was not this the monarch of whom the most eloquent preacher of the age had written, "In the arms of whose justice and wisdom we lie down in safety"?

London flung off her cerements—erased her plaguemarks. The dead-cart's dreadful bell no longer sounded in the silence of an afflicted city. Coffins no longer stood at every other door; the pits at Finsbury, in Tothill Fields, at Islington, were all filled up and trampled down; and the grass was beginning to grow over the forgotten dead. The Judges came back to Westminster. London was alive again—alive and healed; basking in the sunshine of Royalty.

Nowhere was London more alive in the month of March than at Fareham House on the Thames, where

the Fareham liveries of green and gold showed conspicuous upon his lordship's watermen, lounging about
the stone steps that led down to the water, or waiting
in the terraced garden, which was one of the finest on
the river.   Wherries of various weights and sizes filled
one spacious boathouse, and in another handsome stone
edifice with a vaulted roof Lord Fareham's barge lay in
state, glorious in cream colour and gold, with green
velvet cushions and Oriental carpets, as splendid as that
blue-and-gold barge which Charles had sent as a present
to Madame, a vessel to out-glitter Cleopatra's galley,
when her ladyship and her friends and their singing-
boys and musicians filled it for a voyage to Hampton
Court.

The barge was used on festive occasions, or for
country voyages, as to Hampton or Greenwich; the
wherries were in constant requisition.   Along that shining water-way rank and fashion, commerce and business,
were moving backwards and forwards all day long.   That
more novel mode of transit, the hackney coach, was
only resorted to in foul weather; for the Legislature had
handicapped the coaching trade in the interests of the
watermen, and coaches were few and dear.

If Angela had loved the country, she was not less
charmed with London under its altered aspect.   All this
gaiety and splendour, this movement and brightness,
astonished and dazzled her.

"I am afraid I am very shallow-minded," she told
Denzil when he asked her opinion of London.   "It
seems an enchanted place, and I can scarcely believe it
is the same dreadful city I saw a few months ago, when

the dead were lying in the streets. Oh, how clearly it comes back to me—those empty streets, the smoke of the fires, the wretched ragged creatures begging for bread! I looked down a narrow court, and saw a corpse lying there, and a child wailing over it; and a little way farther on a woman flung up a window, and screamed out, 'Dead, dead! The last of my children is dead! Has God no relenting mercy?'"

"It is curious," said Hyacinth, "how little the town seems changed after all those horrors. I miss nobody I know."

"Nay, madam," said Denzil, "there have only died one hundred and sixty thousand people, mostly of the lower classes; or at least that is the record of the bills; but I am told the mortality has been twice as much, for people have had a secret way of dying and burying their dead. If your ladyship could have heard the account that Mr. Milton gave me this morning of the sufferings he saw before he left London, you would not think the visitation a light one."

"I wonder you consort with such a rebellious subject as Mr. Milton," said Hyacinth. "A creature of Cromwell's, who wrote with hideous malevolence and disrespect of the murdered King, who was in hiding for ever so long after his Majesty's return, and who now escapes a prison only by the royal clemency."

"The King lacks only that culminating distinction of having persecuted the greatest poet of the age in order to stand equal to the bigots who murdered Giordano Bruno," said Denzil.

"The greatest poet! Sure you would not compare Milton with Waller?"

"Indeed I would not, Lady Fareham."

"Nor with Cowley, nor Denham — dear cracked-brained Denham?"

"Nor with Denham. To my fancy he stands as high above them as the pole-star over your ladyship's garden lamps."

"A pamphleteer who has scribbled schoolboy Latin verses, and a few short poems; and, let me see, a masque—yes, a masque that he wrote for Lord Bridge-water's children before the troubles. I have heard my father talk of it. I think he called the thing *Comus.*"

"A name that will live, Lady Fareham, when Waller and Denham are shadows, remembered only for an occasional couplet."

"Oh, but who cares what people will think two or three hundred years hence? Waller's verses please us now. The people who come after me can please them-selves, and may read *Comus* to their hearts' content. I know his lordship reads Milton, as he does Shakespeare, and all the cramped old playwrights of Elizabeth's time. Henri, sing us that song of Waller's, 'Go, lovely rose.' I would give all Mr. Milton has written for that per-fection."

They were sitting on the terrace above the river in the golden light of an afternoon that was fair and warm as May, though by the calendar 'twas March. The capricious climate had changed from austere winter to smiling spring. Skylarks were singing over the fields at Hampstead, and over the plague-pits at Islington, and all London was rejoicing in blue skies and sunshine. Trade was awakening from a death-like sleep. The theatres were closed; but there were plays acted now

15*

and then at Court. The New and the Middle Exchange were alive with beribboned fops and painted belles.

It was Lady Fareham's visiting-day. The tall windows of her saloon were open to the terrace, French windows that reached from ceiling to floor, like those at the Hôtel de Rambouillet, and which Hyacinth had substituted for the small Jacobean casements, when she took possession of her husband's ancestral mansion. Saloon and terrace were one on a balmy afternoon like this; and her ladyship's guests wandered in and out at their pleasure. Her lackeys, handing chocolate and cakes on silver or gold salvers, were so many as to seem ubiquitous; and in the saloon, presided over by Angela, there was a still choicer refreshment to be obtained at a tea-table, where tiny cups of the new China drink were dispensed to those who cared for exotic novelties.

"Prythee, take your guitar and sing to us, were it but to change the conversation," cried Hyacinth; and De Malfort took up his guitar and began, in the sweetest of tenors, "Go, lovely rose."

He had all her ladyship's visitors, chiefly feminine, round him before he had finished the first verse. That gift of song, that exquisite touch upon the Spanish guitar, were irresistible.

Lord Fareham landed at the lower flight of steps as the song ended, and came slowly along the terrace, saluting his wife's friends with a grave courtesy. He brought an atmosphere of silence and restraint with him, it seemed to some of his wife's visitors, for the babble that usually follows the end of a song was wanting.

Most of Lady Fareham's friends affected literature, and professed familiarity with two books which had caught the public taste on opposite sides of the Channel. In London people quoted Butler, and vowed there was no wit so racy as the wit in "Hudibras." In Paris the cultured were all striving to talk like Rochefoucauld's "Maxims," which had lately delighted the Gallic mind by the frank cynicism that drew everybody's attention to somebody else's failings.

"Himself the vainest of men, 'tis scarce wonderful that he takes vanity to be the mainspring that moves the human species," said De Malfort, when someone had found fault with the Duke's analysis.

"Oh, now we shall hear nothing but stale Rochefoucauldisms, sneers at love and friendship, disparagement of our ill-used sex! Where has my grave husband been, I wonder?" said Hyacinth. "Upon my honour, Fareham, your brow looks as sombre as if it were burdened with the care of the nation."

"I have been with one who has to carry the greater part of that burden, my lady, and my spirits may have caught some touch of his uneasiness."

"You have been prosing with that pragmatical personage at Dunkirk—nay, I beg the Lord Chancellor's pardon, Clarendon House. Are not his marbles and tapestries much finer than ours? And yet he began life as a sneaking lawyer, the younger son of a small Wiltshire squire——"

"Lady Fareham, you allow your tongue too much licence——"

"Nay, I speak but the common feeling. Everybody is tired of a Minister who is a hundred years behind the age. He should have lived under Elizabeth."

"A pretty woman should never talk politics, Hyacinth."

"Of what else can I talk when the theatres are closed, and you deny me the privilege of seeing the last comedy performed at Whitehall? Is it not rank tyranny in his lordship, Lady Sarah?" turning to one of her intimates, a lady who had been a beauty at the court of Henrietta Maria in the beginning of the troubles, and who from old habit still thought herself lovely and beloved. "I appeal to your ladyship's common sense. Is it not monstrous to deprive me of the only real diversion in the town? I was not allowed to enter a theatre at all last year, except when his favourite Shakespeare or Fletcher was acted, and that was but a dozen times, I believe."

"Oh, hang Shakespeare!" cried a gentleman whose periwig occupied nearly as much space against the blue of a vernal sky as all the rest of his dapper little person. "Gud, my lord, it is vastly old-fashioned in your lordship to taste Shakespeare!" protested Sir Ralph Masaroon, shaking a cloud of pulvilio out of his cataract of curls. "There was a pretty enough play concocted t'other day out of two of his—a tragedy and comedy—*Measure for Measure* and *Much Ado about Nothing,* the interstices filled in with the utmost ingenuity. But Shakespeare unadulterated—faugh!"

"I am a fantastical person, perhaps, Sir Ralph; but I would rather my wife saw ten of Shakespeare's plays —in spite of their occasional coarseness—than one of your modern comedies."

"I should revolt against such tyranny," said Lady Sarah. "I have always appreciated Shakespeare, but I adore a witty comedy, and I never allowed my husband to dictate to me on a question of taste."

"Plays which her Majesty patronises can scarcely be unfit entertainment for her subjects," remarked another lady.

"Our Portuguese Queen is an excellent judge of the niceties of our language," said Fareham. "I question if she understands five sentences in as many acts."

"Nor should *I* understand anything low or vulgar," said Hyacinth.

"Then, madam, you are best at home, for the whole entertainment would be Hebrew to you."

"That cannot be," protested Lady Sarah; "for all our plays are written by gentlemen. The hack writers of King James's time have been shoved aside. It is the mark of a man of quality to write a comedy."

"It is a pity that fine gentlemen should write foul jests. Nay, it is a subject I can scarce speak of with patience, when I remember what the English stage has been, and hear what it is; when I recall what Lord Clarendon has told me of his Majesty's father, for whom Shakespeare was a closet companion, who loved all that was noblest in the drama of the Elizabethan age. Time, which should have refined and improved the stage, has sunk it in ignominy. We stand alone among nations in our worship of the obscene. You have seen plays enough in Paris, Hyacinth. Recall the themes that pleased you at the Marais and the Hôtel de Bourgogne; the stories of classic heroism, of Christian fortitude, of manhood and womanhood lifted to the sublime. You who, in your girlhood, were familiar with the austere genius of Corneille——"

"I am sick of that Frenchman's name," interjected Lady Sarah. "St. Évremond was always praising him, and had the audacity to pronounce him superior to Dryden; to compare *Cinna* with the *Indian Queen.*"

"A comparison which makes one sorry for Mr. Dryden," said Fareham. "I have heard that Condé, when a young man, was affected to tears at the scene between Augustus and his foe."

"He must have been very young," said Lady Fareham. "But I am not going to depreciate Corneille, or to pretend that the French theatre is not vastly superior to our own. I would only protest that if our laughter-loving King prefers farce to tragedy, and rhyme to blank-verse, his subjects should accommodate themselves to his taste, and enjoy the plays he likes. It is a foolish prejudice that deprives me of such a pleasure. I could always go in a mask."

"Can you put a mask upon your mind, and preserve that unstained in an atmosphere of corruption? Indeed, your ladyship does not know what you are asking for. To sit and simper through a comedy in which the filthiest subjects are discussed in the vilest language; to see all that is foolish or lascivious in your own sex exaggerated with a malignant licence, which makes a young and beautiful woman an epitome of all the vices, uniting the extreme of masculine profligacy with the extreme of feminine silliness. Will you encourage by your presence the wretches who libel your sex? Will you sit smiling to see your sisters in the pillory of satire?"

"I should smile as at a fairy tale. There are no such women among my friends——"

"And if the satire hits an enemy, it is all the more pungent," said Lady Sarah.

"An enemy! The man who can so write of women is your worst enemy. The day will come, perhaps, long after we are dust, when the women in *Epsom Wells* will be thought pictures from life. 'Such an one,' people will say, as they stand to read your epitaph, 'was this Lady Sarah, whose virtues are recorded here in Latin superlatives. We know her better in the pages of Shadwell.'"

Lady Sarah paled under her rouge at that image of a tomb, as Fareham's falcon eye singled her out in the light-hearted group of which De Malfort was the central figure, sitting on the marble balustrade, in an easy impertinent attitude, swinging his legs, and dandling his guitar. She was less concerned at the thought of what posterity might say of her morals than at the idea that she must inevitably die.

"Not a word against Shad," protested Sir Ralph. "I have roared with laughter at his last play. Never did anyone so hit the follies of town and country. His rural Put is perfection; his London rook is to the very life."

"And if the generality of his female characters conduct themselves badly there is always one heroine of irreproachable morals," said Lady Sarah.

"Who talks like a moral dragoon," said Fareham.

"Oh, dem, we must have the playhouses!" cried Masaroon. "Consider how dull town is without them. They are the only assemblies that please quality and riffraff alike. Sure 'tis the nature of wit to bubble into licentiousness, as champagne foams over the rim of a glass; and, after all, who listens to the play? Half the time one is talking to some adventurous miss, who will swallow a compliment from a stranger if he offer it with a china orange. Or, perhaps, there is quarrelling; and all our eyes and ears are on the scufflers. One may ogle a pretty actress on the stage; but who listens to the play, except the cits and commonalty?"

"And even they are more eyes than ears," said Lady Sarah, "and are gazing at the King and Queen, or the Duke and Duchess, when they should be following an intrigue by Shadwell or Dryden."

"Pardieu!" exclaimed De Malfort, "there are tragedies and comedies in the boxes deeper and more human than anything that is acted on the stage. To watch the Queen, sitting silent and melancholy, while Madame Barbara lolls across half a dozen people to talk to his Majesty, dazzling him with her brilliant eyes, bewildering him by her daring speech. Or, on other nights to see the same lady out of favour, sitting apart, with an ivory shoulder turned towards Royalty, scowling at the audience like a thunder-cloud."

"Well, it is but natural, perhaps, that such a Court should inspire such a stage," returned Fareham, "and that for the heroic drama of Beaumont and Fletcher, Webster, Massinger, and Ford, we should have a gross caricature of our own follies and our own vices. Nay, so essential is foulness to the modern stage that when the manager ventures a serious play, he takes care to introduce it with some filthy prologue, and to spice the finish with a filthier epilogue."

"Zounds, Fareham!" cried Masaroon, "when one has yawned or slept through five acts of dull heroics, one needs to be stung into wakefulness by a high-spiced epilogue. For my taste your epilogue can't be too pungent to give a flavour to my oysters and Rhenish. Gud, my lord, we must have something to talk about when we leave the playhouse!"

"His lordship is spoilt; we are all spoilt for London after having lived in the most exquisite city in the world," drawled Mrs. Danville, one of Lady Fareham's particular' friends, who had been educated at the Visitandines with the Princess Henrietta, now Duchess of Orleans. "Who can tolerate the coarse manners and sea-coal fires of London after the smokeless skies and exquisite courtesies of Parisian good company in the Rue St. Thomas du Louvre—a society so refined that a fault in grammar shocks as much as a slit nose at Charing Cross? I shudder when I recall the Saturdays in the Rue du Temple, and compare the conversations there, the play of wit and fancy, the elaborate arguments upon platonic love, the graceful raillery, with any assembly in London —except yours, Hyacinth. At Fareham House we breathe a finer air, although his lordship's *esprit moqueur* will not allow us any superiority to the coarse English mob."

"Indeed, Mrs. Danville, even your prejudice cannot deny London fine gentlemen and wits," remonstrated Sir Ralph. "A court that can boast a Buckhurst, a Rochester, an Etherege, a Sedley——"

"There is not one of them can compare with Voiture or Godeau, with Bussy or St. Évremond, still less with Scarron or Molière," said De Malfort. "I have heard more wit in one evening at Scarron's than in a week at Whitehall. Wit in France has its basis in thought and erudition. Here it is the sparkle and froth of empty minds, a trick of speech, a knack of saying brutal things under a pretence of humour, varnishing real impertinence with mock wit. I have heard Rowley laugh at insolences which, addressed to Louis, would have ensured the speaker a year in the Bastille."

"I would not exchange our easy-tempered King for your graceful despot," said Fareham. "Pride is the mainspring that moves Louis' self-absorbed soul. His mother instilled it into his mind almost before he could speak. He was bred in the belief that he has no more parallel or fellow than the sun which he has chosen for his emblem. And then, for moral worth, he is little better than his cousin. Louis has all Charles's elegant vices, plus tyranny."

"Louis is every inch a King. Your easy-tempered gentleman at Whitehall is only a tradition," answered De Malfort. "He is but an extravagantly paid official, whose office is a sinecure, and who sells something of his prerogative every session for a new grant of money. I dare adventure, by the end of his reign, Charles will have done more than Cromwell to increase the liberty of the subject and to demonstrate the insignificance of kings."

"I doubt the easy-tempered sinecurist who trusts the business of the State to the nation's representatives will wear longer than your officious tyrant, who wants to hold all the strings in his own fingers."

"He may do that safely, so long as he has men like Colbert for puppets——"

"Men!" cried Fareham. "A man of so rare an honesty must not be thought of in the plural. Colbert's talent, probity, and honour constitute a phœnix that appears once in a century, and; given those rare qualities in the man, it needs a Richelieu to inspire the minister, and a Mazarin to teach him his craft, and to prepare him for double-dealing in others which his own direct mind could never have imagined. Trained first by one of the greatest, and next by one of the subtlest statesmen the world has ever seen, the provincial woollen-draper's son has all the qualities needed to raise France to the pinnacle of fortune, if his master will but give him a free hand."

"At anyrate, he will make Jacques Bonhomme pay handsomely for his Majesty's new palaces and new loves," said De Malfort. "Colbert adores the King, and is blind to his follies, which are no more economical than the vulgar pleasures of your jovial Rowley."

"Who takes four shillings in every country gentle-man's pound to spend on the pleasures of London," interjected Masaroon. "Royalty is plaguey expensive."

The company sighed a melancholy assent.

"And one can never tell whether the money they squeeze out of us goes to build a new ship, or to pay Lady Castlemaine's gambling debts," said Lady Sarah.

"Oh, no doubt the lady, as Hyde calls her, has her tithes," said De Malfort. "I have observed she always flames in new jewels after a subsidy."

"Royal accounts should be kept so that every tax-payer could look into them," said Masaroon. "The King has spent millions. We were all so foolishly fond of him in the joyful day of his restoration that we allowed him to wallow in extravagance, and asked no questions; and for a man who had worn threadbare velvet and tarnished gold, and lived upon loans and gratuities from foreign princes and particulars, it was a new sensation to draw *ad libitum* upon a national exchequer."

"The exchequer Rowley draws upon should be as deep and wide as the river Pactolus; for he is a spendthrift by instinct," said Fareham.

"Yet his largest expenditure can hardly equal his cousin's drain upon the revenue. Mansart is spending millions on Versailles, with his bastard Italian architecture, his bloated garlands and festoons, his stone lilies and pomegranates. Charles builds no palaces, initiates no war——"

"And will leave neither palace nor monument; will have lived only to have diminished the dignity and importance of his country. Restored to kingdom and power as if by a miracle, he makes it his chief business to show Englishmen how well they could have done without him," said Denzil Warner, who had been hanging over Angela's tea-table until just now, when they both sauntered on to the terrace, the lady's office being fulfilled, the little Chinese teapot emptied of its costly contents, and the tiny teacups distributed among the modish few who relished, or pretended to relish, the new drink.

"You are a Republican, Sir Denzil, fostered by an arrant demagogue!" exclaimed Masaroon, with a contemptuous shake of his shoulder ribbons. "You hate the King because he is a King."

"No, sir, I despise him because he is so much less than a King. Nobody could hate Charles the Second. He is not big enough."

"Oh, dem, we want no meddlesome Kings to quarrel with their neighbours, and set Europe by the ears! The treaty of the Pyrenees may be a fine thing for France, but how many noble gentlemen's lives it cost, to say nothing of the common people! Rowley is the finest gentleman in his kingdom, and the most good-natured. Eh, gud, sirs! what more would you have?"

"A MAN— like Henry the Fifth, or Oliver Cromwell, or Elizabeth."

"Faith, she had need possess the manly virtues, for she must have been an untowardly female—a sour, lantern-jawed spinster, with all the inclinations but none of the qualities of a coquette."

"Greatness has the privilege of small failings, or it would scarce be human. Elizabeth and Julius Cæsar might be excused some harmless vanities."

The spring evenings were now mild enough for promenading St. James's Park, and the Mall was crowded night after night by the finest company in London. Hyacinth walked in the Mall, and appeared occasionally in her coach in Hyde Park; but she repeatedly reminded her friends how inferior was the mill-round of the Ring to the procession of open carriages along the Cours la Reine, by the side of the Seine; the splendour of the women's dress, outshone sometimes by the extravagant decoration of their coaches and the richness of their liveries; the crowds of horsemen, the finest gentlemen in France, riding at the coach doors, and bandying jests and compliments with Beauty, enthroned in her triumphal chariot. Gay, joyous sunsets; light laughter; delicate feasting in Renard's garden, hard by the Tuileries. To remember that fairer and different scene was to recall the freshness of youth, the romance of a first love.

Here in the Mall there was gaiety enough and to spare. A crowd of fine people that sometimes thickened to a mob, hustled by the cits and starveling poets who came to stare at them.

Yet, since St. James's Park was fashion's favourite promenade, Lady Fareham affected it, and took a turn or two nearly every evening, alighting from her chair at one gate and returning to it at another, on her way to rout or dance. She took Angela with her; and De Malfort and Sir Denzil were generally in attendance upon them, Denzil's devotion stopping at nothing except a proposal of marriage, for which he had not mustered courage in a friendship that had lasted half a year.

"Because there was one so favoured as Endymion, am I to hope for the moon to come down and give herself to me?" he said one day, when Lady Fareham rebuked him for his reticence. "I know your sister does not love me; yet I hang on, hoping that love will come suddenly, like the coming of spring, which is ever a surprise. And even if I am never to win her, it is happiness to see her and to talk with her. I will not spoil my chance by rashness; I will not hazard banishment from her dear company."

"She is lucky in such an admirer," sighed Hyacinth. "A silent, respectful passion is the rarest thing nowadays. Well, you deserve to conquer, Denzil; and if my sister were not of the coldest nature I ever met in woman she would have returned your passion ages ago, when you were so much in her company at Chilton."

"I can afford to wait as long as the Greeks waited

before Troy," said Denzil; "and I will be as constant as they were. If I cannot be her lover I can be her friend, and her protector."

"Protector! Nay, surely she needs no protector out-of-doors, when she has Fareham and me within!"

"Beauty has always need of defenders."

"Not such beauty as Angela's. In the first place, her charms are of no dazzling order; and in the second, she has a coldness of temper and an old-fashioned wisdom which would safeguard her amidst the rabble rout of Comus."

"There I believe you are right, Lady Fareham. Temptation could not touch her. Sin, even the subtlest, could not so disguise itself that her purity would not take alarm. Yes; she is like Milton's lady. The tempter could not touch the freedom of her mind. Sinful love would wither at a look from those pure eyes."

He turned away suddenly and walked to the window.

"Denzil! Why, what is the matter? You are weeping!"

"Forgive me!" he said, recovering himself. "Indeed, I am not ashamed of a tributary tear to virtue and beauty like your sister's."

"Dear friend, I shall not be happy till I call you brother."

She gave him both her hands, and he bent down to kiss them.

"I swear you are losing all your Anabaptist stiffness," she said, laughingly. "You will be ruffling it in Covent Garden with Buckhurst and his crew before long."

CHAPTER XIII.

THE SAGE OF SAYES COURT.

ONE of Angela's letters to her convent companion, the chosen friend and confidante of childhood and girlhood, Léonie de Ville, now married to the Baron de Beaulieu, and established in a fine house in the Place Royale, will best depict her life and thoughts and feelings during her first London season.

"You tell me, *chère,* that this London, which I have painted in somewhat brilliant colours, must be a poor place compared with your exquisite city; but, indeed, despite all you say of the Cours la Reine, and your splendour of gilded coaches, fine ladies, and noble gentlemen, who ride at your coach windows, talking to you as they rein in their spirited horses, I cannot think that your fashionable promenade can so much surpass our Ring in Hyde Park, where the Court airs itself daily in the new glass coaches, or outvie for gaiety our Mall in St. James's Park, where all the world of beauty and wit is to be met walking up and down in the gayest, easiest way, everybody familiar and acquainted, with the exception of a few women in masks, who are never to be spoken to or spoken about. Indeed, my sister and I have acquired the art of appearing neither to see nor to hear objectionable company, and pass close beside fine flaunting masks, rub shoulders with them even—and all as if we saw them not. It is for this that Lord Fareham hates London. Here, he says, vice takes the highest place, and flaunts in the sun, while virtue blushes, and steals by with averted head.

But though I wonder at this Court of Whitehall, and the wicked woman who reigns empress there, and the neglected Queen, and the ladies of honour, whose bad conduct is on everyone's lips, I wonder more at the people and the life you describe at the Louvre, and St. Germain, and Fontainebleau, and your new palace of Versailles.

"Indeed, Léonie, the world must be in a strange way when vice can put on all the grace and dignity of virtue, and hold an honourable place among good and noble women. My sister says that Madame de Montausier is a woman of stainless character, and her husband the proudest of men; yet you tell me that both husband and wife are full of kindness and favours for that unhappy Mlle. de la Vallière, whose position at Court is an open insult to your Queen. Have Queens often been so unhappy, I wonder, as her Majesty here, and your own royal mistress? One at least was not. The martyred King was of all husbands the most constant and affectionate, and, in the opinion of many, lost his kingdom chiefly through his fatal indulgence of Queen Henrietta's caprices, and his willingness to be governed by her opinions in circumstances of difficulty, where only the wisest heads in the land should have counselled him. But how I am wandering from my defence of this beautiful city against your assertion of its inferiority! I hope, *chère,* that you will cross the sea some day, and allow my sister to lodge you in this house where I write; and when you look out upon our delightful river, with its gay traffic of boats and barges passing to and fro, and its palaces, rising from gardens and Italian terraces on either side of the stream; when

you see our ancient cathedral of St. Paul; and the
Abbey of St. Peter, lying a little back from the water,
grand and ancient, and somewhat gloomy in its massive
bulk; and eastward, the old fortress-prison, with its four
towers; and the ships lying in the Pool; and fertile
Bermondsey with its gardens; and all the beauty of
verdant shores and citizens' houses between the bridge
and Greenwich, you will own that London and its adjacent villages can compare favourably with any metropolis in the world.

"The only complaint one hears is of its rapid
growth, which is fast encroaching upon the pleasant
fields and rustic lanes behind the Lambs Conduit and
Southampton House; and on the western side spreading
so rapidly that there will soon be no country left between London and Knightsbridge.

"How I wish thou couldst see our river-terrace on
my sister's visiting-day, when De Malfort is lolling on
the marble balustrade, singing one of your favourite
chansons to the guitar which he touches so exquisitely,
and when Hyacinth's fine lady friends and foppish admirers are sitting about in the sunshine! Thou wouldst
confess that even Renard's garden can show no gayer
scene.

"It was only last Tuesday that I had the opportunity
of seeing more of the city than I had seen previously—
and at its best advantage, as seen from the river. Mr.
Evelyn, of Sayes Court, had invited my sister and her
husband to visit his house and gardens. He is a great
gardener and arboriculturist, as you may have heard,
for he has travelled much on the Continent, and ac-

quired a world-wide reputation for his knowledge of
trees and flowers.

"We were all invited—the Farehams, and my niece
Henriette; and even I, whom Mr. Evelyn had seen but
once, was included in the invitation. We were to travel
by water, in his lordship's barge, and Mr. Evelyn's coach
was to meet us at a landing-place not far from his
house. We were to start in the morning, dine with him,
and return to Fareham House before dark. Henriette
was enchanted, and I found her at prayers on Monday
night praying St. Swithin, whom she believes to have
care of the weather, to allow no rain on Tuesday.

"She looked so pretty next morning, dressed for the
journey, in a light blue cloth cloak embroidered with
silver, and a hood of the same; but she brought me
bad news—my sister had a feverish headache, and
begged us to go without her. I went to Hyacinth's
room to try to persuade her to go with us, in the hope
that the fresh air along the river would cure her headache; but she had been at a dance overnight, and was
tired, and would do nothing but rest in a dark room
all day—at least, that was her resolve in the morning;
but later she remembered that it was Lady Lucretia
Topham's visiting-day, and, feeling better, ordered her
chair and went off to Bloomsbury Square, where she
met all the wits, full of a new play which had been
acted at Whitehall, the public theatres being still closed
on account of the late contagion.

"They do not act their plays here as often as
Molière is acted at the Hôtel de Bourgogne. The town
is constant in nothing but wanting perpetual variety,
and the stir and bustle of a new play, which gives

something for the wits to dispute about. I think we
must have three playwrights to one of yours; but I
doubt if there is wit enough in a dozen of our writers
to equal your Molière, whose last comedy seems to surpass all that has gone before. His lordship had a copy
from Paris last week, and read the play to us in the
evening. He has no accent, and reads French beauti-
fully, with spirit and fire, and in the passionate scenes
his great deep voice has a fine effect.

"We left Fareham House at nine o'clock on a lovely
morning, worthy this month of May. The lessening of
fires in the city since the warmer weather has freed our
skies from sea-coal smoke, and the sky last Tuesday
was bluer than the river.

"The cream-coloured and gold barge, with twelve
rowers in the Fareham green velvet liveries, would have
pleased your eyes, which have ever loved splendour;
but you might have thought the master of this splendid
barge too sombre in dress and aspect to become a scene
which recalled Cleopatra's galley. To me there is much
that is interesting in that severe and serious face, with
its olive complexion and dark eyes, shadowed by the
strong, thoughtful brow. People who knew Lord Strafford
say that my brother-in-law has a look of that great, un-
fortunate man—sacrificed to stem the rising flood of
rebellion, and sacrificed in vain. Fareham is his kinsman on the mother's side, and may have perhaps something of his powerful mind, together with the rugged
grandeur of his features and the bent carriage of his
shoulders, which someone the other day called the
Strafford stoop.

"I have been reading some of Lord Strafford's letters,

and the account of his trial. Indeed he was an ill-used man, and the victim of private hatred—from the Vanes and others—as much as of public faction. His trial and condemnation were scarce less unfair—though the form and tribunal may have been legal—than his master's, and indeed did but forecast that most unwarrantable judgment. Is it not strange, Léonie, to consider how much of tragical history you and I have lived through that are yet so young? But to me it is strangest of all to see the people in this city, who abandon themselves as freely to a life of idle pleasures and sinful folly—at least, the majority of them—as if England had never seen the tragedy of the late monarch's murder, or been visited by death in his most horrible aspect, only the year last past. My sister tells everyone, smiling, that she misses no one from the circle of her friends. She never saw the red cross on almost every door, the coffins, and the uncoffined dead, as I saw them one stifling summer day, nor heard the shrieks of the mourners in houses where death was master. Nor does she suspect how near she was to missing her husband, who was hanging between life and death when I found him, forsaken and alone. He never talks to me of those days of sickness and slow recovery; yet I think the memory of them must be in his mind as it is in mine, and that this serves as a link to draw us nearer than many a real brother and sister. I am sending you a little picture which I made of him from memory, for he has one of those striking faces that paint themselves easily upon the mind. Tell me how you, who are clever at reading faces, interpret this one.

"*Hélas*, how I wander from our excursion! My pen

winds like the river which carried us to Deptford. *Pardon, chèrie, si je m'oublie trop; mais c'est si doux de causer avec une amie d'enfance.*

"At the Tower stairs we stopped to take on board a gentleman in a very fine peach-blossom suit, and with a huge periwig, at which Papillon began to laugh, and had to be chid somewhat harshly. He was a very civil-spoken, friendly person, and he brought with him a lad carrying a viol. He is an officer of the Admiralty, called Pepys, and, Fareham tells me, a useful, indefatigable person. My sister met him at Clarendon House two years ago, and wrote to me about him some-what scornfully; but my brother respects him as shrewd and capable, and more honest than such persons usually are. We were to fetch him to Sayes Court, where he also was invited by Mr. Evelyn; and in talking to Henriette and me, he expressed great regret that his wife had not been included, and he paid my niece compliments upon her grace and beauty which I could but think very fulsome and showing want of judgment in addressing a child. And then, seeing me vexed, he hoped I was not jealous; at which I could hardly command my anger, and rose in a huff and left him. But he was a person not easy to keep at a distance, and was following me to the prow of the boat, when Fareham took hold of him by his cannon sleeve and led him to a seat, where he kept him talking of the navy and the great ships now a-building to replace those that have been lost in the Dutch War.

"When we had passed the Pool, and the busy trading ships, and all the noise of sailors and labourers shipping or unloading cargo, and the traffic of small boats hasten-

ing to and fro, and were out on a broad reach of the
river with the green country on either side, the lad tuned
his viol, and played a pretty, pensive air, and he and
Mr. Pepys sang some verses by Herrick, one of our
favourite English poets, set for two voices—

> " 'Gather ye rosebuds, while ye may,
>   Old time still is a-flying;
>   And this same flower that smiles to-day,
>   To-morrow will be dying.'

The boy had a voice like Mère Ursule's lovely soprano,
and Mr. Pepys a pretty tenor; and you can imagine
nothing more silvery sweet than the union of the two
voices to the staccato notes of the viol, dropping in here
and there like music whispered. The setting was Mr.
Pepys' own, and he seemed overcome with pride when
we praised it. When the song was over, Fareham came
to the bench where Papillon and I were sitting, and
asked me what I thought of this fine Admiralty gentleman, whereupon I confessed I liked the song better than
the singer, who at that moment was strutting on the
deck like a peacock, looking at every vessel we passed
as if he were Neptune, and could sink navies with
a nod.

"*Miséricorde!* how my letter grows! But I love to
prattle to you. My sister is all goodness to me; but she
has her ideas and I have mine; and though I love her
none the less because our fancies pull us in opposite
directions, I cannot talk to her as I can write to you;
and if I plague you with too much of my own history
you must not fear to tell me so. Yet if I dare judge by
my own feelings, who am never weary of your letters—
nay, can never hear enough of your thoughts and

doings—I think you will bear with my expatiations, and not deem them too impertinent.

"Mr. Evelyn's coach was waiting at the landing-stage; and that good gentleman received us at his hall door. He is not young, and has gone through much affliction in the loss of his dear children—one, who died of a fever during that wicked reign of the Usurper Cromwell, was a boy of gifts and capacities that seemed almost miraculous, and had more scholarship at five years old than my poor woman's mind could compass were I to live till fifty. Mr. Evelyn took a kind of sad delight in talking to Henriette and me of this gifted child, asking her what she knew of this and that subject, and comparing her extensive ignorance at eleven with his lamented son's vast knowledge at five. I was more sorry for him than I dared to say; for I could but think this dear overtaught child might have died from a perpetual fever of the brain as likely as from a four days' fever of the body; and afterwards when Mr. Evelyn talked to us of a manner of forcing fruits to grow in strange shapes—a process in which he was greatly interested—I thought that this dear infant's mind had been constrained and directed, like the fruits, into a form unnatural to childhood. Picture to yourself, Léonie, at an age when he should have been chasing butterflies or making himself a garden of cut-flowers stuck in the ground, this child was labouring over Greek and Latin, and all his dreams must have been filled with the toilsome perplexities of his daily tasks. It is happy for the bereaved father that he takes a different view, and that his pride in the child's learning is even greater than his grief at having lost him.

"At dinner the conversation was chiefly of public affairs—the navy, the war, the King, the Duke, and the General. Mr. Evelyn told Fareham much of his embarrassments last year, when he had the Dutch prisoners, and the sick and wounded from the fleet, in his charge; and when there was so terrible a scarcity of provision for these poor wretches that he was constrained to draw largely on his own private means in order to keep them from starving.

"Later, during the long dinner, Mr. Pepys made allusions to an unhappy passion of his master and patron, Lord Sandwich, that had diverted his mind from public business, and was likely to bring him to disgrace. Nothing was said plainly about this matter, but rather in hints and innuendoes, and my brother's brow darkened as the conversation went on; and then, at last, after sitting silent for some time while Mr. Evelyn and Mr. Pepys conversed, he broke up their discourse in a rough, abrupt way he has when greatly moved.

" 'He is a wretch—a guilty wretch—to love where he should not, to hazard the world's esteem, to grieve his wife, and to dishonour his name! And yet, I wonder, is he happier in his sinful indulgence than if he had played a Roman part, or, like the Spartan lad we read of, had let the wild-beast passion gnaw his heart out, and yet made no sign? To suffer and die, that is virtue, I take it, Mr. Evelyn; and you Christian sages assure us that virtue is happiness. A strange kind of happiness!'

" 'The Christian's law is a law of sacrifice,' Mr. Evelyn

said, in his melancholic way. 'The harvest of surrender here is to be garnered in a better world.'

" 'But if Sandwich does not believe in the everlasting joys of the heavenly Jerusalem—and prefers to anticipate his harvest of joy!' said Fareham.

" 'Then he is the more to be pitied,' interrupted Mr. Evelyn.

" 'He is as God made him. Nothing can come out of a man but what his Maker put in him. Your gold vase there will not turn vicious and produce copper— nor can all your alchemy turn copper to gold. There are some of us who believe that a man can live only once, and love only once, and be happy only once in that pitiful span of infirmities which we call life; 'and that he is wisest who gathers his roses while he may— as Mr. Pepys sang to us this morning.'

"Mr. Evelyn sighed, and looked at my brother with mild reproof.

" 'If in this life only we have hope in Christ, we are of all men most miserable,' he said. 'My lord, when those you love people the Heavenly City, you will begin to believe and hope as I do.'

"I have transcribed this conversation at full length, Léonie, because it gives you the keynote to Fareham's character, and accounts for much that is strange in his conduct. Alas, that I must say it of so noble a man! He is an infidel! Bred in our Church, he has faith neither in the Church nor in its Divine Founder. His favourite books are metaphysical works by Descartes, Hobbes, Spinoza. I have discovered him reading those pernicious writings whose chief tendency is to make us question the most blessed truths our Church has taught us, or to confuse the mind by leading us to doubt even of our own existence. I was curious to know what there could be in books that so interested a man of his intelligence, and asked to be allowed to read them; but the perusal only served to make me unhappy. This daring attempt to reduce all the mysteries of life to a simple sum in arithmetic, and to make God a mere attribute in the mind of man, disturbed and depressed me. Indeed, there can be no more unhappy moment in any life than that in which for the first time a terrible 'if' flashes upon the mind. *If* God is not the God I have worshipped, and in whose goodness I rest all my hopes of future bliss; *if* in the place of an all-powerful Creator, who gave me my life and governs it, and will renew it after the grave, there is nothing but a quality of my mind, which makes it necessary to me to invent a Superior Being, and to worship the product of my own imagination! Oh, Léonie, beware of these modern thinkers, who assail the creed that has been the stronghold and comfort of humanity for sixteen hundred years, and who employ the reason which God has given them to disprove the existence of their Maker. Fareham insists that Spinoza is a religious man—and has beautiful ideas about God; but I found only doubt and despair in his pages; and I ascribe my poor brother's melancholic disposition in some part to his study of such philosophers.

"I wonder what you would think of Fareham, did you see him daily and hourly, almost, as I do. Would you like or dislike, admire or scorn him? I cannot tell. His manners have none of the velvet softness which is the fashion in London—where all the fine gentlemen shape themselves upon the Parisian model; yet he is

courteous, after his graver mode, to all women, and kind
and thoughtful· of our happiness. To my sister he is
all beneficence; and if he has a fault it is overmuch
indulgence of her whims and extravagances—though
Hyacinth, poor soul, thinks him a tyrant because he
forbids her some places of amusement to which other
women of quality resort freely. Were he my husband,
I should honour him for his desire to spare me all evil
sounds and profligate company; and so would Hyacinth,
perhaps, had she leisure for reflection. But in her London life, surrounded ever with a bevy of friends, moving
like a star amidst a galaxy of great ladies, there is little
time for the free exercise of a sound judgment, and
she can but think as others bid her, who swear that her
husband is a despot.

"Mrs. Evelyn was absent from home on a visit; so
after dinner Henriette and I, having no hostess to
entertain us, walked with our host, who showed us all
the curiosities and beauties of his garden, and condescended to instruct us upon many interesting particulars relating to trees and flowers, and the methods
of cultivation pursued in various countries. His fig trees
are as fine as those in the convent garden at Louvain;
and, indeed, walking with him in a long alley, shut in
by holly hedges of which he is especially proud, and with
orchard trees on either side, I was taken back in fancy
to the old pathway along which you and I have paced
so often with Mother Agnes, talking of the time when
we should go out into the world. You have been more
than three years in that world of which you then knew
so little, but it lacks still a quarter of one year since I
left that quiet and so monotonous life; and already I

look back and wonder if I ever really lived there. I cannot picture myself within those walls. I cannot call back my own feelings or my own image at the time when I had never seen London, when my sister was almost a stranger to me, and my sister's husband only a name. Yet a day of sorrow might come when I should be fain to find a tranquil retreat in that sober place, and to spend my declining years in prayer and meditation, as my dear aunt did spend nearly all her life. May God maintain us in the true faith, sweet friend, so that we may ever have that sanctuary of holy seclusion and prayer to fly to—and, oh, how deep should be our pity for a soul like Fareham's, which knows not the consolations nor the strength of religion, for whom there is no armour against the arrows of death, no City of Refuge in the day of mourning!

"Indeed he is not happy. I question and perplex myself to find a reason for his melancholy. He is rich in money and in powerful friends; has a wife whom all the world admires; houses which might lodge Royalty. Perhaps it is because his life has been over-prosperous that he sickens of it, like one who flings away from a banquet table, satiated by feasting. Life to him may be like the weariness of our English dinners, where one mountain of food is carried away to make room on the board for another; and where after people have sat eating and drinking for over an hour comes a roasted swan, or a peacock, or some other fantastical dish, which the company praise as a pretty surprise. Often, in the midst of such a dinner, I recall our sparing meals in the convent; our soup maigre and snow eggs, our cool salads and black bread—and regret that simple food,

while the reeking joints and hecatombs of fowl nauseate
my senses.

"It was late in the afternoon when we returned to the
barge, for Mr. Pepys had business to transact with our
host, and spent an hour with him in his study, signing
papers, and looking at accounts, while Papillon and I
roamed about the garden with his lordship, conversing
upon various subjects, and about Mr. Evelyn, and his
opinions and politics.

"'The good man has a pretty trivial taste that will
keep him amused and happy till he drops into the grave
—but, lord! what insipid trash it all seems to the heart
on fire with passion!' Fareham said in his impetuous
way, as if he despised Mr. Evelyn for taking pleasure in
bagatelles.

"The sun was setting as we passed Greenwich, and
I thought of those who had lived and made history in
the old palace—Queen Elizabeth, so great, so lonely;
Shakespeare, whom his lordship honours; Bacon, said
to be one of the wisest men who have lived since the
Seven of Greece; Raleigh, so brave, so adventurous, so
unhappy! Surely men and women must have been
made of another stuff a century ago; for what will those
who come after us remember of the wits and beauties
of Whitehall, except that they lived and died?

"Mr. Pepys was somewhat noisy on the evening
voyage, and I was very glad when he left the barge.
He paid me ridiculous compliments mixed with scraps
of French and Spanish, and, finding his conversation
distasteful, he insisted upon attempting several songs—
not one of which he was able to finish, and at last began
one which for some reason made his lordship angry, who

gave him a cuff on his head that scattered all the scented powder in his wig; on which, instead of starting up furious to return the blow, as I feared to see him, Mr. Pepys gave a little whimpering laugh, muttered something to the effect that his lordship was vastly nice, and sank down in a corner of the cushioned seat, where he almost instantly fell asleep.

"Henriette and I were spectators of this scene at some distance, I am glad to say, for all the length of the barge divided us from the noisy singer.

"The sun went down, and the stars stole out of the deep blue vault, and trembled between us and those vast fields of heaven. Papillon watched their reflection in the river, or looked at the houses along the shore, few and far apart, where a solitary candle showed here and there. Fareham came and seated himself near us, but talked little. We drew our cloaks closer, for the air was cold, and Papillon nestled beside me and dropped asleep. Even the dipping of the oars had a ghostly sound in the night stillness; and we seemed so melancholy in this silence, and so far away from one another, that I could but think of Charon's boat laden with the souls of the dead.

"Write to me soon, dearest, and as long a letter as I have written to you.

"*À toi de cœur,*
"ANGELA."

CHAPTER XIV.

THE MILLBANK GHOST.

ONE of the greatest charms of London has ever been the facility of getting away from it to some adjacent rustic or pseudo-rustic spot; and in 1666, though many people declared that the city had outgrown all reason, and was eating up the country, a two-mile journey would carry the Londoner from bricks and mortar to rusticity, and while the tower of St. Paul's Cathedral was still within sight he might lie on the grass on a wild hillside, and hear the skylark warbling in the blue arch above him, and scent the hawthorn blowing in untrimmed hedgerows. And then there were the fashionable resorts—the gardens or the fields which the town had marked as its own. Beauty and wit had their choice of such meeting-grounds between Westminster and Barn Elms, where in the remote solitudes along the river murder might be done in strict accordance with etiquette, and was too seldom punished by law.

Among the rendezvous of fashion there was one retired spot less widely known than Fox Hall or the Mulberry Garden, but which possessed a certain repute, and was affected rather by the exclusives than by the crowd. It was a dilapidated building of immemorial age, known as the "haunted Abbey," being, in fact, the refectory of a Cistercian monastery, of which all other remains had disappeared long ago. The Abbey had flourished in the lifetime of Sir Thomas More, and was mentioned in some of his familiar epistles. The ruined building had been used as a granary in the time of

Charles the First; and it was only within the last decade that it had been redeemed from that degraded
use, and had been in some measure restored and made
habitable for the occupation of an old couple, who
owned the surrounding fields, and who had a small
dairy farm from which they sent fresh milk into London
every morning.

The ghostly repute of the place and the attraction
of new milk, cheese cakes, and syllabubs, had drawn a
certain number of those satiated pleasure-seekers who
were ever on the alert for a new sensation, among whom
there was none more active or more noisy than Lady
Sarah Tewkesbury. She had made the haunted Abbey
in a manner her own, had invited her friends to midnight parties to watch for the ghost, and to morning
parties to eat syllabubs and dance on the grass. She
had brought a shower of gold into the lap of the miserly
freeholder, and had husband and wife completely under
her thumb.

Doler, the husband, had fought in the civil war, and
Mrs. Doler had been a cook in the Fairfax household;
but both had scrupulously sunk all Cromwellian associations since his Majesty's return, and in boasting, as he
often did boast, of having fought desperately and been
left for dead at the battle of Brentford, Mr. Doler had
been careful to suppress the fact that he was a hireling
soldier of the Parliament. He would weep for the
martyred King, and tell the story of his own wounds,
until it is possible he had forgotten which side he had
fought for, in remembering his personal prowess and
sufferings.

So far there had been disappointment as to the

17 *

ghost. Sounds had been heard of a most satisfying
grimness, during those midnight and early morning
watchings, rappings, and scrapings, and scratching on the
wall, groanings and moanings, sighings and whisperings
behind the wainscote; but nothing spectral had been
seen; and Mrs. Doler had been severely reprimanded
by her patrons and patronesses for the unwarrantable
conduct of a spectre which she professed to have seen
as often as she had fingers and toes.

It was the phantom of a nun—a woman of exceed-
ing beauty, but white as the linen which banded her
cheek and brow. There was a dark story of violated
oaths, priestly sin, and the sleepless conscience of the
dead, who could not rest even in that dreadful grave
where the sinner had been immured alive, but must
needs haunt the footsteps of the living, a wandering
shade. Some there were who disbelieved in the traditions of that living grave, and who even went so far as
to doubt the ghost; but the spectre had an established
repute of more than a century, was firmly believed in
by all the children and old women of the neighbourhood, and had been written about by students of the
unseen.

One of Lady Sarah's parties took place at full moon,
not long after the visit to Deptford, and Lord Fareham's
barge was again employed, this time on a nocturnal
expedition up the river to the fields near the haunted
Abbey, to carry Hyacinth, her sister, De Malfort, Lord
Rochester, Sir Ralph Masaroon, Sir Denzil Warner, and
a bevy of wits and beauties—beauties who had, some
of them, been carrying on the beauty-business and trading in eyes and complexion for more than one decade,

and who loved that night season when paint might be laid on thicker than in the glare of day.

The barge wore a much more festive aspect under her ladyship's management than when used by his lordship for a daylight voyage like the trip to Deptford. Satin coverlets and tapestry curtains had been brought from Lady Fareham's own apartments, to be flung with studied carelessness over benches and tabourets. Her ladyship's singing-boys and musicians were grouped picturesquely under a silken canopy in the bows, and a row of lanterns hung on chains festooned from stem to stern, pretty gewgaws, that had no illuminating power under that all-potent moon, but which glittered with coloured light like jewels, and twinkled and trembled in the summer air.

A table in the stern was spread with a light collation, which gave an excuse for the display of parcelgilt cups, silver tankards, and Venetian wine-flasks. A miniature fountain played perfumed waters in the midst of this splendour; and it amused the ladies to pull off their long gloves, dip them in the scented water, and flap them in the faces of their beaux.

The distance was only too short, since Lady Fareham's friends declared the voyage was by far the pleasanter part of the entertainment. Denzil, among others, was of this opinion, for it was his good fortune to have secured the seat next Angela, and to be able to interest her by his account of the buildings they passed, whose historical associations were much better known to him than to most young men of his epoch. He had sat at the feet of a man who scoffed at Pope

and King, and hated Episcopacy, but who revered all
that was noble and excellent in England's past.

"Flams, mere flams!" cried Hyacinth, acknowledging
the praises bestowed on her barge; "but if you like
clary wine better than skimmed milk you had best drink
a brimmer or two before you leave the barge, since 'tis
odds you'll get nothing but syllabubs and gingerbread
from Lady Sarah."

"A substantial supper might frighten away the ghost,
who doubtless parted with sensual propensities when she
died," said De Malfort. "How do we watch for her?
In a severe silence, as if we were at church?"

"Aw would keep silence for a week o' Sawbaths gin
Aw was sure o' seeing a bogle," said Lady Euphemia
Dubbin, a Scotch marquess's daughter, who had married
a wealthy cit, and made it the chief endeavour of her
life to ignore her husband and keep him at a distance.

She hated the man only a little less than his ple-
beian name, which she had not succeeded in persuading
him to change, because, forsooth, there had been Dubbins in Mark Lane for many generations. All previous
Dubbins had lived over their warehouses and offices;
but her ladyship had brought Thomas Dubbin from
Mark Lane to my Lord Bedford's Piazza in the Convent
Garden, where he endured the tedium of existence in a
fine new house in which he was afraid of his fine new
servants, and never had anything to eat that he liked,
his gastronomic taste being for dishes the very names
of which were intolerable to persons of quality.

This evening Mr. Dubbin had been incorrigible, and
had insisted on intruding his clumsy person upon Lady

Fareham's party, arguing with a dull persistence that his
name was on her ladyship's billet of invitation.

"Your name is on a great many invitations only
because it is my misfortune to be called by it," his wife
told him. "To sit on a barge after ten o'clock at night
in June—the coarsest month in summer—is to court
lumbago; and all I hope is ye'll not be punished by a
worse attack than common."

Mr. Dubbin had refused to be discouraged, even by
this churlishness from his lady, and appeared in attendance upon her, wearing a magnificent birthday suit
of crimson velvet and green brocade, which he meant
to present to his favourite actor at the Duke's Theatre,
after he had exhibited himself in it half a dozen times
at Whitehall, for the benefit of the great world, and at
the Mulberry Garden for the admiration of the *bona-
robas*. He was a fat, double-chinned little man, the
essence of good nature, and perfectly unconscious of
being an offence to fine people.

Although not a wit himself, Mr. Dubbin was occasionally the cause of wit in others, if the practice of
bubbling an innocent rustic or citizen can be called wit.
Rochester and Sir Ralph Masaroon, and one Jerry
Spavinger, a gentleman jockey, who was a nobody in
town, but a shining light at Newmarket, took it upon
themselves to draw the harmless citizen, and, as a
preliminary to making him ridiculous, essayed to make
him drunk.

They were clustered together in a little group somewhat apart from the rest of the company, and were
attended upon by a lackey who brought a full tankard
at the first whistle on the empty one, and whom Mr.

Dubbin, after a rapid succession of brimmers, insisted on calling "drawer." It was very seldom that Rochester condescended to take part in any entertainment on which the royal sun shone not, unless it were some post-midnight marauding with Buckhurst, Sedley, and a band of wild coursers from the purlieus of Drury Lane. He could see no pleasure in any medium between Whitehall and Alsatia.

"If I am not fooling on the steps of the throne, let me sprawl in the gutter with pamphleteers and orange-girls," said this precocious profligate. "I abhor a re-putable party among your petty nobility, and if I had not been in love with Lady Fareham off and on, ever since I cut my second teeth, I would have no hand in such a humdrum business as this."

"There's not a neater filly in the London stable than her ladyship," said Jerry, "and I don't blame your taste. I was side-glassing her yesterday in Hi' Park, but she didn't seem to relish the manœuvre, though I was wearing a Chedreux peruke that ought to strike 'em dead."

"You don't give your peruke a chance, Jerry, while you frame that ugly phiz in it."

"Why not buffle the whole company, my lord?" said Masaroon, while Mr. Dubbin talked apart with Lady Euphemia, who had come from the other end of the barge to warn her husband against excess in Rhenish or Burgundy. "You are good at disguises. Why not act the ghost and frighten everybody out of their senses?"

"*Il n'y a pas de quoi,* Ralph. The creatures have no sense to be robbed of. They are second-rate fashion, which is only worked by machinery. They imitate us as monkeys do, without knowing what they aim at. Their women have virtuous instincts, but turn wanton rather than not be like the maids of honour; and because we have our duels their men murder each other for a shrugged shoulder or a casual word. No, I'll not chalk my face or smear myself with phosphorus to amuse such trumpery. It was worth my pains to disguise myself as a German Nostradamus, in order to fool the lovely Jennings and her friend Price—who won't easily forget their adventures as orange-girls in the heart of the city. But I have done with all such follies."

"You are growing old, Wilmot. The years are telling upon your spirits."

"I was nineteen last birthday, and 'tis fit I should feel the burden of time, and think of virtue and a rich wife."

"Like Mrs. Mallet, for example."

"Faith, a man might do worse than win so much beauty and wealth. But the creature is arrogant, and calls me 'child;' and half the peerage is after her. But we'll have our jest with the city scrub, Ralph; not because I bear him malice, but because I hate his wife. And we'll have our masquerading some time after midnight; if you can borrow a little finery."

Mr. Dubbin was released from his lady's *sotto voce* lecture at this instant, and Lord Rochester continued his communication in a whisper, the Honourable Jeremiah assenting with nods and chucklings, while Masaroon whistled for a fresh tankard, and plied the honest merchant with a glass which he never allowed to be empty.

The taste for masquerading was a fashion of the time, as much as combing a periwig, or flirting a fan. While Rochester was planning a trick upon the citizen, Lady Fareham was whispering to De Malfort under cover of the fiddles, which were playing an Italian pazzemano, an air beloved by Henrietta of Orleans, who danced to that music with her royal brother-in-law, in one of the sumptuous ballets at St. Cloud.

"Why should they be disappointed of their ghost," said Hyacinth, "when it would be so easy for me to dress up as the nun and scare them all? This white satin gown of mine, with a few yards of white lawn arranged on my head and shoulders——"

"Ah, but you have not the lawn at hand to-night, or your woman to arrange your head," interjected De Malfort quickly. "It would be a capital joke; but it must be for another occasion and choicer company. The rabble you have to-night is not worth it. Besides, there is Rochester, who is past-master in disguises, and would smoke you at a glance. Let me arrange it some night before the end of the summer—when there is a waning moon. It were a pity the thing were done ill."

"Will you really plan a party for me, and let me appear to them on the stroke of one, with my face whitened? I have as slender a shape as most women."

"There is no such sylph in London."

"And I can make myself look ethereal. Will you draw the nun's habit for me? and I will give your picture to Lewin to copy."

"I will do more. I will get you a real habit."

"But there are no nuns so white as the ghost."

"True, but you may rely upon me. The nun's robes shall be there, the phosphorus, the blue fire, and a selection of the choicest company to tremble at you. Leave the whole business to my care. It will amuse me to plan so exquisite a jest for so lovely a jester."

He bent down to kiss her hand, till his forehead almost touched her knee, and in the few moments that passed before he raised it, she heard him laughing softly to himself, as if with irrepressible delight.

"What a child you are," she said, "to be pleased with such folly!"

"What children we both are, Hyacinth! My sweet soul, let us always be childish, and find pleasure in follies. Life is such a poor thing, that if we had leisure to appraise its value we should have a contagion of suicide that would number more deaths than the plague. Indeed, the wonder is, not that any man should commit *felo de se,* but that so many of us should take the trouble to live."

Lady Sarah received them at the landing-stage, with an escort of fops and fine ladies; and the festival promised to be a success. There was a better supper, and more wine than people expected from her ladyship; and after supper a good many of those who pretended to have come to see the ghost, wandered off in couples to saunter along the willow-shaded bank, while only the more earnest spirits were content to wait and watch and listen in the great vaulted hall, with no light but the moon which sent a flood of silver through the high Gothic window, from which every vestige of glass had long vanished.

There were stone benches along the two side walls, and Lady Sarah's *prévoyance* had secured cushions or carpets for her guests to sit upon; and here the superstitious sat in patient weariness, Angela among them, with Denzil still at her side, scornful of credulous folly, but loving to be with her he adored. Lady Fareham had been tempted out-of-doors by De Malfort to look at the moonlight on the river, and had not returned. Rochester and his crew had also vanished directly after supper; and for company Angela had on her left hand Mr. Dubbin, far advanced in liquor, and trembling at every breath of summer wind that fluttered the ivy round the ruined window, and at every shadow that moved upon the moonlit wall. His wife was on the other side of the hall, whispering with Lady Sarah, and both so deep in a court scandal—in which the "K" and the "D" recurred very often—that they had almost forgotten the purpose of that moonlight sitting.

Suddenly in the distance there sounded a long shrill wailing, as of a soul in agony, whereupon Mr. Dubbin, after clinging wildly to Angela, and being somewhat roughly flung aside by Denzil, collapsed altogether, and rolled upon the ground.

"Lady Euphemia," cried Mrs. Townshend, a young lady who had been sitting next the obnoxious citizen, "be pleased to look after your drunken husband. If you take the low-bred sot into company, you should at least charge yourself with the care of his manners."

The damsel had started to her feet, and indignantly snatched her satin petticoat from contact with the citizen's porpoise figure.

"I hate mixed company," she told Angela, "and old

maids who marry tallow-chandlers. If a woman of rank marries a shopkeeper she ought never to be allowed west of Temple Bar."

This young lady was no believer in ghosts; but others of the company were too scared for speech. All had risen, and were staring in the direction whence that dismal shriek had come. A trick, perhaps, since anybody with strong lungs—dairymaid or cowboy—could shriek. They all wanted to *see* something, a real manifestation of the supernatural.

The unearthly sound was repeated, and the next moment a spectral shape, in flowing white garments, rushed through the great window, and crossed the hall, followed by three other shapes in dark loose robes, with hooded heads. One carried a rope, another a pickaxe, the third a trowel and hod of mortar. They crossed the hall with flying footsteps—shadowlike—the pale shape in distracted flight, the dark shapes pursuing, and came to a stop close against the wall, which had been vacated by the scared assembly, scattering as if the king of terrors had appeared among them—yet with fascinated eyes fixed on those fearsome figures.

"It is the nun herself!" cried Lady Sarah, apprehension and triumph contending in her agitated spirits; for it was surely a feather in her ladyship's cap to have produced such a phantasmal train at her party. "The nun and her executioners!"

The company fell back from the ghostly troop, recoiling till they were all clustered against the opposite wall, leaving a clear space in front of the spectres, whence they looked on, shuddering, at the tragedy of the erring Sister's fate, repeated in dumb show. The white-robed figure knelt and grovelled at the feet of those hooded executioners. One seized and bound her, with strange automatic action, unlike the movements of living creatures, and another smote the wall with a pick-axe that made no sound, while the third waited with his trowel and mortar. It was a gruesome sight to those who knew the story—a gruesome, yet an enjoyable spectacle; since, as Lady Sarah's friends had not had the pleasure of knowing the sinning Sister in the flesh, they watched this ghostly representation of her suffering with as keen an interest as they would have felt had they been privileged to see Claud Duval swing at Tyburn.

The person most terrified by this ghostly show was the only one who had the hardihood to tackle the performers. This was Mr. Dubbin, who sat on the ground watching the shadowy figures, sobered by fear, and his shrewd city senses gradually returning to a brain bemused by Burgundy.

"Look at her boots!" he cried suddenly, scrambling to his feet, and pointing to the nun, who, in sprawling and writhing at the feet of her executioner, had revealed more leg and foot than were consistent with her spectral whiteness. "She wears yaller boots, as substantial as any shoe leather among the company. I'll swear to them yaller boots."

A chorus of laughter followed this attack—laughter which found a smothered echo among the ghosts. The spell was broken; disillusion followed the exquisite thrill of fear; and all Lady Sarah's male visitors made a rush upon the guilty nun. The loose white robe was stripped off, and little Jerry Spavinger, gentleman jock, famous on the Heath, and at Doncaster, stood revealed, in his shirt and breeches, and those light riding-boots which he rarely exchanged for a more courtly chaussure.

The monks, hustled out of their disguise, were Rochester, Masaroon, and Lady Sarah's young brother, George Saddington.

"From my Lord Rochester I expect nothing but pothouse buffoonery; but I take it vastly ill on your part, George, to join in making me a laughing-stock," remonstrated Lady Sarah.

"Indeed, sister, you have to thank his light-headed lordship for giving a spirited end to your assembly. Could you conceive how preposterous you and your friends looked sitting against the walls, mute as stockfish, and suggesting nothing but a Quaker's meeting, you would make us your lowest curtsy, and thank us kindly for having helped you out of a dilemma."

Lady Sarah, who was too much of a woman of the world to quarrel seriously with a Court favourite, furled the fan with which she had been cooling her indignation, and tapped young Wilmot playfully on that oval cheek where the beard had scarce begun to grow.

"Thou art the most incorrigible wretch of thy years in London," she said, "and it is impossible to help being angry with thee or to help forgiving thee."

The saunterers on the willow-shadowed banks came strolling in. Lady Fareham's cornets and fiddles sounded a March in Alceste; and the party broke up in laughter and good temper, Mr. Dubbin being much complimented upon his having detected Spavinger's boots.

"I ought to know 'em," he answered ruefully. "I lost a hundred meggs on him Toosday se'nnight, at Windsor races; and I had time to take the pattern of them boots while he was crawling in, a bad third."

CHAPTER XV.

FALCON AND DOVE.

"Has your ladyship any commands for Paris?" Lord Fareham asked, one August afternoon, when the ghost party at Millbank was almost forgotten amid a succession of entertainments on land and river; a fortnight at Epsom to drink the waters; and a fortnight at Tunbridge—where the Queen and Court were spending the close of summer—to neutralise the bad effects of Epsom chalybeates with a regimen of Kentish sulphur. If nobody at either resort drank deeper of the medicinal springs than Hyacinth—who had ordered her physician to order her that treatment—the risk of harm or the possibility of benefit was of the smallest. But at Epsom there had been a good deal of gay company, and a greater liberty of manners than in London; for, indeed, as Rochester assured Lady Fareham, "the freedom of Epsom allowed almost nothing to be scandalous." And at Tunbridge there were dances by torchlight on the common. "And at the worst," Lady Fareham told her friends, "a fortnight or so at the Wells helps to shorten the summer."

It was the middle of August when they went back to Fareham House, hot, dry weather, and London seemed to be living on the Thames, so thick was the throng of boats going up and down the river, so that with an afternoon tide running up it seemed as if barges, luggers, and wherries were moving in one solid block into the sunset sky.

De Malfort had been attached to her ladyship's party at Epsom, and at Tunbridge Wells. He had his own lodgings, but seldom occupied them, except in that period between four or five in the morning and two in the afternoon, which Rochester and he called night. His days were passed chiefly in attendance upon Lady Fareham—singing and playing, fetching and carrying, combing her favourite spaniel with the same ivory pocket-comb that arranged his own waterfall curls; or reading a French romance to her, or teaching her the newest game of cards, or the last dancing-step imported from Fontainebleau or St. Cloud, or some new grace or fashion in dancing, the holding of the hand lower or higher; the latest manner of passing in a bransle or a coranto, as performed by the French King and Madame Henriette, the two finest dancers in France; Condé, once so famous for his dancing, now appearing in those gay scenes but seldom.

"Have you any commands for Paris, Hyacinth?" repeated Lord Fareham, his wife being for the moment too surprised to answer him. "Or have you, sister? I am starting for France to-morrow. I shall ride to Dover —lying a night at Sittingbourne, perhaps—and cross by the Packet that goes twice a week to Calais."

"Paris! And pray, my lord, what business takes you to Paris?"

"There is a great collection of books to be sold there next week. The library of your old admirer, Nicolas Fouquet, whom you knew in his splendour, but who has been a prisoner at Pignerol for a year and a half."

"Poor wretch!" cried De Malfort, "I was at the Chamber with Madame de Sévigné very often during his long tedious trial. *Mon dieu!* what courage, what talent he showed in defending himself! Every safeguard of the law was violated in order to silence him and prove him guilty; his papers seized in his absence, no friend or servant allowed to protect his interest, no inventory taken—documents suppressed that might have served for his defence, forgeries inserted by his foes. He had an implacable enemy, and he the highest in the land. He was the scapegoat of the past, and had to answer for a system of plunder that made Mazarin the richest man in France."

"I don't wonder that Louis was angry with a servant who had the insolence to entertain his Majesty with a splendour that surpassed his own," said Lady Fareham. "I should like to have been at those *fêtes* at Vaux. But although Fareham talks so lightly of travelling to Paris to choose a few dusty books, he has always discouraged me from going there to see old friends, and my own house—which I grieve to think of—abandoned to the carelessness of servants."

"Dearest, the cleverest woman in the world cannot be in two places at once; and it seems to me you have ever had your days here so full of agreeable engagements that you can have scarcely desired to leave London," answered Fareham, with his grave smile.

"To leave London—no! But there have been long moping months in Oxfordshire when it would have been a relief to change the scene."

"Then, indeed, had you been very earnest in wanting such a change, I am sure you would have taken it. I have never forbidden your going to Paris, nor refused to accompany you there. You may go with me tomorrow, if you can be ready."

"Which you know I cannot, or you would scarce make so liberal an offer."

"*Très chère,* you are pleased to be petulant. But I repeat my question. Is there anything you want at Paris?"

"Anything? A million things! Everything! But they are things which you would not be able to choose—except, perhaps, some of the new lace. I might trust you to buy that, though I'll wager you will bring me a hideous pattern—and some white Cypress powder—and a piece of the ash-coloured velvet Madame wore last winter. I have friends who can choose for you, if I write to them; and you will have but to bring the goods, and see they suffer no harm on the voyage. And you can go to the Rue de Tourain and see whether my servants are keeping the house in tolerable order."

"With your ladyship's permission I will lodge there while I am in Paris, which will be but long enough to attend the sale of books, and see some old friends. If I am detained it will be by finding my friends out of town, and having to make a journey to see them. I shall not go beyond Fontainebleau at furthest."

"Dear Fontainebleau! It is of all French palaces my favourite. I always envy Diana of Poitiers for having her cypher emblazoned all over that lovely gallery— Henri and Diane! Diane and Henri! Ah, me!"

18*

"You envy her a kind of notoriety which I do not covet for my wife!"

"You always take one *au pied de la lettre;* but seriously, Madame de Brézé was an honest woman compared with the lady who lodges by the Holbein Gate."

"I admit that sin wears a bolder front than it did in the last century. Angela, can I find nothing for you in Paris?"

"No; I thank your lordship. You and sister are both so generous to me that I have lost the capacity to wish for anything."

"And as Lewin crosses the Channel three or four times a year, I doubt we positively have the Paris fashions as soon as the Parisians themselves," added Hyacinth.

"That is an agreeable hallucination with which Englishwomen have ever consoled themselves for not being French," said De Malfort, who sat lolling against the marble balustrade, nursing the guitar on which he had been playing when Fareham interrupted their noontide idleness; "but your ladyship may be sure that London milliners are ever a twelvemonth in the rear of Paris fashions. It is not that they do not see the new mode. They see it, and think it hideous; and it takes a year to teach them that it is the one perfect style possible."

"I was not thinking of kerchiefs or petticoats," said Fareham. "You are a book-lover, sister, like myself. Can I bring you no books you wish for?"

"If there were a new comedy by Molière; but I fear it is wrong to read him, since in his late play, performed before the King at Versailles, he is so cruel an enemy to our Church."

"A foe only to hypocrites and pretenders, Angela. I will bring you his *Tartuffe*, if it is printed; or still better, *Le Misanthrope*, which I am told is the finest comedy that was ever written; and the latest romance, in twenty volumes or so, by one of those lady authors Hyacinth so admires, but which I own to finding as tedious as the divine Orinda's verses."

"You can jeer at that poor lady's poetry, yet take pleasure in such balderdash as Hudibras!"

"I love wit, dearest; though I am not witty. But as for your Princesse de Cleves, I find her ineffably dull."

"That is because you do not take the trouble to discover for whom the characters are meant. You lack the key to the imbroglio," said his wife, with a superior air.

"I do not care for a book that is a series of enigmas. Don Quixote needs no such guess-work. Shakespeare's characters are painted not from the petty models of yesterday and to-day, but from mankind in every age and every climate. Molière's and Calderon's personages stand on as solid a basis. In less than half a century your 'Grand Cyrus' will be insufferable jargon."

"Not more so than your *Hamlet* or *Othello*. Shakespeare was but kept in fashion during the late King's reign because his Majesty loved him—and will soon be forgotten, now that we have so many gayer and brisker dramatists."

"Whoever quotes Shakespeare, nowadays?" asked Lady Sarah Tewkesbury, who had been showing a rustic

niece the beauties of the river, as seen from Fareham
House. "Even Mr. Taylor, whose sermons bristle with
elegant allusions, never points one of his passionate
climaxes with a Shakespearian line. And yet there are
some very fine lines in *Hamlet* and *Macbeth,* which
would scarce sound amiss from the pulpit," added her
ladyship, condescendingly. "I have read all the plays,
some of them twice over. And I doubt that though
Shakespeare cannot hold the stage in our more enlightened age, and will be less and less acted as the
town grows more refined, his works will always be tasted
by scholars; among whom, in my modest way, I dare
reckon myself."

Lord Fareham left London on horseback, with but
one servant, in the early August dawn, before the rest
of the household were stirring. Hyacinth lay nearly as
late of a morning as Henrietta Maria, whom Charles
used sometimes to reproach for not being up in time for
the noonday office at her own chapel. Lady Fareham
had not Portuguese Catherine's fervour, who was often
at Mass at seven o'clock; but she did usually contrive
to be present at High Mass at the Queen's chapel; and
this was the beginning of her day. By that time Angela
and her niece and nephew had spent hours on the river,
or in the meadows at Chiswick, or on Putney Heath,
ever glad to escape from the great overgrown city, which
was now licking up every stretch of green sward, and
every flowery hedgerow west of St. James's Street. Soon
there would be no country between the Haymarket and
"The Pillars of Hercules."

Denzil sometimes enjoyed the privilege of accompanying Angela, children, and *gouvernante,* on these rural expeditions by the great waterway; and on such occasions he and Angela would each take an oar and row the boat for some part of the voyage, while the watermen rested, and in this manner Angela, instructed by Sir Denzil, considerably advanced her power as an oarswoman. It was an exercise she loved, as indeed she loved all out-of-door exercises, from riding with hawks and hounds to battledore and shuttlecock. But most of all, perhaps, she loved the river, and the rhythmical dip of oars in the fresh morning air, when every curve of the fertile shores seemed to reveal new beauty.

It had been a hot, dry summer, and the grass in the parks was burnt to a dull brown—had, indeed, almost ceased to be grass—while the atmosphere in town had a fiery taste, and was heavy with the dust which whitened all the roadways, and which the faintest breath of wind dispersed. Here on the flowing tide there was coolness, and the long rank grass upon those low sedgy shores was still green.

Lady Fareham supported the August heats sitting on her terrace, with a cluster of friends about her, and her musicians and singing-boys grouped in the distance, ready to perform at her bidding; but Henriette and her brother soon tired of that luxurious repose, and would urge their aunt to assist in a river expedition. The *gouvernante* was fat and lazy and good-tempered, had attended upon Henriette from babyhood, and always did as she was told.

"Her ladyship says I must have some clever person instead of Priscilla before I am a year older," Henriette told her aunt; "but I have promised poor old Prissy to hate the new person consumedly."

Angela and Denzil laughed as they rowed past the ruined abbey, seen dimly across the low water-meadow, where cows of the same colour were all lying in the same attitude, chewing the cud.

"I think Mr. Spavinger's trick must have cured your sister's fine friends of all belief in ghosts," he said.

"I doubt they would be as ready to believe—or to pretend to believe — to-morrow," answered Angela. "They think of nothing from morning till night but how to amuse themselves; and when every pleasure has been exhausted, I suppose fear comes in as a form of entertainment, and they want the shock of seeing a ghost."

"There have been no more midnight parties since Lady Sarah's assembly, I think?"

"Not among people of quality, perhaps; but there have been citizens' parties. I heard Monsieur de Malfort telling my sister about a supper given by a wealthy wine-cooper's lady from Aldersgate. The city people copy everything that their superiors wear or do."

"Even to their morals," said Denzil. "'Twere happy if the so-called superiors would remember that, and upon what a fertile ground they sow the seed of new vices. It is like the importation of a new weed or a new insect, which, beginning with an accident, may end in ruined crops and a country's famine."

Without deliberate disobedience to her husband, Lady Fareham made the best use of her time during his absence in Paris. The public theatres had not yet reopened after the horror of the plague. Whitehall was a desert, the King and his chief following being at Tunbridge. It was the dullest season of the year, and the recrudescence of the contagion in the low-lying towns along the Thames—Deptford, Greenwich, and the neighbourhood—together with some isolated cases in London, made people more serious than usual, despite of the so-called victory over the Dutch, which, although a mixed benefit, was celebrated piously by a day of General Thanksgiving.

Hyacinth, disgusted at the dulness of the town, was for ordering her coaches and retiring to Chilton.

"It is mortal dull at the Abbey," she said, "but at least we have the hawks, and breezy hills to ride over, instead of this sickly city atmosphere, which to my nostrils smells of the pestilence."

Henri de Malfort argued against such a retreat.

"It were a deliberate suicide," he said. "London, when everybody has left—all the bodies we count worthy to live, *par exemple*—is a more delightful place than you can imagine. There are a host of vulgar amusements which you would not dare to visit when your friends are in town; and which are ten times as amusing as the pleasures you know by heart. Have you ever been to the Bear Garden? I'll warrant you no, though 'tis but across the river at Bankside. We'll go there this afternoon, if you like, and see how the common people taste life. Then there are the gardens at Islington. There are mountebanks, and palmists, and fortune-tellers, who will frighten you out of your wits for a shilling. There's a man at Clerkenwell, a jeweller's journeyman from Venice, who pretends to practise the transmutation of metals, and to make gold. He squeezed hundreds out of that old miser Denham, who was afraid to have the law of him for imposture, lest all London should laugh at his own credulity and applaud the cheat. And you have not seen the Italian puppet-play, which is vastly entertaining. I could find you novelty and amusement for a month."

"Find anything new, even if it fail to amuse me. I am sick of everything I know."

"And then there is our midnight party at Millbank, the ghost-party, at which you are to frighten your dearest friends out of their poor little wits."

"Most of my dearest friends are in the country."

"Nay, there is Lady Lucretia Topham, whom I know you hate; and Lady Sarah and the Dubbins are still in Covent Garden."

"I will have no Dubbin—a toping wretch—and she is a too incongruous mixture, with her Edinburgh lingo and her Whitehall arrogance. Besides, the whole notion of a mock ghost was vulgarised by Wilmot's foolery, who ought to have been born a saltimbanque, and spent his life in a fair. No, I have abandoned the scheme."

"What! after I have been taxing my invention to produce the most terrible illusion that was ever witnessed? Will you let a clown like Spavinger—a well-born stable-boy—baulk us of our triumph? I am sending to Paris for a powder to burn in a corner of the room, which will throw the ghastliest pallor upon your countenance. When I devise a ghost, it shall be no impromptu spectre in yellow riding-boots, but a vision so awful, so true an image of a being returned from the dead, that the stoutest nerves will thrill and tremble at the apparition. The nun's habit is coming from Paris. I have asked my cousin, Madame de Fiesque, to obtain it for me at the Carmelites."

"You are taking a vast deal of trouble. But what kind of assembly can we muster at this dead season?"

"Leave all in my hands. I will find you some of the choicest spirits. It is to be *my* party. I will not even tell you what night I fix upon, till all is ready. So make no engagements for your evenings, and tell nobody anything."

"Who invented that powder?"

"A French chemist. He has it of all colours, and can flood a scene in golden light, or the rose of dawn, or the crimson of sunset, or a pale silvery blueness that you would swear was moonshine. It has been used in all the Court ballets. I saw Madame once look as ghastly as death itself, and all the Court was seized with terror. Some blundering fool had burnt the wrong powder, which cast a greenish tint over the faces, and Henriette's long thin features had a look of death. It seemed the forecast of an early grave; and some of us shuddered, as at a prophecy of evil."

"You might expect the worst in her case, knowing the wretched life she leads with Monsieur."

"Yes, when she is with him; but that is not always. There are compensations."

"If you mean scandal, I will not hear a word. She is adorable. The most sympathetic person I know— good even to her enemies—who are legion."

"You had better not say that, for I doubt she has only one kind of enemy."

"As how?"

"The admirers she has encouraged and disappointed. Yes, she is adorable, wofully thin, and, I fear, consumptive, but royal: and adorable, 'douceur et lumière,' as Bossuet calls her. But to return to my ghost-party."

"If you were wise, you would abandon the notion. I doubt that in spite of your powders your friends will never believe in a ghost."

"Oh yes, they will. It shall be my business to get them in the proper temper."

That idea of figuring in a picturesque habit, and in a halo of churchyard light, was irresistible. Hyacinth promised to conform to Malfort's plans, and to be ready to assume her phantom *rôle* whenever she was called upon.

Angela knew something of the scheme, and that there was to be another assembly at Millbank; but her sister had seemed disinclined to talk of the plan in her presence—a curious reticence in one whose sentiments and caprices were usually given to the world at large with perfect freedom. For once in her life Hyacinth had a secret air, and checked herself suddenly in the midst of her light babble at a look from De Malfort, who had urged her to keep her sister out of their midnight party.

"I pledge my honour that there shall be nothing to offend," he told her, "but I hope to have the wittiest coxcombs in London, and we want no prudes to strangle every jest with a long-drawn lip and an alarmed eye. Your sister has a pale, fragile prettiness which pleases an eye satiated with the exuberant charms of your Rubens and Titian women; but she is not handsome enough to give herself airs; and she is a little inclined that way. By the faith of a gentleman, I have suffered scowls from her that I would scarce have endured from Barbara!"

"Barbara! You are vastly free with her ladyship's name."

"Not freer than she has ever been with her friendship."

"Henri, if I thought——"

"What, dearest?"

"That you had ever cared for that—wanton——"

"Could you think it, when you know my life in England has been one long tragedy of loving in vain—of sighing only to be denied—of secret tears—and public submission."

"Do not talk so," she exclaimed, starting up from her low tabouret, and moving hastily to the open window, to fresh air and sunshine, rippling river and blue sky, escaping from an atmosphere that had become feverish.

"De Malfort, you know I must not listen to foolish raptures."

"I know you have been refusing to hear for the last two years."

They were on the terrace now, she leaning on the broad marble balustrade, he standing beside her, and all the traffic of London moving with the tide below them.

"To return to our party," she said, in a lighter tone, for that spurt of jealousy had betrayed her into seriousness. "It will be very awkward not to invite my sister to go with me."

"If you did she would refuse, belike, for she is

under Fareham's thumb; and he disapproves of everything human."

"Under Fareham's thumb! What nonsense! Indeed I must invite her. She would think it so strange to be omitted."

"Not if you manage things cleverly. The party is to be. a surprise. You can tell her next morning you knew nothing about it beforehand."

"But she will hear me order the barge—or will see me start."

"There will be no barge. I shall carry you to Millbank in my coach, after your evening's entertainment, wherever that may be."

"I had better take my own carriage at least, or my chair."

"You can have a chair, if you are too prudish to use my coach, but it shall be got for you at the moment. We won't have your own chairman and links to chatter and betray you before you have played the ghost. Remember you come to my party not as a guest, but as a performer. If they ask why Lady Fareham is absent I shall say you refused to take part in our foolery."

"Oh, you must invent some better excuse. They will never believe anything rational of me. Say I was disappointed of a hat or a mantua. Well, it shall be as you wish. Angela is apt to be tiresome. I hate a disapproving carriage, especially in a younger sister."

Angela was puzzled by Hyacinth's demeanour. A want of frankness in one so frank by nature aroused her fears. She was puzzled and anxious, and longed for

Fareham's return, lest his giddy-pated wife should be guilty of some innocent indiscretion that might vex him.

"Oh! if she but valued him at his just worth she would value his opinion second only to the approval of conscience," she thought, sadly, ever regretful of her sister's too obvious indifference towards so kind a husband.

END OF VOL. I.

PRINTING OFFICE OF THE PUBLISHER.

Made in the USA
Lexington, KY
13 December 2010